NIXON
OFF THE
RECORD

NIXON
OFF THE
RECORD

MONICA CROWLEY

RANDOM HOUSE

NEW YORK

Library of Congress Cataloging-in-Publication Data
Crowley, Monica, 1968–
Nixon off the record/Monica Crowley.
p.   cm.
Includes index.
ISBN 0-679-45681-3
1. Nixon, Richard M. (Richard Milhous), 1913–1994—Views on
political leadership.   2. Nixon, Richard M. (Richard Milhous), 1913–1994—Views
on presidential candidates.   3. United States—Politics and
government—1989–1993.   4. Presidents—United States—
Election—1992.   5. Political leadership—United States—
History—20th century.   I. Title.
E856.C76   1996
973.924'092—dc20   96-27786

Random House website address: http://www.randomhouse.com/
Printed in the United States of America on acid-free paper
2 3 4 5 6 7 8 9
First Edition
Book design by Victoria Wong

For President Nixon
Mentor and Friend

AUTHOR'S NOTE

I began this project as a single book, a memoir of my four extraordinary years working with President Nixon. As it began to take shape, however, I realized that the story would be better told in two volumes: the first to focus on Nixon's views on American leadership and the political process, and the second to chronicle his evolving thoughts on foreign policy and his final journey toward personal and political resurrection.

This first volume is a guide to twentieth century American politics and the leaders who defined it, past and present. As the country prepares to select another president, Nixon's views will give voters uncommon criteria by which to measure the candidates and their ability to exercise effective leadership.

At the heart of the story is, of course, Nixon. I will be forever grateful to him for giving me such an exceptional opportunity. The Nixon I knew was kind, trusting, magnanimous, warm, and witty, willing to share his wisdom, experiences, joys, and regrets openly and freely. He was a brilliant teacher and a fine man.

A first book is an exciting and daunting enterprise. Nixon often referred to the writing of his first book, *Six Crises*, as his "seventh crisis." I now know what he meant.

I owe a great debt to many individuals who helped me as I developed this project. For his wise counsel and kind support, I wish to thank William Safire. For their early and enthusiastic encouragement, thanks to Frank Gaffney, Roger Robinson, and Rinelda Bliss. For providing superb computer technology and technical support, thanks to Paul Palumbo of Network Integration Consulting, Inc. And for his good-natured patience with a first-time author, thanks to my agent, Carl Brandt.

I extend my deep appreciation to Harold Evans, president of the Random House Trade Group, for his faithful commitment to the project, and to Bob Loomis, for his insightful editorial advice and direction.

I am particularly grateful to my mother, Patricia, my sister, Jocelyn, my grandparents, Stanley and Florence Baron, and my uncle and aunt, Donald and Nancy Blanchette, for their remarkable generosity, guidance, encouragement, and support. They are truly selfless.

Above all, I thank God for blessing me as He has.

—M.C.
Warren, New Jersey
May 17, 1996

CONTENTS

INTRODUCTION

I was born in Arizona in 1968, the year Richard Nixon was elected president. My first memory of Nixon was formed at age five, when I watched him announce his decision to resign on August 8, 1974. I was vacationing with my parents on the New Jersey seashore, and I remember seeing Nixon's face fill the television screen, speaking words that I did not understand. I knew enough to know, based on my parents' reactions, that what he was saying was important, but I could not have grasped that that brief speech was the culmination of a tragic series of events that had brought down his presidency, nor could I know that I would work for him sixteen years later.

On July 3, 1990, I became former president Nixon's foreign policy assistant. I served in this capacity until his death, on April 22, 1994. During those four intervening years, I became a professional confidante of a man who had transformed American politics, changed global balances of power, and become an icon for those seeking both good and evil, brilliance and deceit, selflessness and selfishness, greatness and baseness. Visible and controversial even in death, Nixon remains a source of endless fascination. "In politics," he would say, "the only worse thing than being wrong is being dull." He was sometimes wrong but never dull. His life's journey—completed on such a grand scale—attracts analogies to all that is right and wrong with the world, America, and human nature. Nixon himself had a vague awareness that his life had, in a sense, taken on a life of its own.

My four years with President Nixon were not White House years, vice presidential years, or years in Congress. They were the last of the post-presidency years. What Nixon had accomplished during his years in power determined how others would judge him; what he did during his final years out of power would determine how he ultimately saw himself. Understanding Nixon at the end of his life is crucial to understanding him at the beginning and at his political prime. In many ways, these years offer a richer, more profound and unqualified guide to the man than any other time of his life. This is when Nixon would be most complete.

I came to work with Nixon in an unexpected and extraordinary way. My political values were formed during the Reagan presidency and were based primarily upon Reagan's aggressive approach to the Soviet Union and his determination to restore the military, economic, social, and political forces that had always contributed to America's unique power. Although my primary interest was foreign policy, I was fascinated by the political process and the leaders who had dominated American politics in the late twentieth century, particularly Ronald Reagan and the man who made Reagan possible, Richard Nixon.

When I was a junior and majoring in political science at Colgate University, I was privileged to have Robert Kaufman as a professor of national security issues. He cultivated my interest in foreign and national security affairs, and when I prepared to leave campus for the summer before my senior year, he lent several books to me, one of which was Richard Nixon's *1999: Victory Without War*. That book was the first I chose to read that summer. It had such a tremendous impact on my thinking about such foreign policy issues as the reform process in the Soviet Union, the need to restructure NATO, the nascent pressures for reform in China, and the need for continuing U.S. leadership that I wrote Nixon a lengthy letter in which I agreed with many of his positions, disagreed with others, and expressed gratitude to him for writing a book that clarified my own thinking on these matters. I mailed it and did not expect a reply. Several weeks later, I received a handwritten note from the former president, inviting me to discuss American foreign policy with him at his office in New Jersey.

Nixon and I met for the first time on October 2, 1989, and he was exceedingly generous with the commodity that was most precious to him: his time. That initial meeting—a two-hour conversation about the state of the world—led to a permanent position as his foreign policy assistant.

When I began working for him in 1990, I did not expect to have the access to him that I quickly gained. And surprisingly for a man who had been so often damaged by those he trusted, Nixon trusted me immediately. I became a member of his small circle of advisers. I listened as he confided his views on international affairs and world leaders, American politics and policy, Watergate, his own political career, and human nature. I worked with him on his last two books, *Seize the Moment: America's Challenge in a One-Superpower World* and *Beyond Peace.* With the former president and Mrs. Nixon, I watched, on television, Russian president Boris Yeltsin's address to the U.S. Congress on June 17, 1992. I spent election night 1992 on the telephone with him, analyzing the results as the returns came in. I attended several Nixon-family gatherings, including the former president's annual Halloween festivities. And I traveled with him to Europe and to Asia, where he invited me to attend his private meetings with heads of state and other leaders.

He meant to teach me how "the real world works," as he said, so that I could carry his lessons into the arena myself. Nixon gave me the freedom to sharpen my own political views, the experience and responsibility to act on them, and the challenge of exchanging them with the thirty-seventh president of the United States.

From the beginning, President Nixon was my mentor, employer, and guide to American political history. Granted a rare and highly personal view of the thoughts, actions, and persona of one of the most important and enduring figures of the twentieth century, I kept a daily diary beginning in 1989, of which Nixon was unaware. Immediately after each discussion, I recorded the conversation, the mood, and personal reflections. The quotes herein are the words of former president Nixon verbatim. His professional and personal disclosures were made in confidence but with the implicit understanding that they would be eventually recounted. When William Safire of *The New York Times* encouraged me to write this book in August 1994, he said, "Nixon knew that when he spoke to you, he was speaking to history." Through our conversations, Nixon was ensuring that his message and his vision would live on after he was gone.

Many of his discussions with me contained measured political or diplomatic remarks for public consumption, but most also contained the completely spontaneous and brutally honest reflections of private conversation. I have selected the topics and experiences that most interested, infuriated, gratified, amused, or intrigued Nixon during his last four years. Some reveal the prescient world statesman, others the wily politician, and others the generous and kind but tormented man.

This first volume examines one of the most important aspects of Nixon's philosophy: his views on leadership. Nixon knew what constituted great leadership, what undermined it, and how to qualify for it. His unparalleled experience as a leader who had won power, lost it, then regained the ability to influence placed him in a unique position to judge leaders who preceded and followed him. This book tries to place those judgments in context and bring them alive in the spirit and manner in which they were intended. They were meant not just for me, an audience of one, but for the audience of the ages.

The life of Richard Nixon has become a lens through which we may see the many paradoxes of human nature. Nixon's life is not just complicated; it represents the collision of human potential and human deficiency. If Nixon lived the American dream and then lost it in 1974, he had regained it by 1994 by replacing disappointment with accomplishment. His post-presidential years were filled with activities designed for both political and personal restoration. In the end, by reconciling achievements and mistakes, satisfaction and regret, and hard work and the costs that it exacted, he realized the inner contentment that he had long sought.

The end of life brings the final synthesis of man and experience. Nixon looked back and forward with critical discipline. He passed his lessons to me so that I might pass them to others. He prepared me for my future while preparing the future to be without him. At the final passage, Nixon had a true sense of what his life—and the history through which he lived—had meant.

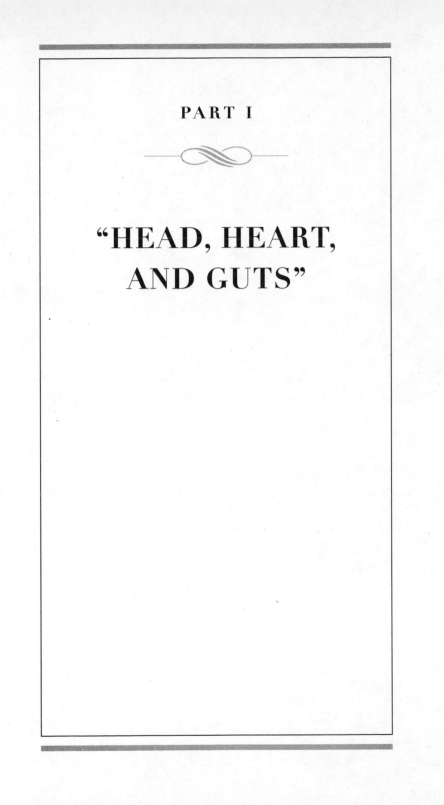

PART I

"HEAD, HEART, AND GUTS"

The first time I met Richard Nixon, I knew I was in the presence of someone who had risen to the pinnacle of power. His posture was ramrod straight, his gaze steady, his voice assured, his gait confident, and his self-discipline obvious. He wore the aura that distinguishes the leader from the led, a cloak of power gained, lost, and regained, a spirit of one who has written dramatic history. Nixon had the intangible yet undeniable dynamic that sets apart true leaders. He understood it and tended to it. He sought leadership and at the same time felt fated for it. If destiny gave him a will to power, his own hard work and mistakes rewrote the script. He believed that the prerequisites of greatness surrounded him: the man, the country, the events. The tragedy that ended his presidency may have robbed him of formal power, but it did not negate the elements that delivered it to him. From that first glimpse, I could see that he considered himself a leader who bore the hallmarks of greatness.

By his own definition, great leadership requires a transcendent vision that inspires the leader and enables him to inspire the nation, for good or ill. People, he said with Machiavellian flair, both love the great leader and hate him; rarely are they indifferent to him. His force and vision, his ability to persuade, move, and lift, and his direction of history grant him loyal followers and bitter enemies. Nixon had both. His thoughts on leadership grew out of years of wielding power, watching others exercise it, and observing the effects. History may yet allow greatness to claim Richard Nixon, but he strove tirelessly to claim it for himself.

"Great leaders must have two main tiers of attributes," he told me on May 9, 1993. "The first is general; the second is more particular." We had been discussing the results of the previous election, and he expressed serious doubts that Bill Clinton was capable of effective presidential leadership. This prompted him to philosophize about great leadership and his own qualifying attributes.

"First, great leaders must have head, heart, and guts," he said, pointing dramatically at his own head, chest, and stomach. "That is, smarts, compassion, and courage. Without these, he cannot be truly great—maybe *great,* but not *good* as well. Look at Russia's Peter the Great or Caesar—they had the brains and the guts but no compassion whatever. And poor Neville Chamberlain had some smarts and compassion but no guts. It's rare for a leader to combine all three. Most great leaders have only two of the three but wielded power so effectively on such a grand scale that they significantly changed the course of history for their nations and for the world. But a great and good leader needs all three. That is the first tier of qualities. The second tier is far more specific."

He emphasized his next points by tapping his fingers in the air. "Great leaders need to be willing to take risks, practice politics well, govern with vision, use pragmatism wisely, be willing to make the hard decisions, and use power effectively.

"It's a tall order. Most leaders aren't up to it. But when they are, that's where the greatness comes in."

He eagerly illustrated his points. "Let's consider each of these attributes one by one." He pointed a finger in the air. "First, risk taking. This is the first element of great leadership. If you are unable to rise to the challenge of a major risk, you will never achieve greatness. In politics more than any other profession, the risks worth taking are those where the odds are enormous. The more you risk, the more you will gain if you win. Consider the Fund speech [popularly known as the Checkers speech]. It could have ended my political career right then and there in 1952. Instead, it saved it. You cannot be obsessed with what you might lose, or you will never move ahead. Life is a gamble anyway. Why not risk it all to gain it all?

"This brings us to my next point about politics. No one should even consider running for anything unless he recognizes from the beginning that politics is a deadly profession. In a democracy, if he loses an election, he can try again or look for another line of work. In nondemocracies, he can lose his head. A leader must be determined to win and put losing out of his mind. The best leaders are those who were pushed up against the wall in a tight race or crisis. Risk brings this out."

Above all for Nixon, leadership demanded a person secure in his abilities and in himself and who was, therefore, willing and able to take those risks. Of the many criticisms leveled at him, the one he found most egregious was that he was insecure. Politics, by its very nature, attracts the supremely secure. Running for office, particularly the presidency, requires subjection to the harshest scrutiny and opposition and the ultimate test of public approval: the judgment of the voters. To lose, face public rejection, and try again requires not just a strong personality but a secure one. Nixon would not have been a human being had he not had personal or political insecurities occasionally, but to suggest that he was chronically insecure is to misread his very nature. When he ran for office or otherwise put himself in the unforgiving public eye, he did so with absolute political confidence and certainty.

"Look," he said, shifting in his chair, "politics is a necessary evil to get the position you need to affect the course of events. It's usually a brawl. It's not for the fainthearted. And it takes guts to get in the arena. But if you are willing to take the risks, politics can push you to levels of greatness.

"Now, uh, what was my third point?" he asked. I looked at my notepad and answered, "Governing."

"Oh, yes. Governing. Campaigning and governing are, of course, two different things. In campaigning, you play to win; in governing, you act to move the nation and, in some cases, the world. A great campaigner does not necessarily make a great leader; look at [President] Clinton. And a great leader can be a terrible campaigner; usually these types don't even make it to the top because they can't get above the political means to the end; look at [former Texas governor John] Connally. Governing is so much more complex and difficult."

"Campaigning serves the needs of one; governing serves the needs of all, right?" I asked.

"Well put, although campaigning is more involved than that implies. But it is, basically, meant to get that one person elected, so that's pretty much on target. And although governing never serves everybody's interest all the time, that's the object."

He paused. "I think my next point was about pragmatism, right? Look, a great leader must know when to stick to his ideals and when to compromise on them. He must know what fights to pick and which to give in to. Principle can be a sturdy leg to stand on, but it can also bring you down if the timing is bad."

He leaned way back in his chair and tilted his head. "I remember meeting [Japanese prime minster Yasuhiro] Nakasone in Tokyo in 1985, and he told me that a leader must have two faces—one smiling and one threatening. What he was saying was that in order for a leader to be effective, he must use pragmatism wisely. Those who use pragmatism as an end in itself and those who view it as a complete evil are both wrong. It can be justified, but only as a means to achieve great goals. Knowing how to get the system to work for your goals is indispensable. But balancing principle against interest is not that easy. Sometimes a leader has to persuade others—and himself—to go against their own interests and principles to achieve those goals. You know that famous quote by Churchill, to the effect that if Hitler had invaded hell, he would have made up something nice to say about the devil in the House of Commons? That cuts right to the point I am trying to make. Idealism and pragmatism go hand in hand; the key to effective leadership is knowing how to balance them."

Nixon leaned forward and with the pen I had placed on the end table, pointed in the air. "Decisions, Monica. Decisions. Every great leader needs to be able to make the hard decisions and come down on one side or another. This goes right along with the ability to take risks; they're both sides of the same coin. You have to be able to take the slings because regardless of how you come down on an issue, even if it is one hundred percent right, half of your constituents—whether in a congressional district or the nation, in the case of the president—are going to oppose and criticize you. Sometimes the right decision is the least popular, in which case all that courage I spoke about helps. People want strength in their leader; that's why [President George] Bush's approval ratings went so high after the Persian Gulf War. He made the hard decisions.

"I remember so well when the North Vietnamese fired on one of our unarmed spy ships and I called a press conference and said, 'The president of the United States only warns once.' They never did it again.

"When it comes to a tough decision, most advisers head for the tall grass or just give wishy-washy opinions because they don't want to be on the losing end. I remember my decision to bomb Haiphong. [Secretary of State William] Rogers said, 'I'm for it if it will work.' Whatever the result of a decision, the final responsibility must rest with the top man. He is the one who made the decision; he is the one who has to live with the consequences, good or bad."

He sipped his tonic water and cleared his throat. "This brings me to my final point about power. Power should never be sought for its own sake but for what may be accomplished with it. Power in the wrong hands can be enormously destructive, but power in the right hands can change history for the better. People accused me of abusing power during Watergate, but let me tell you something: *real* abuse of power involves malicious intent; Watergate was a series of blundering mistakes, not a grand scheme driven by malicious intent. Great leaders know the potential of power and use it wisely, but they also know its limits and obey them." Aware that many believe he had overstepped that line, he continued. "But," he added, "greatness allows for mistakes."

He flashed a mock smile across his face. "People often asked me a silly question: 'Was it *fun* to be president? Were you *happy?*' That's not the point. Leaders take on the office to accomplish something, not to be happy or to have fun. Great leaders, anyway. Leadership requires a view to the future, to bring people up."

"That's true, Mr. President," I replied, "but since most people have little patience for what doesn't affect them immediately, leaders must address everyday concerns as well. Relying on vision alone may get you defeated in the next election."

"Right. You must do both. People always want to know, 'What have you done for me lately?' And if you don't do for them lately, you aren't going to get reelected. But you've *got* to inspire," he said with a clenched fist. "You've got to do the right thing. Look, I only got three percent of the Jewish vote and seven percent of the blacks. But it didn't stop me from reaching out to them and trying to do the right thing."

"Was that, by definition, great leadership?" I asked.

He paused. "Well, I don't know. You just do what you think is best. Selfish goals have to be addressed unselfishly."

"Do you think that when it comes to leadership, either people have the ability or they don't?" I asked.

"I think that's right. Some can rise to the occasion if the events are great and the circumstances are right. But most either have the talent to lead or they don't."

"Some leaders have a strong personal character and a weak political one, like Bush; others have a strong political character and a weak personal one, like Clinton. It's rare for a person to have both, but that's where you find a great leader," I said.

"That's an excellent point. You know, politics has really gone down the tubes since 1960, and frankly it's not much fun to watch. Maybe it's because the characters involved are weak on either the personal or political side—or both. I don't know. I ran in '68 and '72, so I guess that applies to me too." He laughed. "It just seems that good candidates aren't running anymore. It's better not to run anyone at all than a turkey. The top offices in this country require better."

Nixon's thoughts on leadership were so well defined that they represented not just what he thought but who he was. The president, the philosopher, and the man were three inseparable parts of the whole. By laying out his conditions for great leadership, he was qualifying himself for that label. In his book *Leaders,* Nixon identified six foreign statesmen whom he believed met the test of great leadership: Winston Churchill, Charles de Gaulle, Japanese prime minister Shigeru Yoshida, West German chancellor Konrad Adenauer, Nikita Khrushchev, and Chinese premier Chou En-lai. They were great because they had made an enduring difference—by building their nation, by saving it, or by moving the world in some singular way. They were also his contemporaries; he knew them all and therefore had living standards against which to measure himself. He connected his points about leadership to his own political portfolio in the expectation that the audience—and history—would logically place him among the great leaders. He was, perhaps, the last best witness for the defense.

He was not, however, particularly generous with his assessments of the American presidencies that came before and after his own. He gauged other presidents' successes and failures by his own experiences, historical perspective, and of course, bias. America had had few truly great presidents according to Nixon: Washington, Jefferson, Lincoln, Theodore Roosevelt, Woodrow Wilson, Franklin Roosevelt, and implicitly Nixon himself. These men met the test of great leadership: great men in a great country, encountering and directing great events. His inclusion of himself on this list was driven less by determined historical revisionism than by a genuine belief that he belonged in their ranks. His judgments of his predecessors and successors were colored by this view and represented not just discrete opinions but his own historical aspirations.

On February 18, 1991, he handed me *The New York Times* editorial about Presidents' Day, in which he was not mentioned as one of the twentieth century's great presidents. "Well, they had fun with that editorial," he said dryly. His exclusion from such lists provoked mild bitterness and regret, which in turn spurred him to turn a critical eye toward all other American presidents, those on the list and those, like him, excluded.

"I'm reading this biography of Woodrow Wilson," he said to me on November 12, 1991. "Tell me, what do you think of him?"

I turned the question around in my mind before answering, knowing that he was testing my views about a president for whom he had qualified admiration. "His idealism was his greatest strength and his greatest weakness. He was a true leader, but he could not accept the fallibility of human nature and tried to correct it by constructing institutions, like the League [of Nations]. It was futile but admirable."

Nixon smiled. "He was a scholar before he was a politician," he said, drawing an implicit parallel to himself. "He was a man of thought and of action, in his first term anyway. But then he became a man only of thought, and that's why the League failed. He had some great victories and great defeats, which is the sign of a truly great leader. His only fault was that he wasn't a realist enough to know that pragmatism had to be balanced with idealism. Idealism running rampant is impotent.

"And you know, like Lincoln, he was clinically depressed and swung between very high highs and low lows. I know how hard it is when you are president—it takes an iron will not to get down," he said, clenching his fist.

"But Wilson's eloquence dazzles me. His best speeches were 'Leaders of Men' and 'The State.' We really don't see that kind of eloquence today. The invasion of money, the short attention spans of the public, and popular culture have really destroyed eloquent public speaking. Reagan said, 'Make my day,' from a Clint Eastwood movie. Now, I like Clint Eastwood, and it's fine to try to connect with the audience, but you shouldn't replace higher language with that."

"Do you mean that politicians should avoid the temptation to appeal to the lowest common denominator?" I asked.

"Absolutely right. Kennedy, Johnson, Ford, Carter, Reagan, and Bush—none wrote their own speeches. At least I wrote some of my own—and crafted some of the best phrases. Your words as president are what lasts, and they should be—if possible—your own. Look, history boomerangs. The greats—Washington, Jefferson, and Lincoln—stay great. But history does strange things to the others. Kennedy and Reagan ended their presidencies with positive views on them only to have them reconsidered under a much harsher light later on. Those who left under a negative cloud, like Truman, have a shot at a more favorable rating. That's just the way history works. And that's why a president's words endure and why they should be his own. 'The great Silent Majority' phrase was my own. That will live. The point is not to give up and let others call the shots for you. When I lost in 1960, people stayed away, and those in the party said, 'You had your shot.' But I came back and made my case in my own words and won. The greats will always be remembered in their own words. Look at Wilson."

Nixon considered himself a man of thought and action, the Wilson Wilson himself should have been. Against this high standard he measured others who held the office and often criticized them for failing to meet it as he had.

"Franklin Roosevelt was a titan," he said on September 26, 1992. With the presidential election just weeks away, Nixon focused on Clinton's plans to expand the role of government by centralizing health care and other social programs. This led Nixon to comment on Roosevelt. "What he did to bring this country out of the depths of the Depression—even though it didn't remain temporary, as he intended—and to rid the world of fascism will always make him a great leader. The New Deal opened the floodgates of entitlements and government handouts, but I don't think that any other person in that job at that time could have done anything else.

"People often forget, though, that Roosevelt was a superb manipulator. His most useful enemies were those in the upper class, like he was. But he attacked their wealth and privilege and rallied the lower classes to him. Class warfare? Maybe. But the point is that he knew that there were far more have-nots than haves, and so he became their hero. He was a liberal, but it didn't matter because the crises around him were so huge.

"Roosevelt was a good politician. The guy had vision. In the late '30s, he was out there trying to make the case for American efforts to try to block the rise of Japan and Germany, but nobody listened to his warnings. It wasn't his fault; at least he saw the dangers and had the guts to get out there and talk about them. Once Pearl Harbor was bombed, he knew that he had to appeal to the country through idealism. He emphasized moral causes, and that's what inspired the people to support his decision to go to war. He had it all: the ability to take risks, balance pragmatism and idealism, make the hard decisions, and use power for a supreme cause.

"By the way, Teddy Roosevelt is another guy who was just larger than life. He was fearless physically, mentally, emotionally. He knew when to use pragmatism to get to idealistic goals. Uncompromising types like [Wisconsin senator Robert] La Follette attacked him for compromising on principle to get his programs through the Congress. Roosevelt responded by attacking La Follette as an uncompromising 'demagogue.' TR did everything in a big way, and for that he will go down as a great leader."

Nixon's contemporaries received more detailed analysis. On October 27, 1992, inspired again by the politics of the presidential campaign, he spoke about Franklin Roosevelt's successor.

"Harry Truman was very good, but I never read modern history," he said, handing me a copy of David McCullough's biography. "The publisher sent it to me, but I think you'll get more use of it." He was increasingly concerned that Bush was going to lose the election in November, despite Bush's insistence that he would finish with a Trumanesque victory. We sat down in his study for our daily meeting at the Nixon residence; he lifted his glass of tonic water and, instructing me to do the same with mine, offered a toast to an election miracle. After a long pause, he pointed to the book. "Let me tell you a thing or two about Truman, because after all I was in the Congress when he was president.

"Truman was a tough son of a bitch. No real education, but it didn't matter. He had some of the best gut instincts I have ever seen in a president. A major problem most modern presidents have is being exposed to too much information, too much advice—overanalyzing things. I suffered from this to an extent. But not Truman. Truman went with his gut instincts and was usually dead-on. He did have some very good advisers, but really, when it comes down to it, he was the architect of our winning position in the cold war. Truman saw the dangers of Soviet expansionism, and he knew the political risks he had to take to convince the country that we had to compete with the Soviets or peace and freedom would be endangered. He knew the risks, and he went ahead anyway. And even though he could be petty sometimes, the guy had guts. Real guts. He was put in an almost impossible political position when Roosevelt died, you know. Filling those shoes was hard enough. But having to meet the challenges of the early days of the cold war—well, that was history making of the highest order. And Truman rose to the occasion. That was great leadership.

"I know Bush is reading this bio and comparing himself to Truman. That is wrong. There are some parallels politically, but not personally. Truman was a man of the people, but both became president by accident—I mean, Bush through the vice presidency and the Reagan afterglow and Truman through death. The only parallel is that both are fighting from behind, but Truman was made of steel, and Bush is not."

"Do you think that that is based upon their different social and economic backgrounds?" I asked.

"Well," he said, hesitating. "I think so. When you come from privilege, as Bush did, well, you just don't have to try as hard. When you come from a much more modest background, like Truman's, you have to fight for everything you get."

"Fighters, then, are born and not made?" I asked.

"Well, to an extent. Background has a lot to do with making you who you are and your ability to fight for what you want. Having to scrape for everything makes you stronger."

"And more hard-hearted?" I asked.

"Maybe a little. It's difficult not to be. But if anything, it makes you stronger." He was slightly uneasy. "But getting back to the comparisons to Truman—it is wrong to equate the Eightieth Congress with this one. The Eightieth Congress passed the Greek-Turkish aid program, which saved them from the threat of communism; exposed Alger Hiss; and passed Taft-Hartley. [Republican candidate Thomas] Dewey didn't defend it, and he lost. But Clinton is no Dewey. I see that Clinton is also hitting the Truman analogy hard. Truman was 'one of us,' as they say. Neither Clinton nor Bush is. Both are competing for that Truman mantle, and neither deserves it."

On October 30, as the election drew ever closer and Bush seemed destined to lose, Nixon continued his thoughts on Truman. "This election is going to be closer than most people think or even what the polls are showing, but I still think that Bush is going to lose. He's not strong enough to pull a Harry Truman. Although, I remember Bebe [Rebozo] said he voted for Truman in '48 because he felt sorry for him that he was going to lose by so much. If people think it's going to be close, they'll vote. But Truman had that quality that sets apart really effective leaders. I don't see that among many modern politicians: sheer guts and determination.

"I know this is a little off the subject, but I remember so well when Truman sent Ted Williams—the last of the four-hundred batters—to Korea. It was purely political. He was a good friend and a good Republican. If he didn't have to go, he would have broken all the records. Well, Truman did what he had to do. He was just very political, but he was also good—far more visionary than his critics give him credit for."

Nixon's thoughts on Dwight Eisenhower were more complex, layered with gratitude, regret, and cautious criticism. Eisenhower had been his mentor, responsible for launching him into national office and sending him around the world in his first extensive foreign policy lesson. Respect, however, conflicted with a hard judgment; Eisenhower had groomed him and made possible Nixon's presidency, but he had also fallen short of Nixon's standard for loyalty. Nixon simultaneously venerated and resented him. It was an intricate judgmental balancing act that tore into Nixon as much as similar analyses of his own career did.

"Eisenhower was an interesting fellow," he said in his first remarks to me about him during a two-hour conversation on February 27, 1991. "He was very charming and warm socially, but he was a hard-ass. He had to be to lead the Allied victory in Europe. He was a tough son of a bitch. As you know, he didn't endorse me in 1960 until he absolutely had to. That was pretty devastating to my campaign because everyone loved Eisenhower, and here I was, running a *very* close race against Kennedy. Well, I guess he was just protecting himself, but it wasn't really the most loyal thing to do." The sun streamed into the office and fell across his face. He got up, pulled down the shade, and resumed his thoughts on Eisenhower.

"In '52, we talked about cleaning up the mess in Washington; of course that's nothing compared to what they have now, but Eisenhower was such an honest fellow that he insisted, correctly, that we run on that. Eisenhower had me go after Stevenson because I had a core of support, and he knew I'd be good on the attack. Adlai Stevenson was a very intelligent guy but not at all suited to the presidency; he thought things over long and hard before making the wrong decision!" He laughed.

"Eisenhower used me, but he used me well. I remember when he said to me, 'You got Hiss, and you got him fairly.' Then he put me on the ticket and had enough confidence in me to let me defend myself against all the charges they threw at me. He didn't defend me until he knew the truth, but after that, and after he saw the great outpouring of support I got after the Fund speech, he was totally for me.

"Eisenhower respected an honest fight. He wanted to take the high road, so he sent me out to attack the opposition, which was fine. I was pretty good on the attack; Eisenhower knew it. It worked. When I think of the '52 convention—my God! People couldn't *wait* to see Eisenhower! You weren't there, but I lived it. It was a tremendous time. Eisenhower was bigger than life, but he could also be a pretty petty guy. He held grudges and was so protective of himself politically sometimes that he didn't stand up for the people who had served him loyally."

"Are you referring to 1960?" I asked.

"Well, yes, but it wasn't just me. There were others. Eisenhower tried to protect himself, but often at the expense of screwing those closest to him. Well, that's just politics. I don't mean to talk him down; he was a great soldier and a great leader. And he taught me so many things, from foreign policy to working with the Congress to the little things of being president. One of the first things Eisenhower told me was how difficult it was to sign a bad letter. He always said, 'Never begin a letter cold and formally. Make each one different.' He knew how to do all the right things. That was Eisenhower."

Nixon's ambiguous feelings toward Eisenhower were rooted in the premium he placed on loyalty, the damage he sustained from disloyalty, and his incompatible but coexistent feelings of gratitude and resentment. For Nixon, Eisenhower had been an authoritative, disciplinary figure with the power to make or break him. Nixon had been at his mercy and in his shadow. But now, having made his own history, he was able to pass a more honest judgment on him. Eisenhower's capriciousness in his treatment of Nixon had both helped and hurt him, and now Nixon could admit it—to me and to himself.

If Nixon gained experience through Eisenhower's successes, then he gained the presidency through his immediate predecessor's defeats. Although he disagreed with Lyndon Johnson on almost everything and was supremely critical of his handling of domestic and foreign affairs, Nixon respected Johnson's scrappy fighter's instinct, which he also admired in himself. And although he inherited the crippling war in Vietnam from Johnson, Nixon issued a fair judgment of him and considered him an imperious but potent politician.

"Johnson was tough, tough, tough," he said through clenched teeth on May 23, 1991. He had been writing about American leadership for his ninth book, *Seize the Moment,* and after asking me to review a section about our involvement in Vietnam, he issued a frank assessment of Johnson. "He was a patriot, but he was a calculating bastard. You know, not many realize that he used the kind of tactics that they always criticize me for using to sandbag my '68 campaign. Johnson had [vice presidential candidate Spiro] Agnew's plane bugged. [FBI Chief J. Edgar] Hoover told me later that [Johnson] had *my* campaign plane bugged as well. Would you believe it?"

"Did you know it at the time, sir?" I asked.

He looked directly at me. "No, no, of course not. But I should have guessed. Johnson was so obsessed with all of that recording crap. I will never forget the day he had me to the White House after I won the election. We had so much to discuss—the war, the Soviets, and all that. But one of the first things he did was to take me upstairs to show me the bedroom safe, where he kept God knows what, and the recording contraptions that [John] Kennedy had installed under the beds. Johnson got down on the floor, lifted the bedspread, and waved his hand under the bed. 'Dick,' he said, 'they are voice activated.' "

"That must have been an unbelievable scene," I said.

"It really was. He was the one who told me to save every scrap of paper I so much as dribbled on as president. Johnson was obsessed with recording everything. He had every room taped. We know what my problems were with that crap, but Kennedy was the one to put it in, and Johnson worshiped it."

He twirled his pen in the air. "You know, Johnson called the bombing halt to swing the vote for [Vice President Hubert] Humphrey. The Russians were terrified that I'd get elected, so they stepped in to bring the North Vietnamese to the table. He was a schemer, boy, but a pretty good one." A smile crossed his face; he clearly admired Johnson's manipulative talents. "Johnson was a good politician, and I mean 'good' in the sense that he knew what he wanted and usually got it. He was another one who fell into the presidency. And of course after the Kennedy thing there was no way he was going to lose in '64. That was strictly a sympathy vote, and our party was so fractured that we probably would have lost anyway. [Republican candidate Barry] Goldwater was a disaster, but I remember [Herbert] Hoover told me in '64 that with Goldwater, who was *very* weak, it might serve us well to get the party's extremism out of its system. Maybe he was right.

"But when it came to winning, Johnson stopped at nothing. He had guts, but not enough to run again in '68. He left me a mess, but at least he fought the goddamned North Vietnamese. A lesser president may have packed it in.

"He did civil rights, which was his one big achievement. But his expansion of the welfare state in this country was unforgivable. All of that crap about the Great Society was just an excuse to pour money into all the programs and the new ones he created to satisfy his liberal supporters. Don't get me wrong; Johnson was a true-believing liberal. But much of what he did he did for purely political reasons. Johnson was a totally political animal. He told me once, 'People don't support you because they like you. You can count on a person's support only when you can do something for him or to him.' He lived by that rule.

"After he left office, he was bitter, cynical, and hard. As I've said, it's difficult not to be, but Johnson was so sensitive about how he would be portrayed historically that he was just totally shattered when he left. Johnson was not a good man, but he made decisions from his gut, and he tried."

Nixon leaned back in his chair. "There," he said to me, "that's your political lesson for the day."

His thoughts about his more recent contemporaries were less historical judgments than personal opinions. Since Ford's, Carter's, and Reagan's presidencies came after his own, he critiqued them through a finer lens and with less generosity, particularly based upon how they treated him as a former president. Nixon's own policies and achievements would survive or fall depending upon what these men did in the office. His frustrations with being out of power, and with having to watch his successors act in ways he would not have, consumed him. His assessments of these men reflected this disappointment, agitation, and anger and reinforced his own notion that he had been a superior president.

"Poor [Gerald] Ford," he said on July 8, 1992, after a phone conversation with his successor. "You won't even believe why he called me. He was concerned about some presidential photos and about having me sign them. Imagine! He calls me for *that!* Of course he's busy making speeches for big money, like the rest of them." He paused, settling on a point he wanted to emphasize. "You know, I have never taken a dime for a speech since 1952. Of course no one gives me credit for that. Ford was really the first to take money. Roosevelt and Kennedy died; Truman, Eisenhower, Johnson, and I never did. But since Ford, they are out there accumulating a fortune by selling the office—or their experiences in the office, anyway. I know it's tempting, but it's just not right. Besides, when Ford talks, does anyone pay any attention?"

"Well, sir, he did assume the office in a very difficult way and had no choice but to be a steward of existing policies," I said, trying to get a more sympathetic view from him.

"True," he replied. "I don't mean to be so down on him. He was put in a hell of a position. He didn't even want to be president, never mind getting it *that* way. And of course the press and everybody else was going to be rough on him because he was my choice." He hesitated. "No, I feel for the guy. It's not fair to judge him by the same standards. But you know, to see him out there now using the office just doesn't sit well with me."

His disappointment in Ford intensified when he learned that Ford would be attending former secretary of state Henry Kissinger's seventieth birthday party in mid-1993. On April 27, a disgusted Nixon said, "[*Washington Post* board chairman Katharine] Graham will be there. Imagine the nerve of him to invite me too! I will *not* sit in a room with her. Why should I? I'm a pretty forgiving person, but not when it comes to that crowd. Luckily, I can't go anyway because I need to go to [international-affairs expert] Dimitri [Simes]'s wedding on the same day. You know, I would have gone for the first ten minutes because it was for Henry, but when he said Graham would be there—well, forget it! And look at Ford—what is he thinking about, going to the goddamned thing?"

Fortunately for Ford, he was in the presidency for only a limited time, which spared him the full Nixon wrath. Jimmy Carter, however, who won campaigning on the "integrity" he implied Nixon lacked, was an easy and extensive target.

"I can't believe Carter didn't show up at our library opening," he said on July 23, 1990. The Richard Nixon Library and Birthplace in Yorba Linda, California, had been dedicated four days earlier, with former presidents Ford and Reagan and President Bush in attendance. Carter, however, pleading scheduling conflicts, did not attend. Nixon was angry. "Is that the pettiest damn thing you ever heard of?"

I had been working for him for only three weeks and did not know him very well, but I felt compelled to ask, "Sir, have you ever been to *his* library?"

He looked at me, shocked by the question. "Well, no. But that's not right either."

Carter was in the unenviable position of being not just the first full-term president to succeed Nixon but the first Democrat as well. Nixon resented, though understood, the political advantage Carter enjoyed in 1976 by virtue of Nixon's downfall. By showcasing his own moral integrity, Carter had called attention to Nixon's storied moral deficit. With Nixon's tactics discredited as Machiavellian evil, Carter had positioned himself as an idealist who would restore America's virtue and save it from the debris of the Nixon presidency.

"Carter is one of those types who tries to be morally superior but does such small, petty things that it becomes almost hypocritical," he said on April 1, 1992. Carter had been a guest of President Bush's at the White House that morning, prompting Nixon's comments.

"They weren't discussing the Russians, were they?" he asked me.

"Not from what the news reports indicate," I answered.

"Good," he replied, then paused. "Why does Bush invite Carter there? He's a true partisan. He's not there to help Bush." He paused again. "Here is Carter, holier than thou with that toothy grin, but he turns around to slam anyone he passes judgment on, including me. So much for generosity. Look, I understand that he had to do it in '76 and even '80, though to a lesser extent. But to continue to beat the horse after all this time is too much."

In early October 1992, Nixon was concerned that Carter intended to visit Russia when he planned to be there. Several months before, Nixon had taken the lead on the issue of aiding Russia to help solidify the democratic and free-market gains made since the collapse of communism there in 1991. Because of his constant and public prodding, the Bush administration moved forward with an aid program, for which Nixon got the credit. He was protective of the issue and resented Carter's infringement.

"I see that Carter may be there when we are there," he said on October 3. "He's probably going over to build outhouses in Central Asia." He stopped, reconsidered his attitude, and subtracted the sarcasm. "No, that's overdoing it. Look, although I have problems with Carter personally and politically, he has done some very decent things as a former president. While Ford is playing golf, which he should do if that's his idea of retirement, Carter is out there banging nails into houses for the poor. At least Carter puts his money where his mouth is. He practices what he preaches, and for that I give him credit. Basically, he is a decent guy; he was just wrong for the presidency."

"Do you think he was too honest to make an effective president?" I asked.

He smiled. "That's a *very* interesting question. No, I don't know. I think he was too trusting and too naïve, particularly when it came to the Russians."

Carter's involvement in international affairs irritated Nixon immensely. He considered Carter a disruptive intrusion upon other countries' political processes and upon our own in his role as a freelancing and unofficial secretary of state.

Three days after his fellow Democrat Bill Clinton was elected, Carter was called upon by the president-elect, infuriating Nixon. "I see that Clinton intends to use Carter as an informal adviser. He's seeking to validate Carter's foreign policy and distinguish his own 'New Democrat' style. If he's calling on Carter, he won't call on me."

A month later, his agitation intensified when Carter criticized Bush's humanitarian military intervention in Somalia. "Did you hear what he said?" Nixon exclaimed. "I cannot believe it. He said Bush wouldn't have this problem in Somalia now if he had paid attention to Africa in the first place. Goddamn him. He's so irresponsible; he pissed on the Persian Gulf intervention in the middle of the war—and now *this?*" He shook his head. "Clinton indicated that he wants to see all of the former presidents. What bullshit. Carter is already beating his way in the White House and at the same time beating down on Bush, who already lost, for God's sake."

Several weeks later, he discussed Carter's appearance on television without admitting that he had actually seen it. "Mrs. Nixon saw Carter on C-SPAN, and they remarked that he was the best former president because of his work on human rights. Now, please. He does do good work, but let's not confuse our priorities. Nations' interests come first. Then, once those are secure, you can concern yourself with the human rights. Otherwise, you have a situation where idealism runs wild and prevents effective policy."

He leveled his criticism at Carter's role as a foreign policy intermediary. "I can't imagine that the Bush crowd—or even the Clinton crowd—appreciates Carter butting in to all of these places when they are pursuing their own policies. The official U.S. line is one thing, and here is Carter prancing around with his own line. It's confusing for the rest of the world and tempting for ruthless types to take advantage. Dictators around the world can thumb their noses at the U.S. and then try to placate us by waltzing Carter around. They use him. It's dangerous, not just for him but for our foreign policy. It only works when the administration sanctions his visits and then uses him for its own ends. That way, they can deflect the unpleasant side of whatever they want to accomplish onto Carter, who is acting in an unofficial capacity. That's the only way I can see appreciating what he does around the world. You know, he sits in Atlanta or goes gallivanting around the world saying he is monitoring thirty-two wars and intends to monitor elections in Panama, and the media love it! It's ridiculous. The United States already has a secretary of state; we do not need a freelancing one."

His final comments about Carter came on September 21, 1993, when we discussed the massive Chinese campaign to host the 2000 Olympics in Beijing. Nixon felt strongly that despite its human rights violations, China should be given the opportunity to host the Olympics as a way of further opening the door to the pressures for democratic freedom. "The Olympic Committee should give it to the Chinese. Any way we can, we should open them up. I don't believe in abusing the Olympics for political reasons, like Carter did in '80. It's sort of a small thing to do and doesn't amount to anything. Where else are they going to have them? Australia or some other neutral place? Please. I see that the *Times* is against it, but they're wrong. Carter's heart was in the right place, but I think he just picked the wrong fight."

Carter attracted a curious blend of Nixon's admiration and aversion. He respected Carter's integrity, idealism, and sincerity; he disdained his politics, naïveté, and what he perceived as haughty self-righteousness. Incredibly, Nixon saw himself in Carter: a good man led down an incorrect path. For Nixon, it was the path of integrity overrun by the politics of power; for Carter, it was the path of integrity crippled by the realities of power.

Nixon's view of Ronald Reagan was equally as complex a mix of respect, admiration, criticism, and envy. Reagan was closer to him philosophically than any of his other successors, and although he agreed with his policies most of the time, Nixon harbored some marginal resentment against Reagan's enduring popularity. Nixon, like Reagan, had a portfolio of extraordinary foreign policy achievements. Nixon, like Reagan, had an ambitious and often controversial domestic agenda. Nixon, like Reagan, experienced economic recession and rebounded. Nixon, like Reagan, won a landslide reelection. But Nixon, unlike Reagan, suffered a devastating end to his presidency and a more unforgiving historical judgment. Nixon believed he made Reagan possible and therefore felt entitled to some of Reagan's epic glow.

"Reagan is one of the most decent men I have known," he said on January 27, 1991. "He's a good man, a great communicator, as they say, and he made a fine president. He gave us leadership when we really needed it. He was so damn *good*—with the press, with the people, with the Russians, with everybody. But I have mixed feelings on Reagan," he said and, knowing that my political views were grounded in the Reagan presidency, threw a cautious glance in my direction. "He lifted the spirit of the country and he was right-on on the arms buildup, but he ruled from his gut instead of his brain. Now that's not necessarily a bad thing; it worked for Truman. But it was fortunate that he had some very good advisers around him because, frankly, by the end of the second term he wasn't nearly as effective. It wasn't his fault, but his faculties had already begun to decline. We joke about how he fell asleep in a Cabinet meeting, but that's no way to be president. I feel for the guy. He was a very good leader at a time of great events." His voice trailed off.

"You know, as much as I think that Reagan absolutely did the right thing on the arms buildup, I cannot stomach those who go overboard on it and say that that was the only thing responsible for the collapse of communism. We, of course, were going after the Russians that way years before. We fought for the bombers and all the rest. I'm not trying to minimize Reagan, but he was only part of what brought down communism. Communism would have collapsed by its own weight anyway. The Reagan buildup probably accelerated the process because the Russians were forced to match us. But I think the credit belongs to *all* of the cold war presidents, from Truman to Bush."

He paused. "The only reason Reagan went into Grenada was because of Beirut." He stopped and assumed a mocking tone.

"And he proclaimed, 'We rolled back the Communists!' In Grenada? The size of Whittier, California? Now, Reagan had some good foreign policy accomplishments, but Grenada wasn't one of them. He shouldn't trumpet that any more than he has to."

He gave me another sideways glance. "You know, for all of Reagan's talk about 'getting the government off our backs and out of our wallets,' which *was* a great line, his policies weren't very compassionate. It was like capitalism gone hog-wild. He was on to the right philosophy, but his tactics were cold. His critics said that he wanted to throw old people out on the street; well, that's totally inaccurate and unfair, but all of this supply-side stuff his people pushed didn't work. The government has to help those who are truly needy; I'm not talking about those who abuse the system and collect welfare checks under eight different names, but I do believe that we have a responsibility to give a temporary—and I mean *very* temporary—hand to those who really need it. I didn't get that sense from the Reagan policies. All of that go-go-go capitalism seemed to forget about compassion."

He looked down at his hands. "Look, Reagan was the right president at the right time. He did what he thought was best." He looked back up. "As we all did."

On May 12, 1992, Reagan paid Nixon a visit at Nixon's New Jersey office. His Secret Service detail preceded him, and employees from other offices in the building poured out into the lobby to catch a glimpse of the two former presidents together. Before Nixon could hand me the newspaper he was carrying, the Secret Service announced that Reagan's limousine had arrived. Nixon threw the newspaper down on the closest table and hurried into the hallway to greet his successor. Nixon and Reagan entered the office shoulder to shoulder.

"Ron!" I heard Nixon bellow. "Hi! Well, come on in."

"Dick," Reagan replied, "this is the first time I've been to this office. It's great to be here."

They retreated to Nixon's office, and after a one-hour private meeting the two former presidents emerged laughing and joking. Nixon turned to Reagan, and gesturing toward his small staff, he said, "You know, Ron, most of my staff is Irish."

Reagan smiled and crossed his arms. "Well, being Irish, I have a few anecdotes to share." He recounted some humorous stories and then began to regale us with an Irish limerick but stopped halfway through, unable to remember the next line. "Why did I get into this?" he asked, and Nixon gently reached out and took his arm.

"Ron," he said, "would you mind taking some pictures with my staff? I know they would really appreciate it."

Reagan was clearly relieved and delighted to have a diversion. Nixon introduced me. "Ron, this is Monica Crowley. She's one of those rare Ivy Leaguers to come out a conservative! She was too young to vote for you, but she knows all about you!"

Reagan laughed heartily, and the three of us posed for the camera. Reagan was, as I expected, gracious, funny, and warm. Nixon, who did not particularly want to compete with Reagan in his own office, let Reagan be Reagan. When he departed, however, Nixon was frank and a little melancholy.

"We had a good talk. He's more interested in reliving the past, which I really don't like to do, but I got him to talk a little bit about some serious issues. He said he always 'trusted' [former Soviet president Mikhail] Gorbachev. Imagine using that term: 'trust.' Leaders don't 'trust' each other; they are out to protect their nation's interests. He said, 'We arm because we don't trust each other.' It's so naïve. He also told me that he had suggested to Gorbachev that the Soviet Union could come together again. Now that isn't just a misreading of history but incredibly irresponsible. I'm sure Lithuania would love to hear that! Reagan is living in a dream world if he thinks that the Soviet Union can be put back together, and Gorbachev must be delusional.

"But you know, Reagan couldn't have been nicer. I tried to push him in the right direction about Gorbachev and show him that Yeltsin was the one who represented real democratic reform, but he was just being used by this whole Gorbachev trip. He just doesn't see it.

"He does look great, though. He told me he exercises out on the ranch every day. Of course he didn't go through what I went through in the Watergate period, from April 15 to August 8 and 9, the resignation—Watergate, day in and day out. It was rough. Reagan, of course, had the assassination attempt, which was a tremendous physical challenge. Mine may have been rougher because it was emotional. But Reagan just has such a positive outlook that I think that is half the battle."

Nixon looked at the ceiling and then back at me. "He lost his way there, in front of the staff, telling that joke. His memory is not good. I hope they can do something for him. I really do."

Nixon enjoyed Reagan's company for the humor, camaraderie, and goodwill he brought to a visit. They were no longer political competitors but friends, Republican warriors who seemed to belong to a different era. They shared the same generation and many of the same experiences and a spirit borne of a genuine dedication to their country. It was a symbiotic relationship: they looked to each other for the fellowship only the other could provide.

Reagan's condition continued to deteriorate, however, prompting great sadness and empathy in Nixon. In preemptive strikes against those who might also criticize Nixon's advancing age, he attacked viciously those who criticized Reagan's. On November 27, 1992, Clinton visited Reagan, and Nixon remarked scornfully, "He saw Reagan, and the press was really hard on him, saying he was confused and rambling. Why don't they leave the poor guy alone? So he's not as sharp as he used to be. So what? He's eighty-something years old and had all the pressures of being the president of the United States. Let's see if these clowns in the press have it all together at his age!" Nixon was furious that Reagan's deterioration became fodder for a press still reeling from the effects of Reagan's two terms in office. "They are really hitting below the belt on this one," he said. "Criticize his policies, not him."

Before Nixon passed away, he met with Reagan two more times. The first visit was on December 3, 1992, in London, where both were scheduled to give speeches. Two days later, when he returned to New Jersey, he summoned me with a voice filled with sadness.

"Monica, something has happened to Reagan," he said, shaking his head. "I don't know if it's Alzheimer's or what, but he just sits there without speaking a word. I thought his hearing aid wasn't on, but he's just not there. [Atlantic Richfield Company chairman] Lod Cook excused it by saying that he's got jet lag, but of course that's not the case. Nancy [Reagan] talked eighty percent of the time. In fact, all Reagan said was that Clinton 'seemed like a nice guy.' That's the Reagan school of politics based on flattery. Flatter, flatter," he said, waving his hand around. "And Nancy didn't say anything about the Clintons. I'm sure she could give Hillary [Rodham Clinton] a run for her money! Wouldn't *that* be an interesting meeting of the minds!" he said with a wide grin.

"Sir," I said, "if Reagan is really that bad, he must not do any more public events, or they should at least be highly controlled. I think that people should remember him as he was."

"I agree. You know, Mrs. Nixon brings this up with me on occasion. She has so much pain, between her arthritis and emphysema, so she really feels for him. But she may have a point—to stop before you get like that. I don't think it applies to me, not yet anyway, but if it ever does, I'm counting on all of you to stop me."

Nixon's empathy was even more pronounced after he met Reagan for the last time, on September 23, 1993, for lunch in New York. Nixon sat silently across from me in the office for several long minutes before speaking. "Well, Reagan looks good physically, but he is worse mentally than he was the last time. He had a great appetite and loves his desserts. He had three! My God, if I ate one dessert, I'd gain weight! Nancy told him that he has to lose ten pounds. He said, incidentally, that he hates tomatoes; he said when he was a kid, he ate some bad ones out of a patch and ever since can't stand them. That was just about the only thing he said all afternoon. He has great difficulty tracking his thoughts. He begins a story, and Nancy prompts him. It's just very, very sad. You're in his company but feel alone because he is just not there."

He looked down. "Aging is a cruel, cruel process. The problem with Alzheimer's is that usually the body is in such good condition that it becomes a prison for the deteriorating mind. It's awful to go through, although they say that the patient isn't even aware, thank God. It must be awful to watch it happen to somebody else—especially Reagan. I was with him, but it wasn't Reagan."

He paused. "If I ever get that way, God help me."

Reagan's decline prompted Nixon to work harder and longer to maintain his own mental agility. For Nixon, aging was inevitable, but mental decline did not have to be. Immediately after a visit with Reagan, he read more and memorized more, for he feared not only his own deterioration but the pity of those around him. "Exercising the brain" he called it and worked feverishly against the forces of nature he saw ravaging Reagan's mind. The self-discipline Nixon had cultivated throughout his life served him particularly well at the end and led him to a greater appreciation of his own good fortune. His sympathy for Reagan colored a more positive assessment of Reagan's presidency than he might otherwise have had, but he counted Reagan as a friend and a good, if not great, leader.

Of all the cold war presidents Nixon evaluated, however, John F. Kennedy was by far the most often discussed. Although he professed not to be concerned with Kennedy, the name came up in conversation at least once every few weeks. As with most of Kennedy's predecessors and successors, Nixon harbored toward Kennedy a curious blend of admiration, exasperation, esteem, and healthy rivalry. But unlike his opinions of most of the others, his views of Kennedy were complicated by the fact that he competed with Kennedy's ghost. Since untimely death enhances the memory, Nixon knew that it was a losing battle. He did not, however, retreat.

"The 1960 election was probably the greatest election of this century because the candidates were both outstanding," he said on September 4, 1992. The presidential election continued to spiral toward a Clinton victory, causing Nixon to reflect on his

Democratic challenger in 1960. He often referred to Kennedy and himself as "the candidates."

"Bush is down by eight points now. That's too many. Remember in '60 there were never more than two or three points between the candidates in the closing weeks. The debates were crucial. As you know, those who watched the first one on TV thought Kennedy had won while those who heard it on the radio thought I had won because I was better prepared. Appearance made one hell of a difference. Of course that debate began the enormous role of television in national politics.

"I read an article in *Time* recently where the author says something to the effect that Nixon and Kennedy spent all of this time talking about two lumps of rock in the Pacific: Quemoy and Ma-tsu. Now he just missed the whole point. China was still expansionary, and we had to send the proper signal. Even Kennedy changed his position. What most people forget is that Kennedy and I were a lot closer on the foreign policy issues than probably any other candidates this century. It was good for the race and good for the country because it was such a crucial period during the cold war. A softhead on the Russians would never have gotten elected."

He scowled. "Joe Kennedy, the old man, was a tyrant and a real moral scoundrel. He engineered the West Virginia project that destroyed [Hubert] Humphrey and of course the Texas and Illinois vote fraud in 1960. Mrs. Nixon still says we should order a recount!" He laughed. "Yes, headstones were voting in Cook County."

"Did you *really* believe that a recount would have been too disruptive to the country?" I asked.

"Yes, I really did," he replied. "I just thought, 'Let's get on with it.' Instead, we got Vietnam and Watergate—talk about disruptions! I know that it's a parlor game among academics to debate whether there would have been a Vietnam and a Watergate had I been elected in 1960. Vietnam? Absolutely—only done the right way. And Watergate? No way. The cast of characters would have been different, and the circumstances wouldn't have been there. But anyway, the point is irrelevant. History is history.

"The point is that the 1960 election was a turning point. We had two outstanding candidates. We had televised debates that changed the course of politics. We had the cold war. And we had one of the closest elections ever. Nineteen sixty was legendary. Besides, it was my first go at the office and the most satisfying."

When I asked why, he replied, "Well, I would have to say that my first run for the Congress in 1946 was the most satisfying of all of my campaigns only because it was so new. But 1960 was my first run for the presidency, and I was completely on my own. I had Eisenhower, but only in a limited way. It was fresh and exciting, and Kennedy was a fine opponent. The race was clean, of course, until the results started coming in from Cook County! Nineteen sixty-eight and 1972 were much different. Of course I *won* those elections, so what the hell—they were satisfying. But Vietnam was always there, haunting everybody. And the assassinations and social mess made it a very complicated time."

Nixon's life and career were so interwoven with those of the Kennedys that his remarks about them were just as much remarks about himself. When he commented about the Kennedys' activities or behavior, he was often implying that his own had been superior, either politically or morally or both. When he discussed their political ambitions, he was often highlighting his own. When he spoke about Kennedy the man, he vaunted himself, and when he commented on Kennedy the president, he strove to emerge greater by comparison. It was both a conscious and an unconscious exercise. Nixon was not a jealous man, but he did to a degree resent that Kennedy's legacy had been enshrined and his own had been tarnished by different tragic twists of fate.

"To be fair," he had said earlier, on May 15, 1992, "Kennedy really wasn't in there long enough to have an effect. But what can we say he accomplished? The Bay of Pigs was an irresponsible disaster."

I interrupted him. "Have you seen the transcripts from the Cuban missile crisis?"

He claimed that he had not. "Countless passages have been removed," I said. "They have released only a very sanitized version."

Nixon was incredulous. "I knew they deleted some, but not to that extent." He paused. "Well, they want to protect that Kennedy image. I know the curses were removed. You know what a big deal they made out of the whole 'expletive deleted' thing on our tapes. That was nothing compared to the words the Kennedys used! Jack was not nearly as upstanding or honorable as his supporters would have you believe."

He turned his attention back to the Kennedy presidency. "His conduct of East-West relations was disastrous. He was right to send the first combat troops to Vietnam, but the gradualist approach [Defense Secretary Robert] McNamara advised was horrendous. All he did was make a mess of things. Now look," he said, holding up his hands for emphasis, "every president makes mistakes. Kennedy was no exception. But the fact that they gloss over those mistakes when they emphasize everybody else's is simply not fair. Oh well, you know how the liberals are about Kennedy. They love that Kennedy mystique."

His disregard for the Kennedy presidency was outweighed only by his contempt for the family's behavior. "The Kennedys were not admirable people," he said. "They simply were not nice. The legend is that Jack was always gracious, charming, dashing," he said, putting his nose in the air. "Bull. He spit on waiters and ignored or screamed at the help. I remember attending a dinner once and watching Bobby—who was the smartest and also the meanest—throw his meal on the floor and right at a waiter because he didn't like it. Bebe knew the Kennedys, and they used to socialize when they were in Key Biscayne. All of them used to treat the help like crap, and I mean they were *mean*. Most of the help was Cuban, and they treated them like they didn't exist. Bobby was the worst. He illegally bugged more people—and started it—than anyone. He was a bastard."

In early 1992, Bill Clinton's candidacy prompted Nixon to compare Clinton with his own 1960 Democratic challenger in a most unflattering way. "The charges of womanizing against Clinton are of course true," he said on January 17. "It could be a serious liability. But then again, it wasn't for Kennedy. In 1960, though, no one knew because the media protected him. I knew some of it at the time, but of course we couldn't use it. Bebe told me more later, and [Florida senator] George Smathers used to—you know—fix him up. Kennedy was so careless about it, just like Clinton. Kennedy got away with it; I don't think Clinton can. Although he has that same . . ." He paused and pursed his lips, emitting a very poor Massachusetts accent. "Viga." He laughed at his own mocking interpretation.

"You know, it's interesting. Joe Kennedy was a conservative, and I recall one time during the 1960 campaign we were on a train together, and Joe said, 'Dick, you know if Jack weren't running, I'd be for you.' When I noticed a striking woman next to him, he just shrugged and said, 'My niece'! They were really something. They thought because of who they were that they could get away with anything."

"And they usually did," I said.

Nixon smiled. "I know. It's an uphill battle trying to make the point, though. I remember going to Bobby's service and hearing Teddy's talk. It was a good speech, but all of these clichés—'ask why not, not why'—were all bull. But they keep making it into something. And Teddy looked like a matinée idol. Now, I'm sorry to say, he has completely hit the skids."

Nixon knew that his views on the family seemed rather unholy, given the assassinations of both John and Robert Kennedy. He sought, however, to expose the truth about who they were beyond the glare of political celebrity. Smashing the legend was part of his agenda, not out of vindictiveness but out of a desire to level the historical playing field. Assassination had robbed John Kennedy of his life and of a fair, balanced historical judgment. Watergate had robbed Nixon of the same opportunity for a fair assessment, although Nixon himself had propelled it. Kennedy's death, though tragic, was part of the mystique Nixon sought to destroy. His comments on the assassination were prompted by the release of Oliver Stone's movie *JFK* in late 1991.

On December 23, I informed Nixon that I had seen the film. He was shocked. "Why," he asked, "would you give Oliver Stone seven dollars of your money?"

Curiosity had overtaken me when the release of the movie became a major news event. The mysteries surrounding the assassination and Oliver Stone's well-publicized assault on the Warren Commission findings were fascinating to me.

Nixon removed his glasses, sat down in the corner of his office, and asked me for my reaction to the film.

I told him that Stone's thesis is that Kennedy did not die at the hands of a lone assassin but as a victim of a coup d'état carried out by elements in the military and the CIA that opposed Kennedy's plans to withdraw from Vietnam and end the cold war. The coup succeeded. Johnson, who favored intervention, assumed the presidency and, as planned, ordered the continuing escalation in Vietnam, thereby condemning the United States to ten years of war in Southeast Asia and decades of cold war. The success of this coup meant twenty-five years of what Stone implies was "covert government," conspiratorial control of the government by the CIA and the Pentagon ruling in the interests of the military-industrial complex.

Nixon's jaw dropped. "No. He can't be serious about all of this? My God! That is the most outrageous theory I have ever heard in my life. And Stone is going around peddling this goddamned crap? Outrageous."

He sat in silence for a few minutes and continued in a deeper voice. "The Warren Commission findings—that there was a single assassin—came out, and there has never been any solid evidence to prove otherwise. All of these wild theories—to the effect that the CIA was involved, or that there were other gunmen around the grassy knoll, or that the bullet ricocheted at impossible angles around the car and through Kennedy—are absurd. [Lee Harvey] Oswald was a nut; there's no doubt about that. But if Stone or anyone else can show me solid proof—and I mean *solid* proof—that he acted with others—never mind the crazy CIA-conspiracy stuff—then OK. Otherwise, he should stop damaging history in this country with his off-the-wall self-serving anti-Vietnam films."

Nixon was furious. Stone's interpretation of the assassination, including an oblique implication that Nixon knew about the master plot, was reckless and historically irresponsible. Stone claimed artistic license and never denied that the film was a blend of fact and fiction, but the problem, as Nixon saw it, was that those who were not fully informed about this period would walk away from the movie believing it was historical truth.

"It seems to me, from what you told me, that Stone, even though he is trying to glorify Kennedy, is exploiting his death in ways the family has spent all of these years trying to avoid. Grisly obsession does nothing to help Kennedy. What's even worse, I think that his silly Vietnam theme damages Kennedy as well. Only Clinton's generation thinks Kennedy looks responsible by being portrayed as willing to bail out of Vietnam. Now Kennedy's decision to stay in looks better and better. And as you know, the clean withdrawal he was supposedly planning was politically unthinkable at the time. There was just no way."

"This film was not about the assassination at all," I replied, "but rather its sole aim was to vindicate Kennedy on Vietnam. To claim that Kennedy wanted to exit Vietnam after committing the initial troops is wrong. He *was* a cold warrior. For Stone to take that away from him is to distort who Kennedy really was."

"Absolutely right," he said. "It's a well-crafted deception."

"How many in these audiences realize that they are being deceived?"

"Not one," he replied. "This movie is the product of a generation wanting to feel right about its conduct during the war. Vietnam propaganda—dishonest and outrageous! They come after me for Vietnam when Kennedy was responsible for committing the troops. He was right to do it, but let's not forget that he did it."

Two hours later I found a dictated memorandum on my desk regarding Oliver Stone's December 20 *New York Times* column "Who is Rewriting History?" In the column, Stone asserted erroneously that Kennedy refused to send combat troops to Vietnam. In his memorandum to me, Nixon argued that since Kennedy committed the first sixteen thousand troops to Vietnam and since there were over four hundred casualties there prior to his assassination, Stone had his history wrong.

Three days later he handed me a *Los Angeles Times* article, entitled "Why Bother to Conspire Against JFK?". He had scribbled "Monica: Note" and circled the last two paragraphs, which described Kennedy's decisions to send in the initial troops, sponsor the "strategic hamlet" program, launch a series of offensive and covert measures in the south and north, and his failure to entertain the possibility of a negotiated settlement.

Nixon's silent campaign against the movie continued when *Time* published a list of the best movies of 1991 in its January 6, 1992, issue. He circled the paragraph touting *JFK* and wrote underneath it that *Time* owned a piece of the movie. And when *The Wall Street Journal* editorialized that the movie was a dangerous distortion of historical fact, Nixon scribbled above the title of the op-ed article, "Bingo!" The film and its attendant spectacle disturbed him insofar as it warped not only Kennedy's legacy but popular culture's perception of the entire Vietnam period. Although Nixon believed he should have been president in 1961, he agreed with Kennedy's decision to intervene in Southeast Asia. Any attempt to turn back that history was nothing more than a work of fiction.

Above all, however, Nixon was particularly sensitive to any implication that he was envious of John Kennedy, his enshrined memory, or his privileged background. Nixon honored his own humble background, got political mileage out of it, and considered himself a better person because of it. Nixon was "one of us," a self-made political phenomenon. Where Kennedy offered the nation a model of success bestowed, Nixon offered it one of success earned.

"I can't stand it when I hear people say, 'Well, Nixon envied Kennedy.' I never envied Kennedy," he sighed on January 16, 1992, irritated by the uninformed and misdirected psychoanalysis. "Where do they get this stuff? He was brought up one way; I was brought up another. He was a formidable opponent. That's all I ever worried about. We were cordial members of the Congress and ran against each other for president. Our paths crossed a lot, sometimes friendly, sometimes as adversaries, and that was it."

Whether or not Nixon had any real envy of Kennedy or succeeded in burying it, his dismissal of the entire question pointed
to an awareness that their legacies were forever entangled. He
wanted history to record it as a positive competition, not as the
fierce, coarse relationship as so many had succeeded in portray-
ing it. The worst flaws in Kennedy's character forced Nixon to
examine his own more closely. His condemnation of Kennedy's
behavior was perhaps a veiled comparison with his own but
very different deficits. Nixon's mistakes had long been emphasized and his virtues ignored; the opposite was true of Kennedy.
Nixon's remarks about Kennedy were an attempt to rectify the
imbalance.

In his assessments of his predecessors and successors, Nixon
saw much of himself. Their campaigns and policies, successes
and failures, thoughts and actions, and idealism and pragmatism—elements of every presidency—gave Nixon solace as he
considered how history would record his own. Reflecting on the
others offered him relief; not only had they risen like he, but
many had fallen as he had, if not as hard or as far. Ambition and
ability had delivered them to the peak of power; events made
them leaders. When he defined the attributes of great leadership,
he was applying them to himself and to the others, knowing that
he would emerge as a superior president by comparison. Some
leaders had more of the qualities than others; he believed that he
had them all. By outlining the elements of great leadership and
drawing parallels to himself, he wanted the right to be considered in the ranks of those who had achieved greatness by enter-
ing the arena and making an enduring difference. He believed
that he had earned that right, and he made his case.

History, he often said, has its own momentum. His judgment
of other leaders was an attempt to prompt a corrective historical judgment of his own presidency, not to excuse his mistakes
but to place them in context. When he said of Reagan that he
"did what he thought was best, as we all did," he was saying
that *he* had done his best. Mistakes, both profound and minor,
were not exclusive to his presidency. Judge all presidents, he was

pleading, by the same high and realistic standard. His objective was not to tear down the presidencies of those who went before or came after but to make history see that they were inhabited by real, imperfect men who had tried. Nixon was asking for history not to pardon him but to grant him an evenhandedness that so far he had been denied.

PART II

THE 1992 PRESIDENTIAL ELECTION

$\bigwedge$nyone running for office wants to win," Nixon said on November 4, 1992, the day after the election, "but I'd rather lose having run a campaign that had vision than win having run one that did not."

The 1992 presidential election was the twentieth and last of Richard Nixon's life and perhaps the most disheartening. He could not remember a campaign that so lacked the vision and the meaning necessary to inspire great messages and elevate the voting public above the trenches of partisan politics. Nixon was a pragmatic idealist. He ran campaigns that dealt in the legitimate and the dubious, but he always tried to run campaigns that maintained some kind of transcendent meaning for the future. Nixon believed that the races for the presidency should give the voters something to be for instead of something to be simply against. Presidential aspirants must always try to enlighten, act on a grand scale, and project the vision and wisdom required to capture the imagination, and not just the votes, of those they seek to lead. Too much attention was paid in 1992 to the mechanics of the campaign and not enough to what was being said.

"Everyone was talking, and no one was listening," Nixon continued. "A campaign without a profound message means that the candidate is running for the sake of winning and not necessarily for what he could accomplish. A hollow campaign may get votes, but it will inspire no one, and chances are that person will not be reelected. This is what happened to Bush. And although Clinton's and Perot's campaigns were pretty shallow, Bush was the incumbent, and his campaign had to soar. It didn't, and he lost. It's as simple as that."

All campaigns are designed to win elections. Good campaigns, however, teach the candidate what the voters want and how best to represent their interests in office, and in turn voters learn what kind of leader the candidate will be. Nixon believed that the tactics of modern presidential campaigns disrupted both these processes. Candidates talk *to* the people instead of *with* them, rely too heavily on distorted polls and media consultants, and remain insulated from most of the people. The voters, meanwhile, usually hear only the snippets of a candidate's message that have already been filtered and hyperanalyzed by the media. Both the candidate and the voters receive warped interpretations of what the other wants, sees, and expects. A choice between candidates becomes a choice between stylized and often misleading images.

Nixon recoiled from the distortions of modern campaigning. Having run for the Congress twice, the Senate once, the vice presidency twice, the governorship of California once, and the presidency three times, he considered image making a necessary evil. "In the television age, you cannot win unless you present a media-friendly image. I always hated that, and I suppose it showed. I was never what they call media friendly," he laughed on September 15, 1992. "But to me, the image was secondary to the message. I never wanted to put out an image that wasn't me just because, according to some pollster, it played well in Peoria or Los Angeles. I learned that lesson the hard way in that first debate with Kennedy in '60. I was thin and pale because I had been sick, and it didn't even occur to me that I would look ghostly on the tube without makeup. I never even bothered thinking about that stuff because I was so concerned with what I would say. I wanted people to vote for me because I had the best vision for America's future, not because I looked sharp. That was my mistake. Kennedy was tanned and fit and knew how to play to the camera. More important, he knew how *important* it was to play to the camera. I figured my message would carry the day. I was wrong. Sometimes the image is just as important as the message, and sometimes it overrides the message. And I think that is a shame."

The 1992 presidential campaign was, for Nixon, completely devoid of vision and reduced to the myopic political minutiae that the pollsters indicated were popular. The result was a campaign that demonstrated Americans' great dissatisfaction with politics as usual. With three voters in four believing that the United States was on the wrong track, candidates Bill Clinton and H. Ross Perot ran as outsiders, and even the status quo incumbent, President George Bush, was forced to cast himself as the candidate for change. According to the polls, distrust of government was at an all-time high. Less than 40 percent of Americans had at least a fair amount of confidence in the federal government and believed that it created more problems than it solved. Public dissatisfaction was so strong in 1992 that Clinton and Perot fed upon it, claiming that America was in the throes of crisis and decline. Clinton's answer was a vast expansion of government; Perot's was plebiscitary democracy, which takes power away from elected representatives and puts it directly in the hands of the people. Voters responded to both these themes, mistaking agendas for vision.

Nixon observed the campaigns of the candidates with disgust, apathy, frustration, and the latent yearning of a former campaigner. He knew that Bush would have some difficulty getting reelected because he was a crisis manager, not a visionary, and because the media had succeeded in establishing the relatively weak economy as the paramount campaign issue. Despite presiding over the American victory in the Persian Gulf and earning astronomically favorable poll ratings, Bush had failed to project a greater meaning for his presidency that would in-

spire a second term. Nixon likened the Bush presidency to
Ibsen's analogy of the onion in *Peer Gynt:* You peel it off skin by
skin, and at the center you find it's hollow. A year before the
election, Nixon saw that Bush's favorable poll ratings remained
relatively high and predicted that the strongest Democrats
would decide not to run. Bush would win not because he performed extraordinarily well in the first term but because his opposition would be weak.

Nixon's first comment on the 1992 campaign came on October 22, 1991. The tumultuous Senate confirmation hearings on
the nomination of Justice Clarence Thomas as a justice of the
Supreme Court had just ended with a 52–48 vote to confirm.
Nixon turned from the scandalous upheaval of the hearings to
the prospect of a deadly dull presidential campaign.

"I hope to hell that Cuomo runs," he said. "He'll liven up the
damn thing."

That autumn, speculation swirled that the New York governor would try to make his latent ambition to be president a re-
ality. Nixon was intrigued. He and Mario Cuomo disagreed
politically on almost everything, but they seemed to share an
affinity for each other reserved for weathered political warriors.
Nixon stated unequivocally, "He's smart, he's a true believer,
and he's a damn good politician." Cuomo is an unapologetic
old-line liberal who spoke forcefully about his political philosophy and fought just as passionately to institute it as policy.
Cuomo has courage, intelligence, and the ability to inspire an
audience. Unlike most leaders, he had both style *and* substance.
Nixon appreciated the effect he would have on the president
and the campaign: "If he runs, he would force Bush to be a better candidate."

A good opponent could raise the stakes of the race. Even before Bush began his first term, Nixon knew that he would have
a problem convincing the voters that he deserved a second one.
In a memorandum written on November 10, 1988, Nixon foresaw the inevitable political problem. After declaring George
Bush and Mario Cuomo the big winners of the election, he condemned both parties as the losers.

He defended George Bush's decisive victory over Michael Dukakis as evidence that Bush was a political force in his own right, apart from inheriting Reagan's legacy and facing a weak opponent. He did, however, warn that the Republican Party was in danger of losing its relevance in the Congress. If the Republicans did not strengthen their position in the House and Senate, they would be marginalized much as the Democratic Party had been since losing all but one of the previous seven presidential elections.

Foreseeing the possibility of a Democratic win in 1992, Nixon wrote that despite Bush's overwhelming popular and electoral margins over Dukakis, his margin of victory in big states like California, Pennsylvania, and Illinois was so small that a shift of several hundred thousand votes across those states would have given the victory to Dukakis. Nixon intended his warning to be watched by the Democrats and heeded by the Republicans.

Applying electoral logic to the fact that the South would reliably vote Republican, Nixon considered the chances of several potential Democratic presidential candidates for 1992 and dismissed them all except for one: New York governor Mario Cuomo. Nixon predicted that if Cuomo abandoned some of his extreme liberal positions and shored up his foreign policy experience, he would win the Democratic nomination in 1992 and inspire a plausible Democratic northern strategy. And four years before the liberal governor of Arkansas would get the nomination, Nixon wrote that if the Democrats were to nominate a southerner with liberal credentials, he would be too liberal to even win his base: the South. Such a candidate would be, Nixon implied, the toast of the Democratic convention and a pariah in the all-important South during the general election.

Despite the problems within the Democratic Party and the apparent dearth of viable Democratic candidates, Nixon knew days after the 1988 election that Bush would face difficult political odds. Bush's first term put him at an even greater disadvantage for reelection. His accomplishments in the Middle East and his relatively even handling of the end of the cold war were diminished by the constant stream of reports trumpeting an economic recession and neglect of domestic issues such as education, crime, welfare, and health care. Conservatives attacked him from the right, arguing that he was a nondescript moderate who abandoned the Reagan revolution, and liberals attacked him from the left, arguing that he was an establishment conservative who protected affluent interests. Both sides argued that Bush stood for nothing. His presidency showed no discernible pattern of political principle. It had no philosophical rhythm, no conservative cadence, and not enough charismatic style to compensate. Nixon believed that Bush was a good man with good intentions, but that in itself would not win him a second term.

"Leaders need three things," he said on November 8, 1991, restating his familiar mantra, "head, heart, and guts. A good campaigner needs three avenues of appeal: to the head, with issues such as foreign policy (and you can get to the hard-core conservatives this way); to the heart, with issues like crime and education; and to the stomach, through the economy. Bush lost the conservatives because he was too moderate on Gorbachev and the independence struggles of the [former Soviet] republics and because he dealt on the [1990] budget. They don't trust him. The economy is a lost issue too because whoever runs on the Democratic side will hijack the issue for himself. Poor Bush isn't left with much. I'm afraid he was too passive. He was hit over the head with the end of communism, and he really didn't do much with it. There just isn't a lot there to run on."

If Bush's first term made Nixon cautious about predicting his reelection, his campaign style made him nervous. "Bush despises campaigning," he said on August 7, 1992. "You can see it all over him. It's not that he doesn't like people; it's just that he's not very comfortable out there on the stump trying to connect with them. He tries too hard to be one of them, eating pork rinds and the rest, but he is not one of them, and it comes across. He's better off just being himself."

Nixon prided himself on being "one of them" and savored secretly the fact that Bush's patrician upbringing worked against him. Bush tried to diminish the class differences between himself and most of the voters but failed. "People know what's real and what's not," Nixon said. "And Bush is pushing too far away from what he really is. It's demoralizing to him and makes him appear like he doesn't want to win."

Nixon wanted Cuomo to run to "light a fire under Bush." With his intellect and oratory, Cuomo would raise expectations. The result would be a more enlightened and exciting campaign. On October 31, 1991, when the administration downplayed the possibility of a Cuomo candidacy, Nixon snickered, "They are on the defensive. Good! Now maybe they'll get on the ball." Nixon enjoyed watching Cuomo cultivate the press in a coy attempt to create a mystique around his potential candidacy. He read the Cuomo interviews and passed them to me, underlined for emphasis and scribbled with notes.

Someone sent Nixon the November 10, 1991, column by Lally Weymouth of *The Washington Post,* entitled "Cuomo: 'I Can Make the Case'—and Beat Bush." Nixon highlighted several passages, including "What Cuomo didn't say, but his friends confide, is that he has developed what one described as a 'visceral dislike' of President Bush, whom Cuomo sees as a 'bloodless WASP' " and "Asked if Bush is beatable, [Cuomo] replied, 'Of course he is. There's no question about it. The incumbents are getting killed. He's an incumbent. . . . He's responsible for the economy. . . . Should he be beaten? I think so. I think he's a good man, but we need a different direction for the nation.' " Nixon tore John Leo's November 25, 1991, column from *U.S. News and World Report* and underlined a quote from *The Washington Post*'s Mary McGrory: "Cuomo will argue with a reporter for hours over a single sentence in a story." Beside it, he wrote angrily that his own staff was "reluctant" to ever correct members of the press in 1960. Nixon admired Cuomo's willingness to do battle with those who opposed him and his willingness to get advice and opinions from them as well.

Cuomo sought out Nixon about as often as Bush did. Advice given to Bush could just as easily be advice given to Cuomo. "I *want* Cuomo to run," he said in mid-December. "Only with stiff competition will Bush be his best. If he can't rise to the occasion, then Cuomo will win, and he'll deserve to win. And I may have more influence with Cuomo than with Bush." As early as December 1991, Nixon began to think privately about cultivating Bush's opponents in ways that would guarantee Nixon's influence in the next White House.

"The Bush team is about as weak a one as I've ever seen," he said while talking with me in his office on November 15, 1991. "The only two stars are [Housing and Urban Development Secretary Jack] Kemp and [Education Secretary Lamar] Alexander. The rest? I don't know. I like Quayle; he's a good man. But he is perceived as just not up to the job, not yet, anyway. Look at this," he said, handing me a *Wall Street Journal* article in which the vice president said that Vietnam was the greatest failure of the U.S. political system in his lifetime, arguing, "We never made the commitment to win . . . and should have." Nixon had circled the quote and added an exclamation point. "This is where Quayle is coming from. He's just not a heavyweight yet. Anyway, if this is any indication of what his campaign team will be like, he's in big trouble."

Although he believed a Mario Cuomo candidacy would inspire Bush to be a better candidate, he never expected that a challenge from a fellow Republican could serve the same purpose. He had been aghast the day before, when he first heard that Patrick Buchanan might run against Bush for the Republican nomination.

"What in God's name is Buchanan thinking?" he said, throwing his newspaper on the floor next to his desk. He ripped off his eyeglasses, scowled, and slammed his fist on the armrest. "Bush is going to have a hell of a time as it is, and now he has to contend with Pat? My God! He's really going to hurt him."

A former speechwriter for Nixon, a prominent political commentator, an uncompromising conservative, and a brilliant firebrand, Buchanan had the potential to damage Bush's chances for reelection. With no record to defend, Buchanan had the luxury to attack the incumbent with a purist's agenda. Buchanan's platform was "America First": isolationist, protectionist, and pro life. Like Cuomo, Buchanan possesses unshakable core beliefs, passion, and the ability to communicate on an inspirational level. Like Cuomo, he actually believed the strong messages he delivered. And like Cuomo, he sensed a hunger in the nation for a leader and a vision that would bring America back. Bush, who was perceived as a moderate willing to compromise on his rather weak principles, would have suffered from either candidacy. Together, Buchanan and Cuomo would have defeated him.

On November 18, I entered Nixon's office to find him reclining in his chair with his feet propped up on his ottoman. A copy of *The New York Times* lay in his lap under his eyeglasses. He tried to focus on the positive side of a Buchanan primary challenge.

"Well, I suppose Buchanan could galvanize Bush the way Cuomo could," he sighed. "A Buchanan candidacy could force him to articulate clearer ideas and regain some of the conservatives he lost from Reagan when it comes down to the general election, because Buchanan can never win that. But in any case, Bush has got to get moving. Buchanan will kill him early on." He folded his hands in his lap and lowered his voice. "Bush is going to end up moving to the right to try to preempt any damage Buchanan will do to him. This is a mistake. He cannot be a moderate as president for four years and then be a dyed-in-the-wool conservative as a candidate. It will only work against him. He'll look like a political schizophrenic."

Bush's vacillation was most apparent in his handling of a relatively weak U.S. economy. A recession had pushed unemployment up and consumer confidence down. Bush was perceived as negligent not only in allowing it to develop but in allowing it to persist. His mixed messages lent the impression that he was indecisive, too reliant upon conflicting advice, and unwilling to take the lead himself. In mid-November 1991, he had refused to acknowledge the recession and then canceled a scheduled trip to Asia to tend to it. His frenetic insecurity about the economy slipped easily into a self-fulfilling prophecy, upon which candidate Clinton later capitalized. Clinton's devastatingly effective slogan, "It's the economy, stupid!" reinforced the idea that Bush was not only out of touch with the economic problems plaguing the country but also unwilling to solve them. Implied in the slogan was the idea that the American people were *not* better off than they had been four years earlier. Clinton's relentless attacks on Bush's handling of the economy were left largely unanswered by the Bush campaign, giving the challenger the gift of a winning issue.

Nixon was confounded by Bush's apparent and continual mishandling of the economy. "There is really nothing a president can do directly to fix a weak economy. Market economies go up and down in a natural cycle. It's inevitable, and almost every president presides over a recession. The only reason it has become Bush's Achilles' heel is that he is vulnerable in other areas as well," he said on November 21. His frustration with Bush began to degenerate into hostility. He clenched his fists in his characteristic rage and bellowed, "Goddamn it! Why the hell isn't he showing some leadership? I'll tell you something. When the shit hits the fan and his gang comes to me for advice, I am not going to provide it unless they are willing to thank me publicly. Neither Reagan nor Bush did that after all these years of my advice, and frankly I have had it. They'll find me when they need me, but I may not be available."

He did, however, start to offer some advice on the economy to those who he believed might have some influence with the administration. On December 9, he wrote a letter to Herb Stein, then a senior fellow at the American Enterprise Institute, complimenting him on a recent column he had written for *The Wall Street Journal* entitled "Recessions Happen." In his letter to Stein, Nixon argued that the steps the government takes to lift the country out of a recession have only a limited effect on the economy's cycles and can often do greater harm than good.

Nixon also delivered the advice to Stein he hoped would reach Bush. He argued that Bush should issue a statement indicating his awareness of the economic situation and his reluctance to take actions which might further harm the economy, but that he would take some responsible steps in a few significant areas. In this way, Nixon argued, Bush could signal to the voters that he had a consistent and responsible economic policy immune to the politically expedient quick fixes many had advocated.

Nixon knew that Bush was perceived as losing control, not just over the economy but over his subordinates and over policy. Jack Kemp urged a "growth package" while the president was still denying a recession. John Sununu, the chief of staff, blamed for remarking that banks should cut their interest rates on credit cards, which in turn upset the stock market, placed a second round of blame on Bush. And Boyden Gray, the White House counsel, was responsible for turning Bush's sudden approval of a civil-rights bill into a spectacle by trying to undermine it. At the end of 1991, the internal battles for power in the reelection campaign had begun, but Bush gave his subordinates conflicting signals and failed to take the lead himself, thereby turning a rocky period in his presidency into a crisis. Bush's inclination to panic made Nixon want to calm him, either indirectly, with advice to third parties, or, when the opportunity arose, directly to Bush himself.

"I'm afraid that Bush just doesn't have it together," he said on November 22. He had just spoken to the commentator Kevin Phillips, to whom he turned for sobering assessments of the state of the Republican Party. Their conversation must have been particularly pessimistic because Nixon erupted in frustration.

"What the hell is wrong with the administration? They only have a year to go before this election, and they look like they are rearranging the deck chairs on the *Titanic*. They are all scattered. Bush has no loyalists—even in our darkest days, we still had plenty of those—except for Quayle. You know, for all of his problems being taken seriously, he is the only one out there swinging for Bush. That says something about the guy's character. The others are out for themselves. For the first time, I think Bush looks like he's in over his head." He lowered his voice and raised an eyebrow. "You know," he said, "any effective leader has got to be a son of a bitch."

"Truman? Eisen—?" I started to ask. He cut me off.

"Eisenhower was as cold as ice," he snapped. "He had to be to do the damn job. And Johnson? Forget it. You have to instill the fear of God in your people in order to get results. This is Bush's problem. He's nice; everyone likes him. But no one *fears* him."

Three days later, he continued the theme. "Consider what Sununu did. I cannot believe that he got away with blaming Bush for the credit-card disaster. I would have fired his ass. Cabinet members—like the chief of staff—are supposed to be lightning rods *away* from the president. The buck stops with them. By God, Bush has an imperial Cabinet!" Flailing his arms for emphasis, he said, "They're all running around spouting off about God knows what while their boss is drowning. That's not a Cabinet; that's every man for himself." He curled his lip in disgust. "That's the thanks he gets for making them secretaries of whatever. Disgraceful!"

He waved his hand in dismissal. "Bush has got to shake up the personnel. He believes too much in personalizing politics, and it's going to destroy him. Fire the ones who are dragging you down, and replace them with people who will do the goddamned job. Here we are a year away from the election, and he's still screwing around with the same clowns who are making him look ridiculous. He must get the campaign out of the White House, and he can't have [Commerce Secretary Robert] Mosbacher run it. Frankly, he's not up to it. It's just not his bag. He's a money guy, not a strategist. Bush had better do some serious thinking, or he is going to lose."

That afternoon, he asked me to research the Gallup Poll numbers for presidential job approval of him, Reagan, and Bush three years into office. In December 1971, he had the approval of 49 percent of those polled; in December 1983, Reagan had the approval of 54 percent, which the media interpreted as "riding a crest of popularity" after months in the mid–40 percent range; and as of that month, November 1991, Bush had the approval of 51 percent. Nixon compared the numbers, removed his glasses, and tapped the page. "These numbers tell us very little. I had the lowest numbers of the three at this point in the presidency, and I won in a landslide. Reagan's numbers went up and down, mainly due to the economy, and he won in a landslide. Bush's numbers went through the roof after the war, and now they are really starting to fall. But even if he wins, there is no way it will be in a landslide."

A week later, when criticism about Chief of Staff Sununu's overeager use of government aircraft had reached a fever pitch, it seemed clear that Bush would take action.

"Bush must not panic," warned Nixon. "He has worked from the same point of reference for most of his presidency and had high approval ratings. Now those ratings are dropping, and he wants to change the reference point—from foreign affairs to Sununu. He should have fired Sununu for insubordination when he tacked the credit-card fiasco on him, not for the flying thing because the media made something out of it. It's panicky."

He focused on Bush's hemorrhaging popularity. "You know, he's a smart man, and he's a good man, but I just don't see a lot of conviction or direction coming from him. This is why Bush has almost no core support. Even during Watergate and after, I always had twenty to twenty-five percent support. Reagan had it; Bush does not. Maybe if he had been more of a fighter and less of Mr. Nice Guy, it would have been different, but that's not who he is."

At four-thirty on the afternoon of December 3, Nixon took a call from the political consultant Roger Stone, who informed him that Bush planned to fire Sununu, thereby forcing his resignation, and replace him with Transportation Secretary Samuel Skinner.

"Firing Sununu for this was a mistake," he said to me as he hung up the phone. "It's totally defensive. In my case, I accepted [H. R.] Haldeman's and [John] Ehrlichman's resignations reluctantly, and I thought they got a bad rap. The media are like piranhas—once they smell blood, that's it." Having allowed media pressure to dictate his own personnel agenda, Nixon knew it was bad form, even if it was inevitable. Any action that feeds into a perception of presidential vulnerability is to be avoided or at least done and overcome as quickly as possible. This, however, applies only to the actions of those whom the president can control.

Two days after the Sununu resignation, Patrick Buchanan called Nixon to inform him of his final decision to run against Bush for the Republican nomination. This did more to undermine Bush's apparent strength than any minor transportation scandal caused by a subordinate. An intraparty challenge to the incumbent would be devastating to an already vulnerable president. After his conversation with Buchanan, Nixon called me in to his office. He was standing by the window, watching some random snowflakes fall from the sky.

"Well, Buchanan just told me that he is definitely running," he said, turning toward me. "I didn't try to talk him out of it, but I did say that I would support Bush. I am, after all, a company man." He sat down and put his feet up on the ottoman. "But Buchanan is right to say that Bush lost both the Nixon and Reagan conservatives. He feels betrayed by Bush and lost after Reagan. And I really can't blame him. But he is worried because he has been tagged as anti-Semitic, which is totally untrue and unfair. The guy is just not that way. But what it comes down to is this: Buchanan is uncompromising, and he feels that he can make the conservative case far better than Bush." When I asked if he thought Buchanan would see the primary process through to the end, Nixon replied, "I think so. He'll lose, but like Cuomo, he may be good for Bush."

He picked up the latest Gallup Poll numbers, which showed a slight but steady decline in Bush's approval ratings. "These numbers have been wild: way up during and after the war, way down in the midst of a recession. [The White House] should have been suspicious. Bush has no ceiling of support, but no floor either." Nixon considered Bush's campaign team with disappointment. "Mosbacher isn't up to it, [pollster Robert] Teeter is a liberal, and [consultant] Charlie Black is the only SOB in the bunch. This is bad not because they aren't fine people but because they are all like Bush. You have to mix it up a little bit, you know—have people on your campaign who have been out in America and know what the pulse is. These guys have been in Washington so long they don't know what the hell people are thinking out there. And they don't care. You know, like Bush, we were down in the polls too. But we had a good team, and we could relate to the middle class. This is what Buchanan is trying to exploit."

Nixon's frustration with Bush's lack of vision as president and lack of style as a campaigner spilled over into a broader annoyance that despite Bush's serious problems, he had not called upon Nixon as often as the former president would have liked. Nixon knew that Bush needed him, and although he was impatient to dispense advice, he did not want to give it unsolicited. "If Bush wants distance from me, I'll give it to him," he swore on December 11. "Let them lose!" His anger was tempered by the knowledge that came from the presidential experience: the only way to get advice to Bush without offending him was through indirect sources. "One thing I learned as president is to never accept advice from an older politician without being prepared to take it. I do not want to put Bush in that position." But more important, he wanted his message to get to him.

The next day, Nixon received a call from Fred Malek, Bush's campaign strategist. Sitting with him in the office when the call came in, I saw him grimace as he mentally debated whether or not to take the call. His need to give Bush advice won out over his pride.

"Fred! Have you won the election yet?" he asked. "I just have a few suggestions, and the advice is free, which is about what it is worth. I would get six governors, six good congressmen, and six good senators to be surrogates for Bush. He is not comfortable on the attack, as Eisenhower was not. But Eisenhower had me, and he used me for that purpose. Let's be frank; Quayle cannot do it. Sununu might be good. But the campaign must get out of the White House, or you are going to drag the president down into the campaign dirt. Bush's big advantage is that he is president. Keep him above the fray." When he hung up, he said, "So it begins. Bush's spies are on the prowl. Why the hell he doesn't just call me is beyond me."

On December 18, Nixon made his first remark about the governor of Arkansas running for the Democratic nomination. "It's still early, but Clinton seems to be the fair-haired boy," he said.

"Cuomo had better get off the stick and run, or the Democrats are going to end up with Clinton."

Two days later, Cuomo announced that he would not run, leaving Clinton to win or lose the nomination. Nixon was distressed. "So Cuomo is not going to do it. I wonder what it is that we don't know about him. Well, he still might jump in if Clinton or the others stumble. It's too bad; he could have done wonders for the race."

Nixon's disappointment with Cuomo soon translated into a greater disappointment with Bush and, later, with Clinton. In Nixon's view none of the candidates seemed deserving of the office. "There is no question that they are all smart men," he said on December 23, "but you need so much more than smarts to be a good president." Nixon's ninth book, *Seize the Moment*, had just been published, and advance copies were sent to Bush and Cuomo, both of whom replied with generous thanks. "Cuomo will read it; Bush might not have the time, but he should make the time. And he *should* thank me—well, you know . . ."

When Nixon felt that he was neither needed nor appreciated by the administration, he began to break publicly with its policies. Since his support appeared to be unimportant to Bush, he simply began to withdraw it. His first move was a December 1991 piece in *The Wall Street Journal*, urging stronger NATO action in the former Yugoslavia. He also drafted a column attacking the administration's intention to normalize relations with Vietnam and prepared an onslaught on Bush's Russian policy. If he cultivated Nixon, Bush would get valuable advice and a prominent ally; if he ignored him, he would face a troublesome adversary. Nixon knew his power and never failed to use it.

Bush began the new year with a trip to Asia. Nixon hoped it would be a geopolitical tour de force that would allow Bush to showcase his foreign policy skills and provide a needed boost to his sagging image. Instead, Bush took his domestic problems abroad.

"I cannot believe that Bush is in Japan whining about our economy. He should not look like he's running for reelection when he's abroad. Besides, the White House is paying too much attention to Clinton and the Democrats and not enough to Buchanan. He thinks that Buchanan isn't worth the attention, but he will get forty percent of the primary vote in New Hampshire—watch. Bush must not realize that he is vulnerable, and he doesn't have the advisers around to tell him he is. This trip has degenerated into a pathetic appeal for votes. Why the hell is he over there talking about 'jobs'? He should be talking high diplomacy, not whining about the problems of the U.S. economy." Nixon said this after we arrived in Washington on January 6 to promote *Seize the Moment*. He had several television interviews scheduled and was concerned that his private frustration with Bush might become public. "I have to be very careful not to criticize Bush," he said, adding ominously, "at least not until I'm ready."

Two days later, he awoke to the news that Bush had collapsed in Tokyo with an intestinal virus. Nixon summoned me immediately. "Well, Bush seems fine, but his pace is far too frenetic. He's playing tennis with the emperor on this trip? My God! He has got to slow down and build some time into his schedule for rest."

"Sir, as you know, the questions in these interviews today are going to go right down the Dan Quayle alley," I said.

"Monica, you and I both know that he is not up to the top job," he replied. "Despite his good instincts, he will not be elected, at least no time soon. If Bush begs out for health reasons, the Democrats will win. I've been through this three times before—with Eisenhower: stroke, heart attack, and ileitis. But people had the confidence in me to do the job. I don't think that it's there with Quayle. I'll hedge my bets on him if I get any questions."

That afternoon, Nixon went to CNN studios to tape *Larry King Live*. King's first questions concerned Quayle's qualifications to be president should Bush be incapacitated. Nixon hedged. "It is a difficult day for him, and naturally the spotlight will be on him again. . . . I know that the conventional wisdom is 'My, if something happens to George Bush the country is

going to be in a terrible condition,' but let's look at Dan Quayle
for just a moment. He has been through a lot, and when a man
is tested—you don't know what he's made of until he really goes
through the fire. Dan Quayle has been through fire. He has handled himself with poise, with dignity, and with intelligence, and
I think under the circumstances, therefore, that the concern
about whether Quayle would be a good president is not nearly
as much as it would have been early on, when, as you know, he
got very, very bad publicity—almost as bad as I got on occasion." With some perspective and a little humor, Nixon was
able to finesse the issue without contributing to the avalanche of
existing skepticism about the vice president.

Nixon also suppressed his disappointment with Bush's trip to
Asia. "I realize that some are knocking the trip because they feel
that it's too commercial. . . . Let's understand one thing. There
was a very unfortunate statement—which the president didn't
make, but somebody in his Cabinet did—to the effect that the
recession may have been caused, to an extent, by the Japanese.
That's nonsense. . . . We've got to look to ourselves and then
look to them." Nixon was careful not to criticize Bush for traveling with automobile executives, saying that since three-fourths
of the trade deficit with Japan is in automobiles and automobile
parts, "There then comes a reason to try to get the Japanese to
make some sort of arrangement where we could sell more to
them and maybe cut back on what they sell to us. I don't like
that idea. I'm a free trader. . . ."

When King touched upon the sensitive issue of Bush's lack of
conviction and political philosophy, Nixon replied, "I would
never have appointed him to key posts unless I felt that he did
have a philosophy. People say, 'Well, George Bush is not a conservative.' Well, he may not be a conservative according to,
maybe, Pat Buchanan, but on the other hand there's no question
about his conservative credentials. . . . He is what I would call a
responsible conservative, and in the field of foreign policy,
Larry, there's no question. . . . He's a strong leader."

Bush's relative strength or weakness as president concerned
Nixon less than that of his opponents. With Cuomo out of the

race and Buchanan unlikely to wrest the nomination from him, Bush would have to run for reelection against Democratic mediocrity and still might lose.

Bush's failure to solicit help from Nixon meant that Nixon could completely disavow himself from a Bush loss. He therefore considered the perceived distance from Bush as a disguised blessing. This was exemplified by his reaction on the morning of January 11 to the receipt of a "confidential" White House memorandum. It was a two-page national security report handsigned by Bush, who added "warmest personal regards." When Nixon received these standard memos in the past, he erupted in fury. He expected that the sitting president would discuss these issues with him directly rather than send a national security form letter. He despised being grouped with the other former presidents and thought that he should receive special treatment from the president, particularly on foreign policy issues. This time, however, he simply read the letter, scribbled on the top that it was a standard "boiler plate" memorandum, and asked me to write a brief summary of it. His calm reaction indicated a reluctant acceptance of Bush's desire for distance, but it also pointed to a growing disappointment.

Nixon appeared on the *Today* show on the morning of January 16 to promote *Seize the Moment*. When he returned to his office, he was very concerned about his handling of questions pertaining to the Bush presidency. "I hope I sounded all right on Bush," he said. "I'm afraid that I just don't sound credible defending him because I really don't think he's done that great of a job. And his New Hampshire visit is a disaster. He's up there petting cows and raving about God knows what. He just looks so desperate. And you know, he's getting no support from his people; the White House communications people are saying that the New Hampshire trip was triumphant! Oh, boy. They must be dreaming down there." And for Nixon, part of the reason they were in that condition was because they were not consulting him.

The next day, Nixon wanted to discuss the rumors of philandering that had begun to swirl around Bill Clinton. He was not shocked but intrigued by the extent to which such revelations might damage the candidate. "What effect will they have on the voters?" he asked.

"If they are true—" I began to reply.

"They are, without question. He established it early on with the media. I would say this: 'Let's not discuss personal lives. There are plenty of issues that concern us in this country; let us focus on those.' If he cannot avoid it, all he has to say is 'My wife and I have had some problems.' I don't know if the media will be satisfied with that. He is a Democrat, though, so they will be more inclined to protect him. What do you think?"

When I replied that it could be a serious liability, he answered, "It wasn't for JFK. No one knew because those who did protected him and in some cases pimped for him. I just don't know if a moral majority still exists out there where this even matters anymore. But in any case, the Democrats are defusing it now because they believe he's their best hope. The Republicans should bring it up later, when he's the front-runner or nominee, and force a Gary Hart–type withdrawal. But who knows? That type of scandal may be a nothing thing these days."

He shook his head in disbelief and turned his criticism to Bush. "The White House is in total disarray because it still believes it has a communications problem and if it could just put together a slick photo op, he'll be back to seventy percent approval. The problem is deeper; it's something that Lee Atwater [the former and late chairman of the Republican National Committee] could sense. I knew him. He was a tough southern son of a bitch, and we needed him. Bush will miss him this election. He just doesn't have it without Atwater. Frankly, he's a poor campaigner. I really did it for him when I appointed him to the UN; remember, he lost twice for the Senate. He was pretty bad on the Watergate crap, but I guess he had no choice. He was in a hell of a position." Nixon refocused on Bush's immediate problem. "Look, now he is running for reelection. His opposition is weak. His people are not serving him well. People are anesthetized by bad news, and Bush is so closely related to it. Buchanan will cut it close in New Hampshire. Clinton is a pretty boy who doesn't quite have it together. He's a waffler and an opportunist, and I don't think he has much of a chance. This race is Bush's to lose."

On January 22, Nixon began discussing a Nixon Library–sponsored foreign policy conference to be held in Washington in March. The purpose of the conference was to influence the administration's policies toward Russia, Asia, and Europe through debate and discussion. Nixon was scheduled to give a major address, and Bush was invited to deliver the keynote address at a black-tie dinner later the same day. When Nixon discovered that the library had invited Bush directly, he grew frantic. "By issuing the invitation to Bush himself, they have put him in a hell of a position. I understand if he doesn't want to come for political reasons, but he shouldn't have to turn it down himself. I've been there; it's a horrible position. Who else could we get? [Secretary of State James] Baker? No way. We've got Kissinger coming; he can cover the secretaries of state. [Defense Secretary Richard] Cheney? He's a possibility. But I am not expecting Bush. He has kept away, and I don't think he is going to start paying attention to us now." Then he revealed his intention to force Bush to pay attention, saying, "But it will be hard to ignore us come March." His very public criticism of Bush on U.S. policy toward Russia had begun to take shape. Bush was to learn that he ignored Nixon at his own peril.

Nixon's distress with Bush led him to seek out others who would confirm or challenge his concerns about him. Hugh Sidey, presidential observer for *Time* magazine, received an invitation to lunch on January 23 and arrived at the office early. Nixon, not wanting to be seen by Sidey before the appointed hour, grabbed his coat and hid in the mailroom until Sidey was safely ensconced in Nixon's office. As I sat with Sidey, Nixon hurried out unseen and went home to prepare for the discussion.

As he waited, Sidey talked with me about each of the presidents he had covered, from Eisenhower to Bush, whom he knew very well. "Bush, like Kennedy, is basically an elitist who finds it difficult to connect with the average person. It didn't really matter with Kennedy, but Bush will find it harder. And you know," he said, "Kennedy never allowed candid photos; Nixon only reluctantly did—and ended up with the infamous wing tips-on-the-beach picture!", referring to the photograph of Nixon as president strolling in the sand while wearing his formal shoes.

Sidey left the office for Nixon's residence, still smiling at the image of Nixon on the beach, and the former president contacted me after their meeting, relieved that his suspicions about Bush's lack of vision and inept campaign style had been confirmed by a true student of the presidency. "If Sidey thinks the guy needs help, the guy really needs help," he sighed.

If Nixon wanted a livelier campaign, he got his wish the next day, when reports of Clinton's extramarital activities dominated the news. Gennifer Flowers, a cabaret singer, came forward claiming that she had had a twelve-year affair with the governor and had Clinton on tape, begging her not to go public.

Nixon was very interested in the case and its political ramifications. "They've got tapes? Well, then, he covered it up. Just like Watergate?" he asked with a smile. "At least ours was for a good cause. And no one ever profited from it." The smile disappeared. "Anyway," he continued, "Clinton is in a fine mess. What's wrong with him? This is another Gary Hart. Well, Bush must be smiling. It's too bad, because Bush needs to meet the challenge; without a challenger, that's hard to do. He needs to be pushed into a fight. But what's most important to him is to win, not to run a campaign with something to it."

Later that night, Nixon called to follow up. "Monica! How is the media playing this Clinton thing? There is nothing like a love scandal to shake things up!" He laughed out loud. "But seriously, Cuomo may jump in now that Clinton seems vulnerable. I'm still skeptical that this can bring him down, but if he's weakened enough, Cuomo or even someone like [Texas senator Lloyd] Bentsen may run. This thing isn't over."

Nixon relished the scandal and hours later informed me that Clinton would appear with his wife on *60 Minutes* to argue his case. "It's a gutsy move," he said. "This is what is known as major damage control! I've heard from several people who have compared it to the Fund speech. I don't think so. I had the truth on my side. The charges there were political, and I could put the judgment to the people. In Clinton's case, the charges are personal and true. He is going to have a very difficult time making his case. Any comparisons to the '52 Fund speech are misleading. No one was ever able to duplicate that speech and its results."

For Nixon, it was impossible that Clinton would be able to inspire the same type of massive outpouring of national support that had saved Nixon's political career. The public did not yet know enough about Clinton to react with a passionate defense. Most observers believed that the allegations were true. The real test for Clinton would be in how he handled them. He would survive or fall based not on what he said but on how he said it.

On Sunday, January 26, Bill and Hillary Clinton took advantage of the large post–Super Bowl audience to give a live interview on *60 Minutes*. With his wife sitting dutifully by his side, Clinton never denied the allegations of infidelity. Instead, as Nixon had suggested, he admitted to marital difficulties and tried to respond to the questions without incriminating himself; it was a delicate balancing act that amused Nixon. He talked with me after the broadcast.

"I just got off the phone with Julie. She couldn't believe the whole thing. Would you believe what we just saw? He was so defensive—he looked like a Kennedy!" he laughed. "You know, Clinton's wife was a lawyer on the Watergate Committee, so that tells us where she's coming from. How could she sit there next to him knowing what she does about his running around? Humiliating! But she has a higher agenda. She is very smart, and she just wants to win the goddamned election. Take a little humiliation now and get power later."

His next comment came directly from lessons learned in his own experience: "As far as Clinton is concerned, I think he would have been better off admitting he did it and moving on."

Nixon asked me about the benefits of this exposure, remarking, "You know what they say, '*Any* publicity is good publicity.' "

"Mr. President," I answered, "the first impression millions of voters have of him is in defense of his character against charges of infidelity. Even Clinton can't want *this* publicity."

Nixon laughed and said, "I don't think it will help him, but you never know."

The next morning, Nixon gauged the fallout from the Clintons' appearance. "I understand that this Flowers woman is going to hold a press conference and play the tapes. You know, this is really something. The guy didn't just have a fling; he had a twelve-year affair. He's a repeat offender—and as governor, no less. That's arrogance of power! But I still don't think this will destroy him. He seems too slippery to have anything like this stick. And as far as Hillary is concerned, I know I've said this before, but I still can't believe it: she was on the goddamned committee to impeach me. She's a radical. If she gets in, whoa! Everybody had better fasten their seat belts."

He left me in the office for a moment and returned carrying two cups of coffee. He handed one to me. "It's decaf, so don't worry. I wasn't sure how you take it, but I put some cream in it for you," he said, and as I thanked him, I watched him burn himself on the first sip and almost drop the cup. "I should stick with the cold drinks," he said, leaving the coffee untouched through the rest of the conversation.

"Bush gives his State of the Union address tomorrow. Who the hell cares when there is a salacious sex scandal in the news?" He chortled before turning serious. "This whole thing tells you something about America's leadership class. *The New York Times, Wall Street Journal,* [Leslie] Gelb, even [William] Safire are all out for him. These people are intellectual elitists and, except for Safire, a permissive bunch. They all apply a terrible double standard. I want the media to be proved wrong in backing Clinton." He picked up a paper listing some poll numbers. "Clinton has fallen nine percentage points in the last forty-eight hours. This has got to indicate *something*." He picked up the phone and asked his secretary to place a call to his daughter Tricia Nixon Cox. "I spoke to Julie yesterday about the Clinton thing, but not Tricia, and she is so perceptive about these things." When he finished the conversation, he said to me, "Well, Tricia's on target as usual. She said last night's program was one of the most offensive things she has seen. 'Imagine,' she said, 'a presidential candidate having to lower himself like that.' Did you also notice absolutely no affection between Bill and Hillary? They probably can't stand each other. Oh well, that's not really our business, but by going on the tube as they did, they've allowed us to speculate!"

On Bush, he remarked, "The White House must be on a different planet if they think that Bush's image problem is over. We tried to do what they are trying—you know, to change the image during Watergate. It didn't work. Too phony." And after he saw the network news that night, he called me with these remarks: "The media are all shits. Did you see the way they sugarcoated [Clinton's] appearance last night? They are out to save the guy at any cost and to prove they were right on him. They are a lousy damn bunch. It's a wonder that we win any races with the likes of them covering us. The discrepancy between how the elite media and the popular media cover Clinton is amazing. The elitists are all for him; the popular media are calling him an ass. It shows how disconnected those elitists are."

Nixon grew increasingly apprehensive as Bush's State of the Union address approached on the evening of January 28. It would be remembered for Bush's delivery of it, not for its content. Nixon feared that if Bush stumbled or appeared defensive, his political vulnerability would be underscored. "The State of the Union is basically a laundry list of problems, solutions, and accomplishments," he said that afternoon. "In itself, it is not all that important. But what is important is that Bush appear presidential. That is his greatest asset going into this race, and he can't blow it by whining around every little issue. He should stick with foreign policy and the other big issues—the high road. He will have a big audience tonight, and he must use the power and presence of the office. God, I hope he doesn't screw it up."

Nixon hoped that his exasperation with Bush as a candidate would be granted a temporary reprieve by watching Bush speak as president. He was disappointed. "Well, he screwed it up. Actually, he didn't so much screw it up as not make the most of it. He hit a double when he should have hit it out of the park. And I'm worried about his health. He did not look good. He needs weight. I wonder if everything is OK. What did you think?"

I responded with a more optimistic appraisal of the address, saying that Bush succeeded in convincing people that he could take action on the economy with minimal negative effect. The structure of the speech worked to his advantage as well, beginning with his strong suit, foreign policy, and ending with economics and domestic policy. Bush's remarks commending Mrs. Bush and the American family were effective counterpoints to Clinton by reminding his listeners that his integrity surpassed that of the current prominent Democratic challenger. Nixon replied, "Ah, ha! You are right! That went right by me, but, boy, how clever! I wouldn't have given the speech as high marks as you have, but he did do better than I originally thought."

Nixon may have convinced himself of that, because he told Bush himself the next day. The president, in the company of Mrs. Bush and Rev. Billy Graham, placed a call to Nixon after dinner on January 29.

"Mrs. Nixon and I had finished watching the news, and I was walking with her downstairs when I heard my phone ringing. Bush came on the line almost immediately," Nixon said to me, his voice filled with restrained satisfaction. "He admitted outright that Graham told him to call me for advice. He was very concerned about Yeltsin's political and physical health. I didn't have the heart to tell him that I was worried about *his!* He said to me, 'Dick, he doesn't have good backup,' meaning his people are bad. He asked about the Israeli question, and I told him to hang firm and not to give in. This is where using Baker is good. On defense, I told him to go for the cuts now before someone worse gets in. I praised the State of the Union speech, which I think he appreciated. He said, 'We've gotten very positive reactions.' I'll bet! Anyway, Bush put me on with Graham and Barbara, who thanked me for 'all I was doing for George.' That's a laugh. This was the first time in a long time that he's really called for me, and it took Graham to put him up to it. But it might pave the way for me to give advice more freely to Bush himself. It was a fairly good conversation." Nixon tried unsuccessfully to contain a self-satisfied demeanor.

"What's your feeling on Bush now?" he asked. I responded with some qualified praise.

"Why are you so reluctant? Is it because you sense a lack of conviction or principle on Bush's part? That's what I think it is. In all of my interviews these days, I give Bush great support. I go farther for him than what I really think. I have been pretty good to him, haven't I?" He did not stop for an answer. "Call me after you watch Cuomo on *Larry King,*" he continued. "It should be interesting, but I don't want to watch it."

When I rang him after the interview, it was clear that he had seen it. "Cuomo is so impressive. He'd decimate Bush in debate. I wish he would have run," he said, revealing more about his view of Bush than his view of Cuomo. "Bush will probably go up four or five points in the polls as a result of the State of the Union; that's all. Cuomo would have pushed him higher in the polls by polarizing the vote. Clinton doesn't have that ability. There are deeper scars with him than we see now because the media have done a good job of fixing the surface ones. I hope that he *is* the candidate; then we can hit him over the head."

On Sunday, February 2, I spoke to Nixon after the morning shows, which he claimed never to watch. He issued a flurry of hard opinions on the personalities that had appeared. "Of all the Democrats out there running for president, [former Massachusetts senator Paul] Tsongas is the most responsible. I'd actually feel comfortable with him in there. Poor guy doesn't have a chance. This group of Democrats—they are all—what's the word?" He paused. "Weird! They're all weird. And Hillary Clinton is frightening. Her ideas are way out there. The press has been shameless in salvaging Clinton. I'd love to see them eat crow on this one."

Nixon knew, however, that Clinton provided an effective political and personal contrast to Bush. Despite Bush's popular status as a World War II veteran, grandfather, and conservative-leaning moderate in policy, Clinton's New Democrat political liberalism found an energetic voice and rapidly developing support. The clear distinctions between the candidates made a good story, and Nixon sensed that the media buildup of Clinton was tactical as well as political. Unlike the presidential campaigns of the 1980s, a contest between Bush and Clinton held the promise of real debate, real partisan dynamics, and real excitement.

In February, Clinton was engulfed by charges that he had used unethical means to avoid the draft during the Vietnam War. For Nixon, this was the ultimate insult to the American people. A candidate for the presidency, a man seeking to be commander in chief of the armed forces, should have a higher sense of honor than that displayed by Bill Clinton in his young adulthood. His opposition to the war was not the issue. Those who joined the service made the choice and made the sacrifice. Draft resisters who went to jail or into exile made their choice and made sacrifices for their principles. But those children of privilege who defrauded the draft board and, like Clinton, demonstrated against the war on foreign soil evaded the choice, the sacrifice, and the honor. Clinton's letter to Colonel Eugene Holmes, written on December 3, 1969, sought to justify his deception. He had rejected all authority until he had determined that the U.S. government had ceased to be "dangerous and inadequate." At the same time, he plotted his own political advance so that *his* authority would someday be accepted. Nixon believed that Clinton's personal interest came before any sense of national interest or even before any sense of integrity. Ethics that had failed to guide his private life would not suddenly come to guide his public life.

Nixon was disgusted with Clinton, for representing the very worst of his generation, and with the press, which sought to excuse Clinton, since what he did to avoid the draft was accepted practice at the time. Nixon thought that he had closed his own wounds from prosecuting the war only to have them reopened by a presidential candidate's draft evasion. He felt betrayed.

"I cannot believe that this guy is a serious contender for the presidency," he said in his office on February 17. His face was flushed with anger. "I know why he did what he did to dodge the draft: he didn't want to get his ass shot off." He clenched his fist and slammed it onto the armrest. "*Nobody* wants to get their ass shot off, and yet we had tens of thousands of young men who risked and lost their lives because they had more honor and integrity in their little toe than Clinton will ever have, ever. He is a coward and a fraud. He didn't serve his country when it needed him, so why should we have him serve it when *he* is ready? No. The Flowers episode showed that he cheated on his wife. That's his business and his problem. But when he evaded the draft, he cheated the country and the people whose votes he is now asking for. As I was out there trying to end the goddamned war, he was running around, claiming privilege, avoiding service, and demonstrating against it. He was no conscientious objector; he was a selfish, spoiled brat. He made my job so much harder, and he sent God knows how many men to their death in his place. I'll tell you one thing: if he is elected president, I will know that this country has finally gone to hell."

Nixon's fury carried the passion of a personal grudge and the disgust of a former commander in chief betrayed. For Nixon, Clinton's character flaws were not merely peccadilloes, as his advocates claimed, but grave disqualifications for the presidency. The debate over Clinton's fitness for office was a nonissue. The decision he made in 1969 would now have its final result. The lack of an honorable sacrifice then made him an unworthy candidate now.

On February 18, the campaign came alive. New Hampshire hosted the first primary—with shockingly unexpected results. Among Republicans, Bush won, but with a weak 58 percent of the vote; Buchanan stunned the country by matching Nixon's 40 percent prediction. Among Democrats, Tsongas emerged victorious with 35 percent; Clinton placed second with a respectable 26 percent. Nixon remained unmoved. The support for Buchanan was less a vote for him than a protest vote against Bush. Clinton had been badly damaged by the attacks on his past and his perceived vulnerability on "the character issue." Nixon thought that the results were logical, given the political climate surrounding each of the major candidates.

"They are all lacking. Bush is running around looking hysterical. I heard Charlie Black saying that Bush won by a 'comfortable margin.' What the hell is he talking about? My God, he has the one advantage that the others don't: he has the office. Comfortable margin be damned! Buchanan will now be a household name because he stuck it to Bush. Clinton is a nothing, but the press will now go all out to save him since he survived in New Hampshire. Tsongas, poor guy, is simply not electable outside New England. The whole crowd, but especially the Bush gang, is so disappointing it's almost ludicrous."

Two days later, after taking some time to reflect on the significance of the first primary, Nixon was even more discouraged. "I think Bush's handlers are on drugs." This uncharacteristic remark came as I sat down in his office for our daily morning meeting. He noticed that I was stunned and followed up. "Well, I mean they are all so bad. I haven't got the slightest idea as to what they are doing for the man. It's like the inmates are running the asylum. This is one of the most inept campaigns I have ever seen. It's all tactics and no vision. Nothing.

"I reiterate to you once again: I will not give them any advice unless they ask and unless they are willing to thank me publicly. I'm tired of being taken for granted. They all come to me on the sly when they are in big trouble—well, no more. No more going in the back door of the White House—middle of the night—under the cloak-of-darkness crap. Either they want me or they don't. If they think that I am a liability, then so be it. But they won't get a shred from me." His feelings of being underappreciated were leavened by his knowledge that the Bush team would find him when they needed him, and he could then choose whether or not to advise them. Knowing that the Bush campaign would eventually be at his mercy gave him some satisfaction and softened the blow of neglect.

"Clinton is so damn smug," he continued. "How can the guy win? I don't see it, but consider the polls: the nine points between Tsongas and Clinton are very significant. I just don't see how the Democrats can put up either one." He was interrupted by a phone call from former secretary of state Alexander Haig, a close confidant and trusted friend. He allowed me to listen to his side of the conversation.

"Al!" he bellowed. "You going to run for president?"

Haig's laughter came through the receiver, along with his response: "Holy mackerel! It's so bad." He informed Nixon that according to his sources, Secretary of State James Baker was maneuvering to get Bush to replace Quayle with Baker himself.

Nixon was appalled. "Al, he absolutely should not dump Quayle. Even if Quayle is a drag, dumping him will reflect badly on Bush's original decision to put him on the ticket. And for Baker? No way. Al, you know better than I what a deal-cutting opportunist he is."

Nixon's brief encounter with Haig's gossip inspired greater condemnation of Bush's team. "Bush should fire [Office of Management and Budget director Richard] Darman," he said to me. "Someone has got to walk the plank. He fired Sununu on the right, and now he should dispose of Darman on the left. The economy is going to be the big issue, and Bush cannot afford to keep Darman around: he's like an albatross. With regard to our situation, we *had* to let Haldeman and Ehrlichman go, but in retrospect I wouldn't have." He paused. "Well, I suppose sacrifices have to be made. Bush just doesn't know when to do it."

He picked up a copy of *USA Today* and tossed the front section over to me. "Look at this. Bush's approval ratings are down to thirty-nine percent, and if he doesn't get off the dime and do something, *anything*, he's going to be buried alive. You know, never—before the darkest days of Watergate, when I was at twenty-nine percent—did I ever fall below forty-eight percent. Reagan did, in 1982. But Bush has no core convictions to sustain him and no core support." Nixon enjoyed creating his own analogies to his successors, particularly when they reflected favorably upon him.

A new cause quickly animated him. With the end of the Soviet Union in 1991 and the advent of democratic and free-market reform led by Boris Yeltsin, Nixon began advocating large-scale Western aid to Russia in order to preserve the democratic gains already made and advance the process until they were irreversible. His logic was simple: it was better to invest in Russia while there was still a chance for democratic success than to have to meet the far more expensive challenge of a new cold war should the democratic experiment fail. He wrote essays for the major newspapers and news magazines on the subject, but with little effect on the policy makers in the administration. His anger with Bush and Baker for allowing this historic opportunity to pass while tempting a new confrontation was so fierce that it needed to find a new direction, or it would have consumed him completely. The seed was planted on February 21.

"If the situation gets any more desperate in Russia," he said, "the strong hand will have to return, and we will have no one to blame but ourselves. I have been out there talking, but no one in the goddamned administration is listening. Bush and Baker are still hung up on the Gorbachev thing, and even if Baker were inclined to do what I am advising, he still wouldn't do it because the idea originated with me. What else can we do?"

I gave him what I thought was the logical answer. "Sir, perhaps you should consider writing a policy memo to the man himself."

Nixon leveled his gaze at me and asked, "To Yeltsin?"

"No," I said, "to Bush."

Nixon was silent for several moments, pursing his lips and weighing his options. The situation in Russia was so urgent that political pettiness had to be disregarded, and yet Nixon did not want to risk outright rejection by appealing to Bush directly. He knew he had to find a way to get Bush to take the correct policy steps without appearing to be pressuring him. The idea for the notorious Nixon memorandum on Russia was born, though Nixon did not yet indicate his intentions.

"I will consider the idea," he said. "An approach *like that* may be worthwhile."

"If you do decide to go ahead with it, sir, you can then do a mailing so that it reaches a wider audience," I suggested, unaware that he had already reached a similar conclusion.

On February 24, Nixon began to refine his thoughts on how a Democrat could win the election even without the South. "If he picks up the Northeast, Ohio, Illinois, Indiana, and California, he's in—even a candidate other than one from the South, like Clinton. If Cuomo had gotten into the race, I'd bet on him now. Tomorrow's primary [in South Dakota] will be no big surprise; Bob Kerrey will win as a [regional] favorite son, and that will tell us no more about the Democratic race than we knew before."

Nixon's prediction of the results was correct, but he commented instead on Bush. "Bush didn't even win by that much in 1988, when he was much stronger. People forget '88 was *not* a landslide, not like '72." The memory of his own electoral triumph evaporated some of the political frustration he felt with Bush for allowing the Republican presidential momentum to slip away.

"Bush is very vulnerable in Florida, Ohio, and Illinois," he warned me four days before the March 3 primary. "That could be enough to beat him. And every time the Bush crowd goes after Buchanan, they give him air time. The key is to ignore him. Go after his ideas, not him.". Nixon's creeping suspicion that Bush could lose the general election grew more convincing every day, and his hope that the Democrats would nominate someone other than Clinton dissolved. He was disillusioned with the candidates and missed, perhaps more than he would have admitted, the chance to compete.

On February 28, he began to take his revenge on the inattentive Bush administration. In preparation for his appearance at the Nixon Library–sponsored conference, "America's Role in the Emerging World," Nixon wrote a scathing essay, entitled "How the West Lost the Cold War," that attacked the administration's hesitant and frugal policy toward the struggling Russian democracy as "penny-ante" and "pathetically inadequate." If Yeltsin failed and the United States did not aid Russia as it should have, a devastating political debate over who lost Russia would erupt right at Bush's feet.

Well aware of its newsworthiness, Nixon asked his staff to label the essay "secret" and send it to several dozen people on his mailing list. Those closest to the president received the first copies; policy makers, journalists, writers, and commentators got it next. Nixon's strategy was as simple as it was devious: surround Bush with Nixon's criticism and advice, thereby pressuring him to act on it without courting direct confrontation. Nixon knew it was a gamble but calculated that the risk was worth the potential payoff.

"Bush won't be able to ignore us now," he said that morning as he watched the staff fold the copies into their envelopes. "No, this will definitely do the trick."

Later in the afternoon, he summoned me to his residence. I arrived early and climbed silently up the stairs to his third-floor study. The man who never admitted to watching television was watching *The Dick Van Dyke Show,* shoeless feet propped up and remote control in hand. Unseen, I watched him smile at the classic comedy. So rarely did he actually relax that I let him have a few more unspoiled moments to himself before I finally cleared the top of the stairs. Nixon was mortified. Fumbling to simultaneously turn the television off and put his shoes on, he dropped the remote control and struggled to get his feet into the shoes. I apologized for being early, to which Nixon replied, "Well, you caught me. You know I don't watch the tube, but every once in a while I like to see what's out there." Although he would never admit it for fear that he would be considered something less than an *homme sérieux,* even Nixon required some mindless entertainment.

"I wanted you to see this," he said, handing me a letter he had received from Peggy Noonan, former speechwriter for President Reagan. In it she told Nixon that she would be working with President Bush again and asked Nixon if she might approach him for advice.

Nixon retrieved the letter from me. "Thank God Bush has her. He needs someone who is really good with words to get his message across because his communications skills are not the best. Peggy will be superb in that regard, and I like her, but I simply am against handing out private advice. If I advise, there will be nothing private about it."

Nixon's counsel was about to get very public. Bush must have seen a copy of the memorandum, or at least heard about it, because the day before the primary he called to accept Julie Nixon Eisenhower's invitation to speak at the Nixon Library conference. Nixon played it down. "*He* knew he should come to this conference, but I'll bet everyone around him was telling him not to do it, Baker most of all. I think that they probably had a hell of a fight. So Bush is coming. Fine. That's nice," he paused, "for the library."

It was nice for Nixon as well. He had at last attracted Bush's attention long enough to have an impact. Wielding an iron fist in a velvet glove, Nixon would use the conference to force Bush to meet the greatest foreign policy challenge of the end of the century—aiding a newly democratic Russia—and to become a candidate worthy of reelection.

Meanwhile, Buchanan continued to erode Bush's standing among the voters. He landed between 33 percent and 37 percent of the Republican vote in the states holding primaries on March 3, leading Nixon to speculate that Bush would seek to adopt Buchanan's themes as his own. Bush had already shown signs of a more conservative agenda by arguing against abortion more forcefully and by terming his own tax increase "a mistake." Buchanan forced Bush to react instead of act, feeding into the already persistent image of weak leadership. To confirm his instincts that these trends were dooming Bush's candidacy, Nixon called his old friend John Connally, former governor of Texas.

"John! Are you running the campaign? Oh, boy, what a disaster. It's amateur hour down there. Say what you want, we had quite a team!"

Connally told him that Baker was omnipresent, working behind the scenes but "leaving no footprints" and "staying miles away from controversy" because of his own presidential ambitions. Connally, like Nixon, believed that Baker would abandon Bush before he would sink with the ship. "And that is the problem for Bush," Nixon said. "He has no one who would be loyal to him no matter what, with the exception maybe of Quayle."

The Democrats, according to Nixon, fared even worse, with Tsongas having won Utah and Maryland and Clinton, "the horse they are betting on," having just won his first primary in Georgia. "The momentum will now be on his side. He will be on media steroids and probably be unstoppable from now on. Clinton will sweep the South, and he may beat Bush in the fall if the economy doesn't improve significantly."

The day after the March 3 primary results came in, Bush's campaign strategist, Fred Malek, called Nixon. Again, he reluctantly took the call. Malek indicated that they wanted to organize a meeting between Nixon and Bush, but Nixon remained noncommittal. "He tried to squeeze me for advice, but I was careful not to give away the store," he said after the brief conversation. "They're all a bunch of Boy Scouts."

His personal feelings for Bush, however, were warm and in constant conflict with his political appraisals. He knew Bush was a good and thoughtful man of sturdy character but simply lacked a strong political persona. Nixon was torn between liking the man and being displeased with the president.

On March 8, a conversation took place that enflamed this internal conflict. Mrs. Bush called Julie Nixon Eisenhower from Camp David to invite her and her husband, David, to stay at the White House during the Nixon Library conference; President Bush took the receiver and asked Julie whether her father would like to stay there as well.

"Julie is so smart," Nixon told me. "She turned him down so nicely, by saying that I will have many meetings to attend during the conference and that I didn't want to impose on him. It does go to show, though, that the Bushes have class. They are just decent, kind people. It was also shrewd politically, because my staying there would have been a direct slap at Buchanan." Bush's consideration, however, would not be enough to get him reelected.

On March 10, the day before the conference began, Nixon awoke to a front-page story in *The New York Times* that would radically change the course of American foreign policy and his relationship with the administration. Thomas Friedman had acquired a copy of the memorandum and ran portions of it along with positive commentary. The pressure Nixon sought to apply to Bush on Russian policy had now mounted. Bush was forced to reply to Nixon's challenge—at Nixon's conference. Nixon had achieved his objective on a far greater scale than he had anticipated. His immediate concern became his own speech, to be delivered eight hours before Bush's response.

At noon on March 11, Nixon delivered an address that was culled largely from the memorandum but without the recriminations. Entitled "The Promise of Peace," it coupled vision with policy on the Russian question and on the broader issues facing American foreign policy, and it closed with an anecdote that he hoped would be interpreted by Bush as a peace offering.

"In 1947, I vividly recall as if it were yesterday what Harry Truman did," he said, with one eye on history and another on Bush. Despite very low job approval ratings and having to face an overwhelmingly Republican Congress, Truman addressed a joint session of Congress and asked for millions of dollars in aid to Greece and Turkey to prevent Communist subversion. The odds were against him, and yet Truman made his request, got it approved, and won the presidency the next year. Nixon reminded his audience that a Democratic president and a Republican Congress, working together, provided aid to Greece and Turkey, prevented the spread of Communism there, and paved the way for the ultimate victory of democratic freedom in the Soviet Union. Forty-five years later, Nixon said, Bush had a similar historic opportunity.

The attacks of the memorandum had evolved into persuasive historical analogies. Nixon wanted to calm Bush, inspire him to do the right thing through example, and show him that politically unpopular presidents can make relatively unpopular foreign policy decisions and still be elected. If Bush could summon the courage of Truman and move forward with aid to help save the fragile Russian democracy, his place in history would be ensured even if he lost the election.

Bush chose not to take the bait. His speech later that night did not directly address Nixon's call for massive aid to support the efforts of Russian president Boris Yeltsin. "We invested so much to win the cold war. We must invest what is necessary to win the peace," he said. Echoing the Nixon memorandum, he said, "If we fail, we will create new and profound problems for our security and that of Europe and Asia. . . . We must support reform, not only in Russia but throughout the former Soviet Union and Eastern Europe." He sounded like Nixon but without Nixon's sense of urgency and without his commitment to large-scale aid.

Both the president and the former president denied a rift between them on the policy question and praised each other's foreign policy expertise, but the political tension was palpable. Nixon had, in a single stroke, reprimanded the incumbent president in the middle of a difficult reelection campaign. That Bush would forgive and forget was not an option. Nixon's personal and political relationship with Bush might never be the same, but the attention he had focused on the dire Russian situation was worth the sacrifice. "National interest first," he said to me, "political relationships second."

Within the next week, Nixon's message exploded in the press. Every major newspaper in the country, including his old nemesis *The Washington Post,* issued praise for Nixon's arguments for aid to Russia. "He is right," editorialized the *Post.* Nixon, ecstatic, asked me to save all articles pertaining to the memorandum, his speech, Bush's speech, and the media coverage of the issue and the event. He ripped a page out of *The Economist* entitled "A Briefing from Mr. Nixon" and passed it to me with the following passage underlined: "Mr. Nixon said that Mr. Bush was 'uniquely qualified' to meet the challenge [of aiding Russia]. But he also said [both in his private memo and in *Time*] that 'the mark of great political leadership is not simply to support what is popular but to make what is unpopular popular if it is in America's interest.' That hardly sounds like what Mr. Bush has been doing for the past few months." Nixon scribbled underneath, "Monica—we got to all of the editors, but did we get to Bush?"

The question was double-edged: Nixon had affected Bush politically by forcing him to address the highly sensitive and un-

popular issue of aid to Russia, but he could not make Bush act
on it. Whatever the policy result, Nixon had accomplished his
three goals: he had attracted enough attention to the Russian
situation to force a U.S. response, he had done effective political
blocking for Bush on the issue, and he had forced the president
to answer the challenge, if not meet it, and perhaps reenergize
his campaign.

The campaign, however, did not receive the lift Nixon had intended. On March 16, he wrote a memorandum of political advice for Bush in which he told him to ignore Buchanan, prevent
Clinton from setting the agenda, particularly on the economy,
use the media instead of being used by them, emphasize his foreign policy accomplishments while initiating a new one with
Russian aid, and establish a vision for his campaign. It was a
note not only of strategy but of encouragement.

"The poor guy looks like he's really struggling," Nixon said to
me. "I want him to have this before the Michigan and Illinois
primaries tomorrow. It's really a pep talk. Bush is a pragmatic
idealist, but his prudence overruns his ideals. People want
strength in their president. The reason his approval ratings went
so high after the Persian Gulf War was because he made the hard
decisions. Now he's back to being the mushy moderate, and no
one respects that."

Fortunately for Bush, his primary challenger began to fade.
Buchanan's percentages in the primaries were faltering.
"Buchanan is now getting a little less than one third of the vote,
but one third of the voters are kooks anyway," said Nixon on
March 18 after taking a call from Buchanan and agreeing to
meet with him at his office the next Saturday. "I want you there
to meet with him. Talk with him for a few minutes. Try to get a
sense of where he is coming from. I know him too well. Besides,
I'll tell him that you are the house liberal. *That* ought to shake
him up!" He let out a hearty laugh. "He'll probably try to win
over your vote!"

On the press that Buchanan's pilgrimage would undoubtedly
attract, Nixon replied, "I don't care. Let the White House think
whatever they want. I couldn't say no to Buchanan. They know

damn well what I am going to tell him: he should leave the man alone and go after Clinton. Besides, they know that Buchanan can't possibly win. The damage he has done is over. You know what he told me? He said, 'Mr. President, I've stepped up to the plate fifteen times—the primaries—and I struck out fifteen times.' He was laughing, but he knows he has no chance in hell. If the White House wants to worry, they are going to worry anyway, but I suppose I should at least call [Chief of Staff Sam] Skinner and let him know."

The call to Skinner must have instilled some fear in Bush, because the president placed a call to Nixon early the next day, ostensibly to thank him for sending the memorandum of political advice.

"I told him that I am seeing Buchanan on Saturday but not to worry—I wasn't going to give away any valuable campaign secrets!" Nixon told me after the conversation. "I also told him what I was going to tell Pat: I said I would couch it in terms of what is best for him. That's how to appeal to people anyway: play to their vanity. Bush seemed a little nervous that I was seeing Buchanan, so I told him that I would put some pressure on him to get out of the race—for historical purposes. I hope that made Bush feel better, but I don't think Buchanan will buy it." Bush's apprehension, Nixon noted, was rooted in his own vulnerabilities, which had been amplified by Buchanan's electoral inroads. The Democratic race was now down to Clinton and former California governor Jerry Brown, but the Republican race was still animated by the challenge to the incumbent. If Nixon could persuade Buchanan to leave the race, Bush would once again owe him his political life.

"By the way," he said to me, "call John Stacks at *Time,* and alert him to the meeting."

I arrived at the office on March 21 to find Secret Service personnel combing the premises. Nixon was already ensconced in his office, surrounded by the morning papers and fussing with his tie.

"It was dark when I put this on this morning," he said to me. "Does it match?"

After convincing him that his tie did indeed match his suit, I picked up the papers to carry them out of the office.

"No, don't take them," he said, stopping me. "They are good for atmosphere." He took the papers from me and organized them on the table. "Atmosphere. That's all most of these damn things are good for anyway."

Nixon escorted Buchanan and his wife, Shelley, into the office and closed the door behind them. Thirty-five minutes into the conversation, Nixon's voice came through my intercom. "Monica, please come in. I want you to meet the Buchanans."

They were extremely warm and tolerant of my intrusion upon their private audience with Nixon, who asked me to sit across from Buchanan. "Pat," he said jokingly, "she's more conservative than you! Which is a good thing since she helps on the foreign policy issues." Referring to the Russian vice president, he said, "She advises me on the [Aleksandr] Rutskois of the world." I took their laughter as a cue to leave.

Nixon stopped me with an unexpected question: "Monica, why don't you tell Pat what *you* think he should do?" A half-smile crossed his face as I turned toward the three of them. He clearly wanted me to back up his message that Buchanan should leave the race.

"Mr. Buchanan, let me preface this by saying that I respect what you have done for this campaign. You have the courage of your convictions and a commitment to principle that is very rare on the American political scene today. And you have provided a vital service to the country by elevating the debate." I looked tentatively at Nixon, who nodded almost imperceptibly. "I think, however, that by pursuing this further, your message is in danger of losing its effectiveness. You have given a full airing of the conservative dissent, and now it may be time to end it, particularly if you want to run again in the future." I held my breath until Nixon broke the silence with a follow-up question.

"How about in terms of what it means for him?" he asked.

"Well, it may be that staying in the race is doing more harm than good. With the Tsongas withdrawal, the media is showing that the Democrats have united behind one candidate, and yet the Republicans can't even unite behind an incumbent president. I fear that it will leave President Bush in a weakened position in November, and you will be blamed, at least in part, for it. You might consider that if you plan to run again." Buchanan nodded, undoubtedly having heard this advice before.

Nixon smiled with approval and escorted the Buchanans out to the waiting press conference. He immediately placed a brief call to Skinner at the White House to inform him of the conversation's content. "I told Buchanan to get out of the race," he told Skinner and, nodding at me, said, "and I had some support on that point. I also told him to go after Clinton and the Congress instead of relentlessly attacking Bush and to hit the Russian-aid question hard. I think he listened."

Nixon replaced the receiver and said, "He'll tell Bush, but it won't stop Bush from worrying. Although he's way out there on most issues, Buchanan is a damn impressive candidate; he just has to straighten out his foreign policy. Isolationism simply doesn't work in this world. At least Bush has that working for him. And Buchanan's not even getting ink anymore."

In March, Clinton was broadsided by allegations of financial wrongdoing as governor of Arkansas. The nationwide savings and loan scandals had reached into Arkansas, where Clinton had allegedly benefited from misused funds involving a defunct land-development deal. As serious as the complex yet uninvestigated charges were, Nixon sensed that as a Democratic candidate, Clinton would receive mild treatment from the press.

"This S-and-L scandal or whatever it is—these sweetheart deals he made are big, and they are treating him with kid gloves. Imagine if this had been us—or Reagan or Bush! Look what the press did to me—the Herblock cartoons and whatnot. The way they are treating Clinton is disgusting. And I know that what we have seen so far on this financial stuff is just the tip of the iceberg. The problem is that the press doesn't want you to see the rest of the iceberg."

On March 29, Tricia Nixon Cox called her father with more disturbing news: Clinton had admitted to the recreational use of marijuana during his days as a Rhodes scholar in Great Britain.

"Clinton said, 'I didn't break the law *of my own country,*' "
Nixon said to me in disgust. "He's a clever bastard."

Scandal after scandal engulfed candidate Clinton only to fail
to have any discernible impact on his campaign. Issues that
would have discredited any other candidate seemed to give new
life to Clinton, defying the odds of politics and granting momentum to the Democrat. He was now winning primaries consistently, in spite of the scandals, and clearly would be the
nominee.

Nixon's own fate with regard to the Republican National
Convention was less certain. The party establishment had not
formally invited him since his resignation, though each election
year the topic was actively debated, and each year Nixon professed his unwillingness to go. "I am *not* going to the convention. It is just not in my interests. It will be a dog-and-pony show
with the three former presidents; besides, who wants to see three
old men sitting up there anyway? It will be fine for Reagan to
go—and logical since Bush was his vice president. But for me?
No way. The conference was such a huge success that I don't
want to detract from that. And anyway, I don't want to make a
politically partisan speech because, one, if Bush loses, I'll look
bad, and two, I need to preserve the bipartisan support required
for Russian aid. No convention for me."

Nixon's disavowal of a convention invitation before the actual invitation was issued was more of a defense mechanism
than a principled decision. He had become so used to protecting
himself from the political rejection brought on by his resignation that he often preempted it before it could hurt him.
Whether or not an invitation to the convention were delivered,
Nixon would not attend.

Nixon tossed two items at me the morning of April 8: the
first, Strobe Talbott's *Time* article defending Clinton's draft evasion and the other, Garry Kasparov's piece in *The Wall Street
Journal,* "Campaign '92 and the Rest of the World." The Talbott piece looked as if it had been ripped with a vengeance from
the rest of the magazine and did not even merit Nixon's under-
lining.

"Would you believe this?" he asked, pointing furiously at the article in my hands. "Clinton is a goddamned liar."

I glanced at Kasparov's article and noticed that Nixon had highlighted certain lines and scribbled on the top that it was "brilliant." Referring to Kasparov's argument that isolating rather than engaging Communist states would accelerate liberalization, Nixon wrote that China was clearly the exception.

"The campaign," he said to me, "is on the domestic track, and Bush is going to suffer because of it. If he doesn't bring foreign policy back into the discussion, even though it is unpopular, he will be doing a grave disservice to the country."

Bush's lack of vision made Nixon anxious every time Bush made a campaign-related appearance. He knew that a directionless president was apt to make mistakes not only in relating to voters but in campaign strategy. Bush held a press conference on April 10 in which he failed to state clearly what the objective of a second term would be. The effects were devastating. The president was suddenly more vulnerable on questions of his political character. More interested in personal relationships than ideas, he had been consistently willing to change his public positions to suit the needs of the moment and later discard them under competing pressures. Equivocation on the issues was one matter; hesitation on why he deserved a second term was another. His inability to give the voters a compelling reason to choose him again doomed his candidacy to a mundane rehash of his past achievements. The fresh ideas seemed to belong to his Democratic opponent.

"This is going to be a mean-spirited, dirty campaign, maybe even dirtier than most," Nixon said on April 13, shaking his head. "I'm sorry. I wanted to show you the ins and outs of campaign politics, and this campaign—my model—is dull as hell, not to mention ludicrous." He nodded to me. "This is bad. Let's see if I can put it in historical perspective. In '44 I was overseas. In '48, Truman was great; he really defied the odds. Nineteen fifty-two was exciting because we had Eisenhower versus [Senator Robert] Taft, two titans fighting it out. Nineteen fifty-six was just a replay. Nineteen sixty was probably the greatest election of the century because we had *two very good candidates,*" he said slowly. "In '64, everyone knew it was going to be a land-slide. The GOP speeches were good, but they were talking to themselves. Nineteen sixty-eight was interesting; '72 less so, but [Senator George] McGovern was an interesting angle. Nineteen seventy-six was dull because neither Ford nor Carter was very interesting. Nineteen eighty was interesting because of the Rea-gan breakthrough. Nineteen eighty-four was fairly empty, and '88 wasn't very interesting—it was just the Reagan afterglow. So here we are, watching maybe the dullest of them all, with the most vapid candidates."

Early in April, another candidate entered the scene, threaten-ing the two-party balance. H. Ross Perot, the self-made billion-aire from Texas, stated publicly that he was weighing a campaign as an independent candidate. Petition drives began in all fifty states to get him on the November ballot, and specula-tion began that a Perot candidacy could become a significant force in the rest of the campaign. Voter apathy and dissatisfac-tion with a nondescript incumbent and a flawed challenger con-tributed to an enormous groundswell of support for Perot, who had not yet advanced any positions on the issues but offered a novel alternative to the traditional two candidates.

Nixon read an early poll conducted by the Prodigy online ser-vice that showed Perot with 36 percent of the vote to Bush's 28 percent and *Nixon* having attracted some write-in votes. "Mon-ica—amusing!" he wrote at the top of the article and dismissed the poll findings. "[Perot] won't run. He'll be less attractive as voters see more of him."

Independent candidates traditionally cannot get more than 20 percent of the popular vote in a general election because they cannot overcome the enormous financial and organizational ad-vantages enjoyed by the two major parties. Perot, however, had a massive personal fortune, which he was willing to spend, and a corps of volunteers nationwide that had already organized it-self into an efficient framework. Perot was an outsider, a party-less candidate who appealed to a volatile and frustrated electorate. What Perot stood for was less important than the fact that he stood alone. Perot set out to banish politics as usual, the effects of which would not be felt significantly until the primary season ended.

Meanwhile, social unrest marred the domestic landscape. After the Los Angeles police officers accused of beating the motorist Rodney King were acquitted of the most serious charges, widespread riots erupted on April 30 and engulfed the city in racially violent chaos. It became an opportunity for Bush to regain control, project presidential authority, and demonstrate leadership by appealing for calm in a forceful and dispassionate way.

Despite the inevitable criticism that Bush had failed to mend racial divides, eliminate economic class conflicts, and restore civic health to urban areas, Nixon believed that Bush could make the politics of the riots work for him. After Bush's Oval Office speech on the matter, he responded with praise. "The speech was one of Bush's best. He was strong and decisive; it must have been Peggy Noonan. At least he delivered it with some conviction. It will help him in the image department."

He reflected on his own experience with domestic unrest. "Bush thinks this is bad," he said. "My God, we had millions in the streets. Thousands were rioting over the damn war over many years. You were born years after Watts in '65. It was a hell of a time. But both times, the upheaval was totally senseless. In this case, the jury saw things that we did not, but it didn't give the cops the right to beat him. I don't know; I wasn't there. But the videotape sealed the fate of this situation in any event. I'm afraid that we have gotten to the point where in the major cities our police chiefs must be black to project positive black authority.

"And as far as Jesse Jackson is concerned with this whole mess, he is out there talking to the blacks in Watts, but you don't see him living with them. He just likes to pose around controversy. I think he is just posturing for the number-two spot on the ticket, but Clinton will never go for it. He wants the presidency too much. He's shrewd. And he already knows that he has the black vote. I'm just glad that Bush stepped up to this. He looks like a president again."

On May 4, Nixon began to turn his attention to the potential of a Perot candidacy. He had sprained his ankle in Florida several days before and was at home recuperating when he first analyzed Perot's chances with me.

"Ignore the foot," he said as he lifted it in its soft cast onto the ottoman. "I hate to have anyone see me disabled like this. So much for running for president this year!"

He picked up copies of poll results from May 3 in Arizona and Colorado showing Perot ahead of both Bush and Clinton. "These," he said, tapping the page, "are disturbing. Perot is showing strength when no one knows what the hell he stands for. He could be a contender if he wins a Bush state like Texas or Florida. California should be a Bush state, but with everything going on there, it will go to Clinton."

"Without California, can Bush still win?" I asked.

"He can," he said, looking down at his cast, "but it will be a very close run thing."

Several days later, when *The New York Times* ran a front-page story about Perot's visit to the Nixon White House, Nixon's face betrayed cynicism. "That story is nothing. He never gave us anything. [Former ambassador Walter] Annenberg called me this morning peeved because Perot pledged to our library and never came through, and he did the same to the Reagans. Anyway, that's sort of petty stuff, but it does point to a bigger issue: he doesn't keep his word, and he doesn't say what he means. Radical change is Perot's appeal. The fiscal-responsibility issues of cutting spending and reining in the deficit help him tremendously. I may be wrong to discount him. Politics may have changed too much. People like his straight talk. They sense that neither Bush nor Clinton has any convictions. Perot will at least shake the place up. Look at the incredible numbers he's polling! We had [Alabama governor George] Wallace in '68, but he only polled seventeen percent. And [Hubert] Humphrey and I had core constituencies; Bush doesn't. He's not up for the 'big play.' We have to remember that he wouldn't have gone into the Persian Gulf if [British prime minister Margaret] Thatcher hadn't been there with him, and he wouldn't have stepped up to the Russian-aid issue if I hadn't pushed him into it. Bush is vulnerable, and he shouldn't be, god-damn it."

Nixon's frustration with Bush's lack of leadership translated into a fascination with Perot's appeal. Although he could not win the election, Perot had the resources and the timing to re-shape the political landscape. On May 20, however, headlines were stolen from Perot by an unlikely bandit: Dan Quayle.

He had delivered a speech in San Francisco in which he crit-icized the fictional television character Murphy Brown for hav-ing a child out of wedlock. The speech was more pointedly about the decay of family values in America and the moral codes and ethical conduct that guide behavior and determine right and wrong. The day-after press coverage of the speech at-tacked Quayle and the speech as representative of the radical conservative right, a direct appeal to the conservative faithful two weeks before the California primary, and a broad defense of Republican ideology. Conservatives considered the taunting and the mockery of Quayle's message a reflection of intoler-ance of traditional values and basic morality. For the Demo-crats, it was neither fashionable nor politically correct to address these topics; for Bush, it was too risky. By default, then, the chore fell to Dan Quayle, who had little to lose and possi-bly much to gain.

The decline of moral culture may have brought derision upon the messenger, but the message seemed to resonate with voters angry about the loss of traditional virtues and noble, decent, and good ways of life. The debate was not, as Quayle's detrac-tors argued, about intolerance of alternative families, uncondi-tional acceptance of traditional ones, and political gauges of moral life. It was about the propriety of public discussion of the sensitive issues of right and wrong, good and bad, morality, im-morality, and amorality. They are not subjects that lend them-selves easily to objective assessments. Quayle intended to call attention to the decline in moral culture and offer the renewal of individual values as a way to reverse the trend. It was both a brash political move to give Bush a campaign vision based upon values and a shrewd broadside to Clinton's apparent lack of them. Nixon appreciated the maneuver.

"Did you see the play that Quayle got?" he asked me. "One thing is for sure: the guy's got guts. It took a hell of a lot of courage to stand up and say what he did, especially out there in California. Poor Quayle. He is trying so hard—he's the only one carrying any water for Bush—and Bush just seems to use him without supporting him. I cannot believe that [press secretary Marlin] Fitzwater said that Bush agreed with Quayle on this only to turn around and backpedal after he saw the elite reaction. To hell with the elite reaction. Quayle was right-on. Can't they get it together down there, goddamn it!" He paused and lowered his voice. "Look, Bush should have supported Quayle and taken on the issue himself. He should be the primary spokesman on the values thing for two main reasons: one, Clinton is a moral disaster, and the contrast between them is stark, and two, because he is still the president, and he has a traditional family. There is a lot of political mileage to be had here if Bush could only get it together instead of hanging poor Quayle out to dry."

He changed his tone again and said, "Murphy Brown sounds like a man. Is that that Candice Bergen show?" I answered him, and he continued, "I met her once when she was about sixteen and I went to a party at the Bergens'. Anyway, I cannot believe that a fictional character made it into the Oval Office. The press was wrong to ask Bush about it as he was standing there with [Canadian prime minister Brian] Mulroney. 'Oh, gee,' I would have said, 'I don't follow the show. Next question.' "

Bush's equivocation on the family-values theme and his failure to support Quayle created a sense that the president's lack of convictions was more serious than many thought. A California poll conducted right after the Murphy Brown debate showed Perot with 39 percent, Clinton with 26 percent, and Bush with 25 percent. Nixon, considering the political landscape of his home state, shook his head in disbelief. "Well, there you have it. My God, it is worse than I thought."

"I think that the Perot appeal goes far beyond the deficiencies of Bush and Clinton," I said.

"Right. He has tapped into an undercurrent of society that craves some kind of renewal, some kind of meaning. The man at the top is not providing the necessary leadership. And Clinton is as weak as piss on a rock. What choice do voters have but to look in another direction?"

The apparently clear answer disturbed him. "The Perot phenomenon—there is no other word for it, is there?—has really taken off," he said on June 7, upon his return from Russia. "I honestly didn't think it would, but the guy is just damn good at his rallies and interviews. He brings the house down. In all of the newspapers abroad, Perot was everywhere. I see that the media is off cultivating him. Interesting. And by the way, what the hell was Clinton doing on *The Arsenio Hall Show*? What *is* that show, anyway?" Since Nixon professed not to watch television, I assumed in my answer that he did not know it was a talk show.

"First of all," he said, "I didn't know what to expect from this guy Arsenio Hall until I saw Clinton standing there with him, playing the goddamned saxophone. Oh, boy! Is that desperation to be liked or what?"

He grew serious. "Both Clinton and Bush are so frantic to regain the spotlight from Perot that they seem willing to do anything. Their negatives are so high. I see Bush has fallen to thirty percent approval. My God! That's where we were in the middle of Watergate: twenty-five to twenty-eight percent. That's really bad for a sitting president. His major problem, apart from not showing any ideological backbone, is that he has some real difficulty communicating with regular people. I heard him the other day say 'a splash of Tabasco.' A 'splash'? That's so elitist. In my day, I heard everyone saying 'Wait a sec.' What the hell is a 'sec'? I'd never say it because I'd look ridiculous. It's the same for Bush. He needs to just be himself. He is an elitist, and that's fine, but he can't fake *not* being one. And he also can't fake the fact that he doesn't look like he has the spirit to win." Nixon was so torn between wanting and refusing to give Bush advice that he resorted to giving the advice to me.

Three days later, when I asked whether his public advice to Bush—to say what is right with himself, not wrong with the others—was still possible, he whispered, "No, I don't think he can do it." He leaned back and pointed his finger in the air. "You know, Perot should ignore Bush and Clinton, and neither of them should attack Perot."

The advice was about to find its way to the third-party candidate himself. Perot called Nixon and told him that he would arrive for a private discussion the next day. Nixon was thrilled at the prospect of being called upon by a presidential candidate who might actually listen to him. His advice to Bush was filtered through Baker and others with their own agendas, and his counsel to Buchanan to leave the race had gone unheeded. Perot, however, began with a clean slate, and Nixon sought to use the opportunity to advance his own profile as well as to advise Perot.

Nixon paced in his office the morning of June 11 as he waited for Perot's arrival. "This is called 'waiting for Perot.' " He laughed. "You know, like *Waiting for Godot?*" he said, referring to the play by Samuel Beckett.

"Only Godot never arrives in the play, sir," I said.

"Well, he's already a half hour late. Maybe Perot won't show up either."

To Nixon's great irritation, Perot arrived two hours late, pleading traffic delays. The candidate bounded into the office and shook hands with the staff members, proclaiming, "Ross Perot! How are you? Good to see you!" He led Nixon around his own office, bellowing questions without waiting for the answers. His words rolled over everyone in his presence, including Nixon, who quickly escorted him to the waiting limousine and over to his residence for lunch. After Perot's departure one and a half hours later, Nixon met with me.

"Well, he is something else, isn't he? You can see why voters are attracted to him. He's dynamic and loud and seems full of ideas. I'm glad I saw him. We'll leak it, of course. It's a hot story. The press will hate it, especially when they are set to beat the hell out of me next week for the Watergate anniversary. But they'll have to admit that Perot is seeking my advice. I really got a kick out of all of this. I'll tell you what we spoke about; I think you'll find it interesting." He picked up the legal pad upon which he had scribbled his notes and put his eyeglasses on.

"Perot wanted my suggestions on foreign policy and advisers. I told him that the number-one issue of our time is the survival of the Russian democratic experiment and that he must do everything he can to ensure that Yeltsin and his reformers survive. I gave him my suggestion for a special committee under one person designed to coordinate and unify all aid to Russia; no one else has picked it up, so what the hell. I gave it to Perot. I also told him that he had better surround himself with some qualified foreign policy types to reassure voters that he wouldn't get us into a hell of a mess."

Nixon removed the glasses. "I couldn't believe it. He says to me, 'Who would have thought that a short, ugly Texan would be ahead of the pack?' At least he's good at the self-deprecating stuff. He's going to need it." The glasses went back on, and he continued.

"I told him that the source of his appeal is that he is real and not airbrushed. That silly book *The Making of the President* by [Joe] McGinniss—or whoever that was—said that about me," he said, confusing unwittingly McGinnis's *The Selling of the President, 1968,* with Theodore White's book about John Kennedy. "I never even met the guy. I relate more to the hard-hat types and those in the Silent Majority than probably anyone else.

"Anyway, I told Perot that if he wins Texas and California, he would deny the election to Bush, whom he dislikes. Perot's fear is that no one decent will ever want to run since the system is so screwed up. He told me that he wanted to change that. I said that since our conventions will be dull as hell, he should stage something big either right before or right after the Republican convention. He seemed to take to that idea. I said his campaign should be clean and not negative. Perot agreed. What impresses me most is that the guy's got guts." He removed the glasses a final time and tapped the legal pad. "This will antagonize the hell out of the Bushies. To hell with them. If they want my advice, they can ask and stand in line these days!"

For Nixon, the Perot visit was significant on several levels. It put the former president back in the arena of campaign politics. It forced Bush to seek him out more aggressively than he had initially. It had the potential to motivate Bush to campaign more energetically and in a more anti-Perot and anti-Clinton way. It animated Perot's campaign and granted it greater legitimacy. And it showed that since Nixon was playing all sides, his confidence in a Bush win was slim. This made Clinton hopeful, Perot optimistic, and Bush anxious. Nixon did more than simply advise another presidential candidate; he lit a fire under the campaign.

Three days later, on June 14, Bush called Nixon, apparently reeling from the Nixon-Perot summit. "Before I tell you what the Bush call was all about," he said to me, "what is your latest line on Perot?"

"The more exposure he gets, the less popular he will be," I replied.

"I agree, because he got his highest popularity numbers when he first began his effort. But they have only gone down slightly. I think that they will once people see that he doesn't know a lot about most things. Good!

"Well, this is what I told Bush. Let me fill you in. I dictated a memo on the conversation—in full—which I will let you see tomorrow. He called at ten-thirty, and we talked for twenty-five minutes. It went that long at his request. It was the most substantive talk since the Gulf War. He began talking about the Earth Summit [the UN Conference on Environment and Development] in Rio [de Janeiro] and said that the tear gas episode he endured in Panama was nothing like what I went through in '58, but the Panamanians just overreacted. We talked about Yeltsin, and I hit the Baker thing hard. I told him that Yeltsin likes *him* and will bring some surprises for him when he arrives this week, but he doesn't like Baker and will not work through him. Bush was silent, but he needed to hear it. Baker is his blind spot.

"As you know, the last subject of any conversation is always the main point. He turned to Perot, and he was fit to be tied. He called him a phony and said he'll flame out. He didn't even mention Clinton. But, boy, he's sensitive about Perot. He says that the guy has changed his positions so many times. That, of course, is defensive. Perot is not going to flame out. He is not going to fall into the single digits; his support is broader, deeper, and more sustainable than anyone else's third-party candidacy. [George] Wallace ran on the race issue and only carried four hard-core states. But Wallace was single issue and Perot covers many of the important ones, particularly on the economy. He's far more mainstream.

"If Perot hangs on through the summer, where does the Clinton vote go? Could go to Bush. It will dwindle to a two-person race, and it seems that the odd man out may be Clinton. Bush was looking to be reassured that I would support him. Skinner called after I saw Buchanan to do the same. Remember? Instead of worrying about whom I am talking to, they should be worried about themselves. Anyway, when I asked Bush if he had seen my Friday op-ed on Russia in the *Times,* he said that he hadn't. I couldn't believe it. Baker probably kept it from him. It was a good conversation. He is just so nervous about Perot. It's eating him up."

Nixon's satisfaction with his own role in advising the candidates was tempered by his sympathy for Bush. His personal fondness for Bush could not overcome the political disappointment he felt. He experienced some guilt by wishing challengers on Bush but knew that that was the only way to make Bush a better candidate. Even a traditional guarantee of higher approval ratings—a summit with a Russian leader—did not elevate Bush's sagging poll numbers.

"Take a look at this," Nixon said on June 15, handing me a column by George Will he had ripped from *Newsweek*. "No, no. Don't read the whole article. Just look at what I circled." He had drawn a line around a passage describing Bush as one of the weakest presidents, Clinton as one of the weakest challengers, and Perot as a "bantamweight" who only looked strong because the others were so weak. Nixon had written next to the passage, "Interesting." "I suppose that we have seen mediocrity in presidents and challengers before," he said, "but never in both in the same election."

By the end of June, Nixon believed that Bush was almost destined to lose the election. Seventy percent of the electorate believed that the country was on the wrong track and that Bush was largely at fault. If he were to win, according to Nixon, he would have to change his campaign strategy. The campaign and the White House had to become more confrontational and less accommodating. Only by relentlessly attacking the enemies of Bush's policies with a sharply defined ideological message could the campaign construct a winning conservative plurality. The right-of-center plurality could be won in enough states to win both a popular-vote plurality and an electoral-college majority. The question was not how to defeat Perot but how to keep Perot's disaffected voters from defeating Bush with Clinton.

Nixon knew that Clinton was far better positioned to win than either Bush or Perot. The essence of Bush's strategy had to be to shore up his natural right-of-center coalition and prevent Clinton from emerging successfully from a battle with Perot as the candidate for change. Bush himself had to take the offensive and define the election ideologically. He needed a sharp-edged campaign, which so far he had chosen not to run. Attacks would bring free media coverage. Ideological assaults would win votes. Bush had to start criticizing Clinton and his liberal base, particularly the Congress, and begin a debate not unlike Quayle's message of right and wrong. Nixon felt that Bush must not waver on this message. Discipline and leadership were required. If Bush could achieve this, he still might have a chance to win in November.

"I'm concerned about his recent press coverage," Nixon said on June 25. "It's pretty bad. They are beating the hell out of Bush and Perot and ignoring Clinton because they want him. He'll gain by a feud between Bush and Perot. The attacks on Perot are pretty intense, although nowhere near the intensity of Watergate. They're into bashing Perot now because they have created a monster. All this stuff about Perot being dictatorial, et cetera—it's nonsense. Perot was always Perot. The media is just running scared now. The only way Perot can survive is if he can lead a popular charge against the press, and wouldn't *that* be something! But you know," he said, "they are all such whiners. Bush, Clinton, Perot—they are all complaining about below-the-belt tactics as if they didn't anticipate them in a presidential race. Now, please!"

Bush honestly believed that he had been a good president and that since he had given his country such honorable and lengthy service, he deserved a second term. He was clearly hurt and confused that the voters did not agree. "I've worked my heart out as president!" Bush cried at the end of the month.

Nixon was in disbelief. Instead of wallowing in destructive self-analysis, Bush should have been engaging in the type of politics that would help him win the campaign. For Nixon, the campaign was not zero-sum. If Bush and Perot lost ground, it did not necessarily mean that Clinton gained it. This was crucial if Bush planned to lift himself out of third place in the polls and win by default.

Malek called again on the last day of June. "He's so desperate," Nixon said to me after the conversation. "He said that I *really* knew how to run things. He's scared. The fact that he called me is significant."

Nixon's vow to withhold advice from the Bush team proved meaningless. Despite the early wounds to his personal pride left by Bush's neglect, Nixon felt obligated to help his party stay in power. More important, with the primaries over and the Democratic convention days away, he could not accept the idea of Bill Clinton in the White House. Bush, the lesser of the two evils, needed Nixon's counsel even if Nixon felt that he did not deserve it.

On July 7, Nixon considered the upcoming convention and the inevitable nominee. He tried to prepare himself for the Clinton candidacy and turned back my assessment that he was too damaged to win the general election. "On the political side, I disagree with you on Clinton. He's the real opponent for Bush. Perot will remain in it, although there's no question but that he has been damaged. His support is a fraction of what mine was—the Silent Majority. Clinton will get a lift out of his convention but not much.

"Of course, Bush should be able to exploit his foreign policy experience, like the G7 [Group of Seven industrial states] meeting, but he won't. He will start flailing around, saying that he's ready to fight. And he *was* up to it last time. But last time he had a formidable campaign team: [Roger] Ailes, Noonan, and Atwater. This time he's really behind the eight ball. I do think, though, that Perot's entry is good for the country because it still may sharpen the campaign. Perot's ability to attract heavyweight talent depends on his popular support level. If it stays high, he could get some decent people to work for him."

He refocused on Bush through a different lens. "Eisenhower, as you know, thought highly of Bush. He was very impressed by business types—most military men are—and with the class thing. Bush was old money, and Eisenhower related to that."

"Did you think that Bush would have performed better as president?" I asked.

"No. I knew that he wasn't a strong man politically," he replied, pointing a finger to himself. "A good man, but not strong. And goodness does not necessarily make for an effective leader."

Clinton, aware of his own vulnerabilities on the character issue, sought out the respected Tennessee senator Al Gore as his running mate on July 9. Gore would provide the ticket with character balance if not regional balance. Nixon thought it was a good choice. "Gore is smart. He got there with help from his father, but he's still smart. He's very strong on the environment, which Clinton wants. And he's been all right on foreign policy. The only problem, for both sides, will come in the debates. Quayle *and* Gore? These are two slick, handsome, career politicians—"

"Vying for VP at a time when Americans are rejecting that type of airbrushed professional candidate," I said, finishing his sentence.

"Right. This is why Perot must choose someone like *him:* folksy, plain-speaking. The image will be powerful.

"The Gore choice was solid. I've thought for a long time that regional balance on a ticket doesn't matter anymore. But Gore will help him in the border states. Clinton will get a five- to six-point lift with this. And as far as Bush is concerned, he must not talk about the good he's done in the past. People don't want that. They want to know what you will do in the future. Especially now. The media is making things look pretty bad, and Bush is asking, 'Look at all the good I've done.' It's a mistake."

Early the next morning, Nixon walked into my office, opened his briefcase on my desk, and handed me two articles. The first, from *The Wall Street Journal,* suggested that Perot was too inexperienced to run the nation's foreign policy. The other, a yellowed copy of the *New York Herald Tribune* from August 1, 1952, had been pulled from Nixon's personal archives. "Compare this with the rhetoric put out by Quayle and the others," he said. "I had no speechwriters, no staff, no one to help me, and yet I managed to make some decent speeches as a candidate. I notice that Quayle's negatives are higher than ever. None of his speeches on the cultural elite did any good. The damage on him is irreversible, at least as far as this election is concerned. And Perot must fear slippage in the polls above all. The other two can slip, but for Perot it would be fatal. He must assemble a good group of responsible people and forget about political operatives. In the end, Clinton is the man to beat."

Nixon had always spoken freely over the phone about highly sensitive political issues because he was confident that his lines were secure. Every once in a while, FBI agents arrived at the office and swept Nixon's phones for listening devices. Though they never indicated whether or not they found any, Nixon believed that the only ones remaining after such a visit would have been put there by the FBI itself. This did not concern him. During the primary season, however, we both heard peculiar sounds on his office and home telephones; suspecting that they were tapped, he decided, three days before the Democratic convention, to take action.

"Monica, I want to flush out anyone listening in on my conversations, so this is the plan: I am going to call you and tell you that I am coming out for Perot. Keep a straight face and a straight voice. If anyone is eavesdropping, it will make it to the press, and we will know."

The next morning, my phone rang. "I have decided to endorse Perot, maybe this week when I'm in California. Does that bother you?" he asked.

Playing along in this surreal episode, I replied, "No, sir, it doesn't, but it will certainly be a political bombshell."

Either no one was tapping Nixon's phones, or no one cared enough to leak Nixon's planted tidbit to the press, because his scheme produced no result. Relieved that he could now talk freely and confidentially, he began a running commentary with me on the Democratic convention in calls from California, where he was to deliver a speech to the annual summer retreat of San Francisco's private Bohemian Club.

When Jesse Jackson took the podium at the convention on July 14, three days after he had endorsed Clinton, the party was almost whole. There were continuing negotiations between the party leadership and the last holdout for the job, former California governor Jerry Brown. The message, however, was unity. The baby boom "social" liberals had risen up to claim the mantle of government but had included the "redistributive" liberals and others under their banner of the New Democrat. The complacent, centrist mood was reminiscent of the end of the 1950s, when the Democratic Party, as it swept to power, seemed able to encompass the hopes of every radical, disaffected group in the country. In a half dozen years, it found it could not. Clinton and his supporting cast would meet a similar fate if elected, Nixon believed, and that in itself would be vindication.

"Today I drove up to Santa Monica, where I campaigned in 1950," he said when he called me on July 14. "Everywhere I went, people said that I should be running for president and that no one is as smart and as politically savvy as I am—and whatnot. It was something!" He brimmed with satisfaction. "But I'll tell you one thing. It does go to show that people are looking for real leadership—someone to fill the void that neither Bush, nor Perot, nor Clinton seems up to filling."

Perot apparently was no longer willing to be the self-styled political savior. On July 16, I called Nixon to tell him that Perot had dropped out of the race. Before I could impart my news, he said, "Well, I go away for a few days, and the world falls apart," referring to the fact that Perot strategist Ed Rollins had quit the campaign the day before.

"Mr. President, have you been watching Perot?" I asked.

"Watching him?" he repeated.

"Sir, he dropped out of the race."

Nixon paused for a long moment. "My God! Well, I guess it was logical. Rollins quit, and now he's finished as an adviser. And [international-affairs expert] Paul Nitze quit because Perot wanted to disengage from Europe. He's way out there on foreign policy. Well! I was wrong on Perot. I really thought he'd see it through. What was his reason?"

I told him that Perot said that he didn't want to disrupt the process by having the election thrown into the House in the event of a three-way split.

"Isn't that the damnedest reason? He seemed to have it together, but he was really just boiling over," he said. "After tonight, Clinton will be twelve to fifteen points ahead of Bush, and Bush will have to rise to the occasion. Look, Clinton has given the Bush team all of the material they need: the draft dodging, the lying, and the rest. Bush just needs to remind voters of that. He doesn't even have to lie. It's all there. Both of them will pick up from Perot, maybe Bush more than Clinton because Perot took more away from him."

Later that evening, he wanted to discuss the Clinton and Gore speeches at the convention. He expressed profound disappointment, not only with the speeches but with the broader fact that Clinton and Gore were the candidates. "First of all," he said, "Clinton made a mistake by talking about his state. Talking about Arkansas really doesn't help him. Second, Hillary's eyes were ice-cold. She doesn't help him either. And third, his speech wasn't very good. It was too verbose and too long. He didn't show command. And he lost a few people with this 'New Covenant' crap. What the hell is *that*? It's as bad as Bush's

'New Paradigm.' These Ivy Leaguers who come up with this stuff have no real connection to real people. That 'New Covenant' stuff fell flat. New Deal, New Frontier—fine. But this doesn't work. Nobody knows what the hell it is. And as far as the personal anecdotes go in acceptance speeches, I always used them sparingly. I talked about Yorba Linda and my mother. But these guys went overboard."

Nixon's gravest concern, however, was that neither Clinton nor Gore focused enough on the big issues of foreign policy. "Each of them spent only four minutes talking about foreign policy. I know that it isn't popular, but goddamn it, they are asking for votes, and they had better show that they are responsible."

The Democratic National Convention had produced a nominee who Nixon thought several months before was completely unelectable. The firebrand independent had quit. And the incumbent president remained weak electorally. The unresolved question was to whom the Perot voters would defect. Nixon thought that since Clinton had positioned himself as the candidate for change, the Perot malcontents would likely gravitate toward him. Bush could benefit only if the Perot supporters decided that they were safer with the devil they knew in the White House than with the devil they did not know. If, however, these voters were willing to support the renegade Perot in the first place, they might risk voting for Clinton.

The day after Perot's announcement, CNN ran a poll showing that 53 percent of the Perot supporters said they would lean toward Clinton while only 35 percent said they would support Bush. Fear again pervaded the Bush White House, and Skinner called Nixon in California. Unfortunately, Nixon missed the call and was forced to speculate. "I hope to God they don't want me to speak at the convention. I won't do it. It's a loser all around." He believed more strongly, however, that Skinner knew Baker was about to assume control, which in turn was producing a grand fight between the White House and the State Department. "Baker loves his job with that cushy office in Foggy Bottom. No way he'll want to give that up unless Bush personally forces him to do it. Baker has the Mideast peace talks coming up with [Israeli prime minister Yitzhak] Rabin, and there may be a new chance to make a breakthrough, so he really doesn't want to leave State. But Bush really wants to win, and that's that."

Nixon knew that Bush would prevail in convincing Baker to command the reelection effort from the White House, but it would be a move long resented by Baker. As one of Bush's oldest friends and a former campaign strategist, Baker had the trust of the president and the credentials to lead the campaign. It would not, however, be a job to which Baker would go willingly. To confirm his suspicions about the Baker transfer, Nixon called Haig on July 23 and had me listen to his side of the conversation.

"You say, Al, that they are despondent down there and very depressed. Bush should let Darman and [Treasury Secretary Nicholas] Brady go and introduce his new team for the second term," he said with a wry smile. "So Baker is coming over to run the campaign. . . . You know, he's very overrated as a campaign director. But the best reason to get Baker to run the campaign is because it keeps him the hell out of foreign policy!"

Haig's verification of the Baker rumor confirmed Nixon's view that Baker would run the campaign for the purely selfish reason of preserving his position as secretary of state in a second Bush administration. Problems would inevitably arise, however, when it became clear to voters that Bush's team wanted the president's reelection more for themselves than for the president or the country.

On July 21, Nixon, along with the other former presidents, had received another foreign policy form letter from Bush. Bush had crossed out the salutation "Dear President Nixon" and replaced it with a handwritten "Dear Dick." At the bottom of the last page, Bush added a postscript: "Ray Price is being *very* helpful." Price had been Nixon's chief speechwriter and remained his close confidant, particularly on domestic political matters. He was a brilliant wordsmith, and Nixon had suggested that he collaborate with Bush on the important speeches in order to project a more finely tuned vision for the campaign. Nixon liked and admired Price, called him a true gentleman, and knew that Bush would benefit from his counsel. Bush's note seemed to indicate that he was at least calling on Price, which meant that his speeches and their content would improve. Polls would reflect whether they were making a difference with the voters.

"As you know," Nixon said to me two days later, "in politics everything that goes up comes down. You have to get out there confidently, fighting. Otherwise, you are lost. You have to show that you are made of steel. And cheerful!" he said, plastering a fake smile on his face. "Not ha-ha-ha cheerful, but determined." He made these remarks after seeing a shocking *Washington Post*–ABC News Poll placing Clinton ahead of Bush by thirty percentage points. That substantial a lead is almost insurmountable. Price could help at the margins with Bush's speeches, but ultimately Bush would win or lose on his own merits. The president mouthed the right conservative platitudes about family values, economic growth, and abortion, but voters could tell that he did not mean them. If he did, he would not have decided to turn over the campaign to Baker, a man whom conservatives distrusted. If voters felt that Bush were running a campaign bereft of ideas and conviction, they had an alternative.

Nixon spoke to Skinner several times before the Republican convention and each time stressed the need for Bush to discuss foreign policy in campaign appearances. During one conversation, on July 27, he told Skinner, "I know that the polls show that foreign policy isn't important to the voters, but you have to make it important with some mountaintop stuff, not necessarily the Persian Gulf—that's not a winner. But stress Russia."

He replaced the receiver and said to me, "He didn't respond to that advice at all. There is just no vision there. But what was most shocking is that Skinner repeatedly brought up the possibility of dumping Quayle. That, of course, is not a real possibility. I think he's just desperate for his own job." Desperation had turned to panic, and staff dislocation had developed into staff trauma. The destructive cycle of blame had begun.

Bush, meanwhile, had been working quietly with Price, to whom he turned for help with the increasingly crucial acceptance speech. Price called Nixon on July 30 and reported his shock at finding the pollster Robert Teeter, Fred Malek, and Richard Darman at his first campaign-strategy meeting.

"Darman!" Nixon cried. "What in God's name was *he* doing there?" Nixon stressed to Price the importance of having others attack Clinton so that Bush could remain presidential. "The problem is, however, that you don't really have anyone to do it. Bush will give a good speech, and he will deliver it well, but it won't be enough."

Nixon, however, was reassured with Price now close to Bush, knowing that he would be a perfect channel to the president. He said to me, "It's like going straight to the man. I'm going to send him a memo tomorrow and include some state strategy too. They've got to write off California. That's gone. Don't send Barbara [Bush] there; it's a waste of time. The strategy now is to point out why Clinton must not win, not what is right with Bush. He is now behind in thirty-one states and ahead in only one. It may take a miracle."

Nixon sent his latest contribution to the miracle effort to Ray Price the next day. Entitled "Reflections on the Acceptance Speech," the memorandum was a comprehensive plan for Bush's acceptance speech and the attitude required to make it successful. He reminded Price that Bush spoke now as president, which meant that he should avoid giving his challenger equal time in the media by attacking him by name.

Nixon offered some pointed suggestions on content, arguing that 25 percent of the speech should focus on foreign policy and how it relates to domestic policy. In this way, he could preempt Clinton's singular message that only domestic policy matters.

Bush should, he wrote, play to his strengths: his character and his advocacy of family values. But he argued forcefully to Price to omit a reference to a right-to-life amendment. The abortion issue was divisive enough without the President emphasizing it in a speech that was supposed to win him centrist votes. He told Price to focus instead on the economy, law and order, health care, and education, and to avoid any mention of a tax cut or increase. He should avoid dwelling too long and too hard on the economic problems and making entrapping predictions about economic recovery. Instead, Nixon argued that Bush should turn his fire on the entire Congress.

On foreign policy, Nixon advised Price to have Bush take the high road: avoid attacking Clinton directly for his lack of foreign policy expertise and concentrate instead on the challenges of the new era. While taking muted credit for leading the peaceful transition to a post–cold war world, Bush should allude to his service to the country in both war and peace. He should emphasize his pride in America and in its noble efforts for peace and freedom during World War II and the cold war. This, Nixon argued, was a subtle yet direct way of criticizing Clinton for failing to serve his country and of forcing him to acknowledge or deny the same pride in America's efforts.

Nixon's suggestions were designed to give Price some guidance on how best to help the Bush campaign without appearing to do so. Bush was lagging far behind in most polls, and the herculean effort needed to lift him from last to first would have to be both subtle and powerful. The acceptance speech would at least give him the opportunity to speak directly to the American people in words unfiltered by the press and unencumbered by the opposition.

By early August, the opposition included not only the inevitable Democrats but Bush's own former supporters as well. Nixon was aghast when informed that *The Orange County* (California) *Register* intended to print an editorial urging Bush not to run. "My God!" Nixon gasped. "That's his base. Northern California is going for Clinton. Bush needs to carry Orange County by at least one million votes. This is disastrous."

Bush's support was crumbling beneath him each day. The acceptance speech and fine performances in the debates were Bush's last hopes.

"Bush thinks pragmatically, not conceptually. I hope Ray takes my advice. A laundry list of achievements will be the kiss of death on TV. Ray tells me that Bush is in better spirits, but he still thinks he can win California. Monica, he can't. It's gone. They are in a depression. He shouldn't waste his time there; concentrate on Ohio, Illinois.

"And I'm afraid that now his only hope to defeat Clinton is to tear the guy down and go negative. The best weapon we have against him is the truth, if we can use it properly. But I think that Americans have become desensitized to the infidelity and drug-use stuff because of the Kennedy thing. Ray said that Bush particularly took to my advice on handling the Congress. Go after all of them; never mind alienating [Senate majority leader George] Mitchell or [House Republican whip Newt] Gingrich. Truman didn't care—and he won!

"Unfortunately, unlike Truman, Bush has not really had to go through the fire as president. I saw a quote the other day where he compared himself to Lincoln and said 'I've been tested by fire.' What is he talking about? Tested? He's never *really* been tested. And Lincoln? He's not in the real world. Panama was a nothing thing, and Iraq turned out to be a loser. Besides, he had the UN to fall back on. Imagine if he had to make the decisions I did: the May 8 or Christmas bombings? Oh, boy! I don't mean to cut him down—he's a good man—but he's deceiving himself."

Nixon, aware that his own experiences as president set him apart from Bush, often used comparisons to prop up his own image of himself. Gauging the weight of presidential decisions and ranking them next to his own were sport for him. According to his own appraisals, none of his successors faced decisions as monumental as those he had faced, and none of them had been tested as he had been. He therefore felt that he was uniquely qualified to pass judgment on each of them. Bush was a particularly easy target.

On August 11, Senate minority leader Robert Dole sent Nixon a request for his suggestions on a draft of his speech introducing Bush at the convention. Dole indicated that his remarks were to be "positive and issue-oriented" and leavened with just a few subtle attacks on the Democratic challengers. His goal, he wrote to Nixon, was to persuade undecided voters and those leaning away from Bush "to stop, look, and listen." Nixon read it overnight and sent Dole a lengthy response.

After commending him on its content, Nixon recommended that Dole refer to President Bush's leadership during the Gulf War and ask the American people outright if they would have wanted a man who had avoided service to have acted as their commander-in-chief. It was, Nixon wrote to Dole, the most effective way to attack Clinton on his avoidance of military service in Vietnam. By implying that Clinton is unqualified to send troops into a hostile situation, Dole would draw attention to Bush's—and his own—honorable military service and sense of integrity.

Nixon's advice to Dole, like the advice to Price before him, was to make the contrast between Bush's and Clinton's characters so stark that voters would be compelled to vote for Bush, even if they were dissatisfied with his performance as president. Subtle distinctions, such as the one Nixon implied to Dole, would work best. Bush's last hope was that people would vote for him based not on the fact that he was the better candidate, but that he was the better man.

Nixon left to vacation in Montauk, New York, at the start of the Republican National Convention, the week of August 16. Despite his vow not to watch the proceedings, it was apparent from his comments that he followed them closely each day.

He was reassured temporarily by hearing Bush's first speech, on August 17. "He was out there fighting, but he was affirmative—combative, but not shrill. He has come alive."

On Buchanan's speech, he was less enthusiastic: "He's so extreme; he's over there with the nuts. I didn't like his attack on the gays. It's important that they consolidate the core—the evangelicals, the anti-abortion crowd, et cetera. But that's not enough. Attacking the gays was wrong, wrong, wrong. Besides, they vote too."

On Reagan's speech, Nixon hesitated before saying, "Monica, he's not up to this. They put him on last, at eleven o'clock, and he didn't look good. His voice was gone, and he was losing his concentration. I know everyone went crazy for him, but I don't think he should have done it." Nixon's envy of Reagan's continuing popularity colored his view of Reagan's performance, and his comments were a transparent attempt to justify his own absence from the convention.

"I'm glad that I'm not there! I suppose Reagan was OK," he admitted grudgingly. "He still has that way with an audience. But then he brought Nancy on. Well, that's just his style, but if he hadn't, she would have killed him!"

Overall, he said, it was a good night, though "Reagan talked in vague terms about the world, and Buchanan gave a fighting speech on social issues, but no one mentioned the only issue voters care about: the economy. No one appealed to the Silent Majority types."

The speeches of August 18 also failed to meet that standard. Nixon thought that Newt Gingrich's remarks were "a disappointment—but he's a bomb thrower, and we need him," and he thought Texas senator Phil Gramm's speech was "too long and too tiresome. In the TV age, he just doesn't have it." Jack Kemp's speech was "the best of the night. Kemp had meat to his message. He went beyond sniping at Clinton and cheerleading the party. He's compassionate. Let's face it, Buchanan, like Goldwater, is cold. Kemp was better than Reagan on the Reagan issues."

On the rumor that Bush was immersed in the David McCullough biography of Truman, Nixon snorted, "Now, please. Bush is not really a reader, especially during the convention! No way. He wants to know how Truman did it. Hell, he should remember! And as far as these calls for a Republican Congress are concerned, they are dreaming."

August 19 was "family-values night" at the convention. Nixon was unimpressed by Marilyn Quayle, who he said reminded him of Hillary Clinton, and he was completely impressed by Barbara Bush. "Julie likes her, and so do I. We all thought that she was terrific. She's warm and classy and funny. She's Bush's greatest asset. I did think that bringing Bush's grandson on to read that letter from him was a bit much. But Bush looked good, and it served him well to have his family by his side.

"The big mistake of the evening was when [Labor Secretary] Lynn Martin, who is usually so good, asked whether we are better off now than we were four years ago. No one reacted. Did you catch that tepid response? If she followed it up and preceded it with foreign policy, it would have been OK, but she talked about the economy, and let's face it, we are not better off in that regard."

He was most moved by Mary Fisher, the HIV-positive daughter of his good friend Max Fisher, who spoke eloquently about tolerance and managed to counter some of the damage done by Buchanan's speech. "She is a lovely girl. And it took guts to speak out like this, particularly on behalf of the party. She did it with dignity, and she really brought a lot to the convention tonight. Look here, the Republicans feel that if they had her talk, then they would cover the tolerance issue. But that is missing the point. We have too much bashing of everyone in this party. It's an embarrassment. So many people are gay—or go both ways. I don't care. I don't want to hear about it. And I don't want to hear about abortion. That's people's own business. Tolerance in this party is far too low. Fifty percent of all families are single parent; sixty-five percent of all women work. We can't crap on them. We've got to reach out—and mean it." The family-values theme put Bush's differences with Clinton into bold relief and made the choice between them even clearer. The unanswered question was whether the voters would respond.

Bush's speech was the centerpiece of the final day of the convention. Nixon was curious to see whether Price had been able to persuade Bush to include any of his suggestions and whether Bush would deliver the speech with the conviction of someone who wanted to be reelected.

I spoke with Nixon immediately after the speech. "I want to discuss Bush," he said, "but first, did you see Ford? Ho, ho! He's never been a speaker, but tonight he was particularly bad. Did you hear those two jokes at the beginning? They fell flat. Oh, horrible!" He took some perverse pleasure in seeing the other former presidents stumble, but his assessment of Bush was far more generous than it had been in months.

"First, he won me over when I saw that the reference to me survived. It took guts for him to say that the cold war was won by the efforts of Richard Nixon, Jerry Ford, and Ronald Reagan. It's the first time that anyone has referred to me at a convention. Reagan never did. It was gutsy." When I told him that the crowd applauded wildly at the segment on him in the introductory movie and at Bush's reference to him, he responded unconvincingly, "Really? I didn't hear."

Perhaps affected by his own breakthrough at the convention, he gave Bush's speech a relatively positive review. "I don't think that much of my advice survived—well, maybe to an extent. But he gave a fighting speech, and that's what the people want. His mea culpa on the tax increase neutralized the issue, which was really his Achilles' heel. I do think, however, that he is overusing the Truman analogy. The only parallel is that they are fighting from behind. One comparison with Truman would have been enough, but I think we are the only ones to pick up on this. Sometimes, you know, Bush is a little too flippant in his language—all those disconnected phrases to Elvis and not inhaling and Millie the dog. I didn't understand half of what he was getting at. Those references just don't make him look presidential, but I guess it goes over well with the general public.

"I wish he had more visionary stuff. He tried to include it at the end, about being on a submarine in the navy, but he's just not very comfortable with it. I wish he had more of a lift; it would have made it more memorable."

Nixon waited to see whether Bush would get any leverage from the convention. Traditionally, candidates move up in the polls, and any meaningful gaps between them start to narrow after the final convention. Two days after the close of the convention, Clinton's lead had diminished significantly. A *Los Angeles Times* poll showed him eight points ahead, CBS News and *Newsweek* put him eleven points ahead, and Gallup showed him twelve points ahead.

"The lowest poll numbers are artificial," he said. "They are immediate reactions to the convention. But the spread is what we thought. Winning the election can almost be done. The convention gave him a boost, but only because he tore down Clinton, not built up himself. They can win, but only if they continue doing this. I don't know. I'm a great advocate of attacking, but he's president now, not a challenger. And he should *not* be campaigning in an open-necked shirt. I don't think I'm old-fashioned on this one. Clinton can get away with it because he's Dogpatch." Bush's image problem required more than the removal of a tie. Public antipathy toward him could be overcome only by greater fear of his opponent.

By the end of August, Baker had assumed control of the campaign from the White House. Nixon was concerned that Baker had neither the savvy nor the unselfish temperament to run the campaign successfully.

"I don't think that Baker can pull this off," he said on August 28. "The crew he is bringing with him is just like him—opportunists and tacticians. But without a message, he has nothing to sell. Two things motivate people: hope or fear—and love, but I don't mean that in a sappy sense."

Nixon was now anxiously following the polls, which were consistently showing Bush trailing Clinton by eight to twelve points. "Baker will be sure to fix those polls so that the margin is at least narrowed. But he won't be doing it for Bush; he'll be doing it to show what a talented campaign manager he is. The pollsters make the news when their polls change, so they cook them. Gallup is the most reliable, but I'm afraid that some of these organizations are closing the gap purposely to set Bush up. These polls may be not so much *for* Bush as people revising their opinion of Clinton. The pollsters just have to watch it: by placing Bush closer to Clinton, there is the danger of creating momentum for Bush. Of course, they all want to avoid that. It's like when [*New York Times* editor Jack] Rosenthal wrote in '72 that McGovern was picking up steam. Ha! Picking up steam— my God!

"I wonder if Baker will have him debate. It's a gamble. Clinton is a damn good campaigner. He's energetic, confident, and robust; Bush looks lethargic. Debates will hurt him; they always help the challenger, anyway. But I don't see how he can avoid them. The only way we can win now is if Clinton collapses, and I think he is too smart to do that. The only things that would be self-destructive would be bombshells, like a letter showing that he asked to renounce his American citizenship during Vietnam, an illegitimate child, things like that. But we've got hacks, let's face it. Malek, Teeter—they're smart, but they are babes in the woods when it comes to politics. The Democrats aren't giants, but we're midgets. And as far as the polls are concerned, as I see it, Bush went through three phases: denial, blame of the media and Congress, and combative. He's fighting for his political life."

Just after Labor Day, the traditional beginning of presidential campaigns, the prevailing sense of the election was already obvious. The electorate trembled with dissatisfaction. Its mood reflected not just a weak economy but the perceived loss of the American dream. After the frenetic 1980s and the collapse of Communism, the United States was not soaring, as had been expected, but mired in the mundane concerns of jobs, crime, and the debates over values and character. In the run-up to Labor Day, the public's discontent naturally focused on the incumbent. Even after a lifetime of public service, Bush remained to much of the public a peculiar combination of leadership and inadequacy, goodwill and apparent pettiness.

In the post–Labor Day race, however, voters were more inclined to consider Clinton and the party he would bring into power. The Carter presidency might have left enough concern about a little-known southern governor to prevent a Clinton victory. And for twenty years, voters had roundly rejected the big-government, higher-taxes, appeasement platforms of the Democrats. Clinton, however, presented himself as a New Democrat, concerned with limiting spending and reducing the deficit, advocating free trade, workfare, and aid to Russia. He seemed to be a fresh alternative, even though most of his record as governor reflected traditional Democratic principles. The fall campaign would ultimately turn on the voters' capacity to dispense with political illusion. If allowed to blur the realities of the candidates, discontent could be a dangerous sentiment.

On September 8, Nixon spoke to several people whose political judgment he respected and later gave me their predictions on the election. "The only one who was optimistic was Ray [Price]. He still thinks that it can be won. [John] Connally says that Bush is losing in Texas, and without it he cannot win. Kevin Phillips says that the draft evasion hurts Clinton in the South. Roger Stone is very negative on Bush's chances. [Former Reagan director of political affairs] Lyn Nofziger says that the Bush campaign won't even let him in to advise. [Former Reagan campaign manager] John Sears says that Bush will lose. [Former Nixon press secretary] Ron Ziegler told me that Bush has had it. [Senator Warren] Rudman said that we could lose the White House for years. [Former Reagan chief of staff] Ken Duberstein said that Clinton could be exposed on the economy, and Bush might pick up some speed.

"They all agree that the convention was a disaster. By appealing to the nuts, we lost so many in the middle. It was an enormous cost. I think that the election is done—lacking a breakthrough, even with Baker and his organization. Our only hope is that Clinton's vulnerabilities are exposed—like the draft issue. We have some difficulty on that score, though, because of Quayle and Cheney and the rest of them. The key to exploiting it is in *how* he handled avoiding the draft. It's not that he was against the war then—almost everyone his age was. It's the fact that he says he's *still* against it. Well, our involvement in Vietnam has been vindicated by what has happened since."

Two days later, he continued with the theme. "Look at this article about [Senator Bob] Kerrey's speech defending Clinton's pathetic performance with the draft," he said, handing it to me. He had underlined a passage in which Kerrey was quoted as saying that Bush, as a congressman and later as a member of the Nixon and Ford administrations, was among the political leaders who helped "create this painful ordeal" of Vietnam. Nixon had written underneath, "What about Kennedy and Johnson?"

"This is what we are up against," he said. "Democrats never take responsibility on the Vietnam issue, so how can they condemn Clinton for avoiding it? The Vietnam antiwar movement was not the first, but it was the first in which millions of leaders and followers embraced the idea that the United States should not be at war *and* that our enemies should win because their cause was more just. Clinton still thinks that North Vietnam's cause was more just. I wish that someone would ask him if he does or not. That would say more about the candidate than anything else."

On September 14, Connally gave Nixon some explosive information. "Just between us," he said to me, "Connally told me that Perot is getting back in the race October 1 after asking both candidates to step up to the deficit issue. When they hedge, as they will, he is going to jump back in." Nixon was neither shocked nor concerned. Bush was currently losing the election, and if Perot's reentry could alter the campaign dynamics, Bush might benefit. A losing two-man race might be coaxed into a winning three-man one.

By mid-September, Nixon thought that Bush, consistently eight to twelve points behind Clinton, had "bottomed out. He'll rise some, but not enough to win. We can't put it together electorally—popularly, maybe; electorally, no way. And Clinton's coasting is dangerous. I don't know why he's sitting on his lead. You always must run as if you are behind."

At the mention that Bush had attracted only one thousand people to a recent rally, Nixon gasped, "My God! The president of the United States should *never* have difficulty attracting crowds. Monica, long ago, you could have whistle-stop rallies, outdoor events, and they worked. Not in the television age. We did this in 1960, '68, and '72—get a hall, and fill the son of a bitch. Even with two thousand people, the noise reverberates, and it looks and sounds like a crowd. Outdoors, the noise fritters away. If you want the picture, go with outside. But you cannot communicate with an outdoor crowd—they're eating hotdogs and so forth. Holding rallies inside is much more efficient. I don't know who is doing Bush's campaign schedule, but their heads should roll.

"My major concern is that a Bush loss will bring down the whole party. I lost—well, not really—in 1960, but I was still a major figure. And as president, until Watergate, my approval polls were never really below fifty percent. Neither were Eisenhower's. If Bush loses, it will be a repudiation of the party. We can't afford that."

If the election became a referendum on the party and the party lost the White House, the conservative majority that Nixon began building and Reagan solidified would crack and perhaps lead a trend toward a more liberal consciousness. Nixon began to consider seriously whether the conservative cycle had come to its natural end.

"I don't think that the voters are just rejecting the candidate," he said on September 25. "I think they are rejecting everything he stands for. It may be that the country is just ready to turn in another direction. But that doesn't mean that Bush shouldn't fight it like hell. Holding new ideas and fresh language back for the last two weeks of the campaign is good strategy. I hope someone is telling him that. It's hard to say if people only focus on the election two weeks before. People are attuned all the time. Even when they don't think they are paying attention, they are paying attention. I think that six weeks before, people have made up their minds. That's why with Bush it may be too late. There are, however, a great many undecideds. He's got to fight for those with everything he's got. And because he is so far behind now, I've changed my mind on the debates. I now think that he should have six! They might help him.

"The major issue is the economy. He must hit it again and again and show people that he is on top of it. The only numbers that matter come out next Friday—the unemployment figures. Ford was helped in '76 by the economy coming up. Today, it is not improving. But anyway, those unemployment numbers are cooked like the rest of them. The Labor Department bureaucracy is a bunch of liberals. Let's face it, would a smart conservative want to work in the Labor Department? The president really only affects the economy at the margins. The economy shifts regardless of who is in power. The only way in which a president has an effect is on morale—consumer confidence. Roosevelt's New Deal made things worse but improved morale. The *war* ended the Depression. No, presidents can do damn little."

The perception was, however, that the little Bush had done to manage the economy had neither solved the problem nor related to voters' plights. The result was a volatile electorate leaning toward Clinton.

With a little over a month to the election, Nixon composed a "personal and confidential" memorandum on the campaign for our private use. He analyzed the latest poll numbers from across the country and developed four categories: "Probable Clinton," which included California, New York, Pennsylvania, New Jersey, and Illinois; "Probable Bush," which included Virginia, Indiana, and Ohio; "Even," which included Texas and Florida; and "Leaning Clinton," which included Michigan, Georgia, and Missouri.

In his analysis, he wrote that despite his formidable lead, Clinton was making a significant mistake by running not to lose rather than to win. His shallow support continued to be undermined by liabilities related to his personal life and character. And although those issues were not reflected in the current polls, they could influence undecided voters in the immediate run-up to the election. Perot, wrote Nixon, was "a wild card" who could damage Clinton in the even states.

He argued that Bush should concentrate only on the key states where victory was possible. He could win without any of the states in the Clinton "probables" list if he focused his efforts on the "even" states and on the "Clinton leaning" states, where he could deny Clinton crucial votes. Bush's strategy would have to incorporate these political realities if he were going to win in November.

The memorandum reflected not Nixon's optimism but his disappointment that the race had degenerated into such a close contest. What should have been a relatively easy reelection bid for Bush had evolved into a political upset by a challenger who was one of his party's last choices. With the hope that it would inspire new strategy and optimism in the downtrodden presidential-campaign team, Nixon sent the memorandum to the national security adviser, General Brent Scowcroft, who he knew would forward it to Bush.

"Perot should not get back in the race," he said on September 29. "I used to think he was helpful, but now I just think he's disruptive. The only way that he could help is by making the others look good with his slang and clichés—you know, the 'we've got to fix this' stuff. I spoke to David Gergen [a journalist, commentator, and strategist for Nixon, Ford, and Reagan], who also agrees that the Bush image has not improved. He's really in deep trouble. In the memo, I purposely put some states in Bush's column that I don't feel belong there because I had to build him up. That whole Bush crowd is going to go crazy when Perot gets back in, but you know what they say—'Love is like a cigar. If it goes out, you can light it again, but it's never the same.' Isn't that great? The same applies to Perot."

As the election drew closer, Nixon grew increasingly concerned about how Bush would perform in debate. Clinton was an excellent speaker and enjoyed the banter of political debate. Perot was a plainspoken populist and could bring the house down with a single remark. Bush was a flat speaker and courted trouble each time he spoke without a script. Dangling phrases and non sequiturs peppered his language, leaving his audiences perplexed and amused when they should have been inspired and encouraged. On the last day of September, Nixon laid out Bush's strategy for the best possible return on the debate investment.

"First, he cannot have them on Sundays because there are ball games on every Sunday in the fall—there goes the audience. And if they preempt for a debate, the viewers will be annoyed. Second, the debates aren't going to help him that much. A gain of two or three points won't help when he's down by ten. In 1960, Kennedy gained one point—that was it! Since then, people assumed he gained more because he won, but it wasn't the case. In this election, there won't be an instant effect—like people sitting around the tube saying 'He won.' No, the media will declare a winner, and then they'll poll. That's the effect. The media want a story, so they'll give Bush some—not much, but some." The philosophical and generational distinctions among the candidates would become even more meaningful in debate, as they stood, shoulder to shoulder, answering the same questions and appealing to the same audience.

As expected, Perot reentered the race on October 1, prompting Nixon to remark, "Can you believe this guy? He's such an egomaniac. A debate with him will be a goddamned circus. The rise of Perot happened because the other two are so bad. Clinton stands for the wrong things, and no one knows what Bush stands for. Perot is just a demagogue—right message on deficit, wrong messenger." Perot's last-minute third-party candidacy would cause anxiety for everyone but Perot. He knew that he could not win the election, but he could certainly deny it to Bush. The possibility that Clinton could win by default was a prospect that all three candidates now faced.

"As you know," Nixon said on October 2, "I'm strong on law and order, but I don't go for these kooky ideas on abortion and isolationism. Buchanan whipped everyone into a frenzy over the anti-abortion and 'America first' crap. The Phyllis Schlaflys and the Buchanans are, frankly, frightening. Bush has attached himself—sort of—to the nut-head social types and may lose the election as a result.

"Even talking about the economy doesn't help." He handed me several newspapers, including *The New York Times*. "Here. The latest unemployment numbers are not bad: down point one percent. It's a wash for Bush. The media will kill it, but imagine what they would have done if it had gone *up!*"

He grew quieter and more reflective. "Clinton should not be president. He's damaged merchandise. He's got the McGovern crowd as advisers. Assuming he wins, we'll have Warren Christopher as secretary of state, which will be very bad. My God, Henry [Kissinger] will climb the walls! And he'll put others in there—the [former secretary of state Cyrus] Vance–[George] McGovern type, which is what Clinton *really* is, not the [former secretary of state Zbigniew] Brzezinski–[Senator Henry] Jackson type. We will see the end of the Reagan-Bush era and, really, the era I began in '68. So we'll have Clinton and his New Covenant, and he'll build an ark for his covenant, and we won't hear from them at all. He believes in the wrong things. But he *is* good out there on the stump. He's positive and optimistic. I saw him yesterday at a pig roast, or some damn thing, and while he's not a good man, he's a great campaigner.

"I suppose my greatest concern is that at our moment of victory in the cold war we could do so much better. This campaign has been disappointing in that regard. The party will Goldwaterize. The extremists will take over. It's so destructive, and we'll have to wait until the year 2000 for a comeback. Bush has a credibility gap, which even though the other two have it as well, he will not be able to overcome.

"We could have a situation—and you can write this down—in which Clinton could have a popular-vote landslide and a close or narrow electoral-vote victory."

In early October, someone sent Nixon a copy of Bob Woodward's October 4, 1992, *Washington Post* article on "Origins of the Tax Pledge," which detailed the sources and ramifications of Bush's 1988 "no new taxes" pledge. Nixon threw it at my feet. "Woodward! As if I would read anything by him. The point is that Bush showed no leadership on the economy then and little leadership since. I don't need that asshole to tell me that!" he exclaimed. "Put it in your file if you want, but please keep it away from me."

The latest scandal involving Clinton, a charge that he was in Moscow in 1969 as a guest of the KGB, which allegedly cultivated him to oppose the war in Vietnam more aggressively, swirled on October 8. The story disappeared before it could become real news, and Nixon was disappointed. "Well, it may not even matter anymore. The cold war stuff is yesterday's news, I'm afraid. The number-one issue is the economy. No one gives a horse's ass about anything else. If Bush loses, he will have erased the '72 victory, because that was a referendum on Vietnam. A Clinton victory will reverse that by saying that it was OK to have actively opposed the war."

I asked how he would have run the campaign differently. "At the outset," he replied, "I would have leveled with the American people about the economy. By not doing so, Bush didn't look engaged. I would have sacked Darman and Brady and kept Sununu. They miss him now. I would have had more surrogates going after Clinton. Where are they? Baker dazzles the media, but there are only so many daggers that he is going to take for Bush.

"I would have hit the Russian-aid thing hard by saying 'I know that it's not popular, but it must be done.' And it makes me sick to my stomach to see *The New York Times*—*The New York Times,* for God's sake—calling for force in Bosnia. He's allowed too many of the wrong people to get to the right of him. They talk about changing the team in a second term, but they've got to win first!"

The first debate was held on October 11. Nixon viewed it with a mix of curiosity, apathy, and apprehension. Even if Bush performed extremely well and Clinton and Perot stumbled, it was doubtful that the president could make up his eight-point national-poll deficit. Bush's strategy had to be to ignore the others and keep the audience focused on his positive achievements, experience, and character. If he could do that, he might not win the debate, but he might plant a seed of doubt about the others in voters' minds.

"All of them were good," Nixon told me immediately after the debate, "but Perot won hands down. The guy is just interesting. And I've always said that the only thing worse than being wrong in politics is being dull. If Perot weren't there, it would have been dullsville. It won't affect a damn thing, though. It was a letdown in terms of interest. There wasn't enough controversy. Clinton looked too contrived, too rehearsed; Bush was too casual and conversational, like he didn't want to be there, which of course he didn't, but you don't show that. The whole episode wasn't memorable enough to make an impact, certainly not enough to give Bush a five-point lift. Let me know if you hear anything else; I'm going to watch the ball game."

The first debate accomplished little. The candidates' stock answers to questions on domestic and foreign policy issues, which were essentially versions of their stump speeches, left little room for an election-winning performance, Perot's comic-foil status notwithstanding. If it sent Nixon to dullsville, it certainly did not persuade any other viewers to change their minds.

Two days later, the vice presidential candidates engaged in their debate, which introduced the country to Vice Admiral James Stockdale, Perot's running mate. Quayle's performance surprised Nixon. "He was great! He was on the attack, confident, aggressive—and it worked. The only problem is that sometimes he is not serious enough. He tends to get overenthusiastic and go overboard. And Gore—ugh. He's really one-dimensional. Poor Stockdale. I felt so bad for him; he was just unprepared. When he flailed around in that opening statement, I put my face in my hands and thought, 'Oh, no!' But I loved what he said on abortion—'It's none of the government's business. Period.' He was refreshing, but he's not prepared to be vice president. He may have damaged Perot. I think it was tragic that there was absolutely no mention of foreign policy whatever. That was a huge mistake."

He was also disappointed with the format. "The one-moderator format was bad. I know Hal Bruno; he covered me in '68, and he's fairer than most of the others. But he was too soft with them. It became undisciplined and bad mannered."

When he saw the media declare Gore the winner the following day, he shook his head. "Unbelievable. Quayle was so obviously the winner. They don't give that guy a break. He's a damn good fighter. They should bring him out more. They should put him in the marginal states; people will come out to see him in droves. For better or for worse, he's interesting. And where the hell is Baker?"

Baker, the man who commanded the press at the State Department, seemed to have dropped from view as chief of staff. Distancing himself from a losing campaign, Baker pleaded ignorance of campaign mistakes and refused to give campaign speeches in behalf of Bush. "The White House chief of staff is not the campaign manager," he snapped. When promising campaign themes did not immediately move the polls, Baker had them dropped, and when the multiple and short-lived attacks on Clinton failed to discredit him, Baker feared looking cynical. His decision to place distance between himself and the president even as he was running the campaign pointed to his own preoccupation with saving his reputation. A sacrifice of the Bush presidency might mean the preservation of a potential Baker presidency. In their final gambit for power, they remained friends and mutually suspicious associates. In his panic, Bush revealed his dependency on Baker, and in his lackluster campaign management Baker revealed his opportunism. Ultimately, neither would escape a losing campaign unscathed. Bush's failure would be, undeniably, Baker's failure.

The second presidential debate was held on October 15, probably, Nixon thought, against the wishes of Bush and Baker. It was conducted in a talk-show format, with the three candidates fielding questions from a live studio audience.

Nixon was horrified. "Wasn't that format miserable? It made them *all* look bad. They claimed that it was an 'audience of undecideds.' Undecideds? Selected by whom? Come on. Undecideds don't know very much because they don't care! And I don't like it when they cut audience reaction; they should be allowed to react. It breaks up the damn thing. It really bored me to tears. They remarked that Bush looked at his watch and shouldn't have; hell, *I* looked at my watch! Bush meandered around, like he was bored, which he probably was, but you can't look it! And Clinton is so good at being a phony baloney that he loves this type of format. The questions were all weighted against Bush, starting with the first one that dismissed the character issue. Bush looked depressed to me; he must have seen the polls putting him up to twenty points behind in key states. As far as Perot goes, he didn't help himself. He didn't say anything new." Perot, however, served Clinton by irritating viewers about the status quo so that they would rage against the incumbent.

"Perot must really hate Bush personally. Connally told me that it is a petty little feud between them, and Perot has dragged it into the national arena." Nixon considered the latest polls.

"The ABC Poll showing Bush down by seven points is wrong. They're doing it so that when he loses by more, it will be big news. The Terrence Poll showing him down by seven is also wrong, but for a different reason. They are lying the other way because they are Republicans. All of these polls are cooked. You can't be down twenty points in key states and only seven nationwide."

Nixon believed that Clinton's substantial lead was rooted primarily in a projection of vitality and energy that Bush failed to match. The contrasts were striking: Clinton answered the questions with vigor and optimism; Bush looked at his watch. Clinton proclaimed a "New Covenant"; Bush had buried his "New Paradigm" long before. Clinton looked like he wanted the job; Bush looked like a spent incumbent.

"Bush is a pragmatist," Nixon said the next day. "Youth— and most of the rest of the country—want inspiration, vision, lift. Clinton, even if he is wrong on almost everything, has it. Young people want inspiration. Women are more idealistic than men. If you are guilty, you want women on the jury. Men compromise, cut deals; women don't. All this stuff about women being softhearted is nonsense," he said, admiring women's ability to be both idealistic and tough. "Women are hard-nosed. Hillary is an example. She really believes this liberal crap; I don't know if Clinton does to the extent that he won't compromise on it. He connects with people. Mrs. Nixon observed the way he worked the crowd and thought he was great. I worked crowds pretty well; I looked at each person, and even if you give them thirty seconds, you are theirs alone. Bush is so mechanical," he said as he mimicked Bush shaking hands and looking around wildly. "You've got to hurry, but you can't look as if you are hurrying. I wish him well. It's just so sad. I've always said on a campaign that you must be realistic but upbeat when it looks bad. And the people around the candidate should try to bring him up, but with the truth. This is where Baker is AWOL. [Roger] Stone says they are still hopeful. Imagine—twenty-four points behind in California and still hopeful! Oh well, only one more debate to suffer through." He cleared his throat.

"After Bush loses, the media will all be crying that the party is dead. The question isn't the party; the days of parties are over. We must think beyond parties to responsible government; then the parties and their candidates won't matter as much. Our people shouldn't be chanting 'four more years.' It doesn't work for Bush. They should say, 'four *different* years' or 'four *new* years.' Poor Bush is caught up in larger trends and events. He represents an older generation when America is changing and most people *like* Murphy Brown. Some revisionists have seen this with [Herbert] Hoover. Hoover was a brilliant guy. You probably learned that he said during the depths of the Depression that 'prosperity is just around the corner.' He never said that. Anyway, Hoover was just caught up in forces larger than himself. Bush doesn't see them. And no one around him is fighting against the tide. Reagan and Ford have been quiet. Reagan is probably annoyed because Bush squandered the Reagan revolution, but we have to face the fact that the country went overboard in the '80s, and any president following Reagan would have to meet the consequences. Bush was there at the wrong time.

"Clinton, however, will be a disaster. But it will give me leeway to criticize him on Russian aid and everything else he screws up. With Bush, I had to be restrained, but with Clinton it will be no-holds-barred." Nixon savored the possibilities. "I think he'll take some strong foreign policy action, like in Bosnia, to prove his manhood like Kennedy did. Bush screwed it up from the beginning. On Russian aid—after the Persian Gulf War, he could have gotten anything through the Congress at ninety percent approval, which was unprecedented; even Johnson, after the Kennedy thing, was never that high. And he missed a golden opportunity to come out swinging early last year, when all the Democrats were lily-livered and didn't run, so we ended up with second raters, like [Jerry] Brown. Come *on,*" he said, shooting me a disgusted look. "At least Cuomo was a heavyweight, but he didn't do anything about it. Bush could have come back with his acceptance speech if it had more lift to it. If Clinton wins, he might want to open a channel to me, but Hillary won't allow it. He will screw up China policy and set it way back. And he's dying to normalize relations with Vietnam, which will totally vindicate his behavior during the war."

Nixon's last remaining hope for a Bush victory had already evolved into a strategy for dealing with and criticizing the new president. The reservoir of goodwill that Nixon had tapped in relating to Republican White Houses would run dry on January 20, 1993.

The final presidential debate, held on October 19, gave Nixon pause. Bush performed well, and although his performance was not strong enough to win the election, it may have narrowed the margin. Nixon knew that a strong Bush appearance two weeks before the election could attract undecided voters and some support from voters leaning toward Perot.

"Bush was far more aggressive, coherent, and presidential this time around. At least he showed some convictions on the issues. Clinton stayed quiet because he didn't want to risk a mistake and he didn't expect the Bush fight. Perot was more serious, but he'll go down as an also-ran. This won't be enough to give Bush the win, but at least he will have gone down fighting and, frankly, dignified. This is shaping up to be another '56-type situation. In '72, the last poll showed twenty-four points, and we ended up with twenty-three. In Reagan's case in '84, it was nineteen, and they predicted that right on the nose. Bush may come down to ten. When the campaign says that its internal polls show five points, that's bullshit. They are lying to protect him."

Early the next morning, Nixon's sympathy for Bush found its way into a handwritten note of friendship and political camaraderie. His opening line was an enthusiastic political stroke: "You hit a home run last night!" Nixon encouraged him to keep his spirit up and to take comfort from the honorable example he was providing for others to follow. He told Bush that he was proud of him and of his "character and courage."

It was very important, he told me, "to buck the guy up. I know he must be depressed. Losing is one thing, but losing to someone like Clinton is really something else. It's disheartening. Perot, whose conspiracy theories show that he's really off his rocker, seems to be gaining from Clinton, but Bush isn't gaining at all."

Bush was depending on three things: that the economy would improve, that Clinton's vulnerabilities would destroy him, and that Perot would self-destruct. None happened. Bush had to win Pennsylvania, New Jersey, and Ohio and sweep the South to get the requisite 270 electoral votes, which by the end of October was unlikely. The polls narrowed as Nixon had predicted, but he was inclined to disbelieve them. He easily discounted the more promising polls and focused instead on the ones showing a wider gap, as if he were hoping that Bush would lose—or willing it to happen.

"These narrower polls will give heart to the troops, but we are still not going to win. At the very least, a closer race will deprive Clinton of a mandate, and it may make a difference in the House and Senate races. But the electoral votes are just not there. Election night," Nixon said, "will be a short evening."

The polls continued to swing wildly between one and seven points. One week before the election, Nixon revised the list of states in his four categories, with the "Probable Clinton" category containing the necessary electoral votes to win, including California, New York, Illinois, and Missouri. The "Probable Bush" column had dwindled to a handful of states, including Virginia, Indiana, and South Carolina. The "Even" states included Texas and Florida, which were still too close to call.

Clinton's internal polls showed a three-point spread on October 30, and Nixon was surprised. "That's close for an internal poll. Maybe the gap is really narrowing. If so, it will be the greatest upset of the century. Everyone in the media will be discredited, and all those liberals who have apartments in the Watergate and in Georgetown will be thrown for a loop!" He was amused, but I suspect that he preferred Bush not win, lest a dramatic end-run victory outshine Nixon's own election performances.

"These polls mean nothing," he said that day as he scanned the latest numbers. We sat in his office, contemplating Bush's fate. "All the pollsters lie, but I had a few great ones. In 1960, particularly, my pollster was right on the money." He opened his briefcase on his lap, put his glasses on, and removed his polls from 1960. "This one," he said, handing me a yellowed page, "showed Kennedy at fifty-four percent and me at forty-five. That was October and the last one they published. They didn't publish the November one showing fifty-one–forty-nine. Bastards! That last published one created the winner psychology for Kennedy. They manipulate the numbers now because there are too many polls to keep them under wraps."

I asked him what went through his mind the night before his own presidential elections.

With a soft smile he responded, "It's really tough. They are the longest hours of your life. You are so tired. You just want the goddamned thing over. The most grueling campaign was 1960 because of the mistake I made with the fifty-state strategy. Bush started to do the same thing. In '68, I just drove around on election day. The day is the worst because there isn't a goddamned thing you can do. I watched people drive by, and I thought, 'How many of these people did I reach?' You really wonder because inside you are paralyzed with worry. You want to think that all of the effort was worth something to somebody."

As he leaned forward to continue, a bird flew into the window above his head, hitting the glass with such force that the former president, startled, threw his hand over his heart. "My God! What the hell was that?" he asked.

"A bird hit the window, Mr. President," I answered.

"Oh," he said. "Did it fall to the ground?"

"No, it was stunned for a moment but then recovered and flew away," I said.

"That's good," he said, a distant look in his eyes. The status of the bird seemed to reassure him, as if its injury and recovery were metaphors for the current campaign drama involving the Republican president.

"Bush sent me a thank-you for that pick-me-up note I sent. Politicians are generally cold. They back winners. When you are down, they all desert. They are not a very nice bunch. So I think he really appreciated my note. I guess it sort of stood out amidst all that pessimism." His face brightened. "Well, hope springs eternal. Pray!"

Election day 1992 dawned cool and damp in the Northeast. Nixon awoke at his customary five o'clock in the morning and telephoned me at six-fifteen.

"Did you vote yet?" he asked with a laugh. "It's election day, and we are going to lose, goddamn it. Get your vote registered as soon as you can. Maybe you can start a landslide for Bush!"

He was in remarkably good spirits, considering that he believed that the probable Bush loss meant a dismantling of the Republican popular majority he had begun. He had resigned himself to a Clinton presidency and began to contemplate the most prudent ways of attracting Clinton's attention. His influence with Bush was limited; his influence with Clinton, a man with no foreign policy experience and even less confidence in the international arena, could be meaningful. Republican presidents had to distance themselves publicly from the scandal-damaged Nixon; Clinton was free from those political burdens and might be more willing to seek his advice. Nixon, therefore, approached election day with a mix of empathic disappointment and hopeful anticipation. His party might lose, but his influence with the new president might grow.

To avoid the lines at the polling sites, the Nixons voted by absentee ballot and devoted the day to anticipating the returns. When I entered the former president's office that morning, Nixon was rifling through his briefcase. I closed the door behind me and alerted him to my presence. Without looking up, he admonished me not to be upset when the results come in. "Being on the losing side isn't pleasant, but you have to know the disappointment of loss so that you can appreciate the triumph of victory. Politics, like life, isn't fair. But everything happens for a reason, so look at the returns with a grain of salt, and let's see what we can *do* with them rather than wallow in them."

He handed me a copy of the final Bush internal poll, which showed a possible win. "I admire their arithmetic, but I just don't see it," Nixon remarked. "Some states—like Tennessee, Connecticut, Montana, New Hampshire, New Mexico, South Dakota, Louisiana, and Wisconsin—in their formulation will go to Bush. If Bush loses just one of any of his states, it's over. It can be done, but it doesn't look good."

He redeposited the polls in his briefcase and produced a letter sent to him from Thomas E. Dewey on election day 1960. It was in pristine condition, and Nixon held it with gentle hands. "Take a look," he said, giving the letter to me. It was handwritten and dated. Dewey wrote that either Nixon would be elected to the greatest "responsibility in the world" or he would be "liberated." He told Nixon to disregard those who would critique his campaign after the election and to know that whatever the result, Nixon had served his country with an admirable campaign and loyal service. The United States, Dewey wrote, owed Nixon great gratitude.

I placed the letter on the table next to Nixon and waited for him to speak. Several moments elapsed, and he cleared his throat. "Dewey," he said, "was a class act. That letter made getting through that day much easier; it wasn't easy, but it was easier. Here—read this." He handed me another sheet of paper marked with his handwriting.

His note to Bush was short and compassionate. He shared with Bush a copy of the Dewey letter and wrote that he "could not state it better" as he wished him good luck on election day.

He looked straight at me. "I sent a copy of the Dewey letter to Bush yesterday for historical purposes—and also to give him a lift. Dewey made me feel better thirty-two years ago, and I thought it might do the same for Bush." He closed the briefcase and removed his glasses.

"In politics, if you are losing, you never hear from anyone. I think Bush will appreciate this. He's been set up for a hell of a fall." He informed me of his plans to watch the returns come in with Mrs. Nixon and his daughters, sons-in-law, and grandchildren but said that he would contact me continually throughout the night for updates and reactions. The first call came several minutes after eight o'clock that evening.

"Well, it's shaping up to be a landslide, according to Dole, who is really worried about his Senate candidates. [Granddaughter] Melanie was really cute. She's only eight years old, you know, and she told Julie that she was worried about me because she knew I was for Bush and 'if Bush loses, it's like Pa losing.' Isn't that something? Of course I do feel for the guy. Losing to Clinton is pretty bad."

Early returns from the East Coast indicated a Clinton victory, and Nixon rang again. "It looks like this is it. Although the polls were way out there, they did show Clinton ahead. Bush must be crushed."

When I told him that CBS News's Dan Rather could not contain his glee at the apparent Clinton victory, Nixon said, "My God! Does that guy have to be so damn smug? Here, tell Julie."

I relayed the story to her, and she handed the receiver to her husband, David Eisenhower, who said, "People took another look at Bush last week and didn't like what they saw."

Nixon called me again later in the evening, after Clinton's victory had been announced. He was surprisingly unemotional and clearly concerned with analyzing the results for the immediate and long-term future. "Dole did the smart thing," he said. "Because Clinton only got about forty-three percent, he said that the Republicans represent the fifty-seven percent that did not want him. It's great spin, but it also happens to be true. Perot should have gotten out. His was a protest vote, and it hurt Bush."

Nixon saw Bush's concession speech and was moved by its spirit and content. "It was sad but classy. Concession speeches are the most difficult speeches to make because you are so wounded and so heartbroken that you are dying inside. And yet you have to keep your chin up and your voice steady and your eyes dry and concede defeat for an office you have spent your entire life trying to get—or hold on to. Bush did it well, but I can tell you that inside he is devastated.

"By the way, did you notice that Baker protected himself to the bitter end with a weak introduction of Bush? He was an *ass*. Couldn't he have said something—*anything*—nice? He was up there smiling like a Cheshire cat, and what he *did* say—my God, could he spare it?"

I asked him how he was handling the news, and he replied without emotion. "Oh, fine. It's discouraging, but we are realistic people. We have been through this so many times before. What can you do?"

As he ended his day, Nixon was already planning what he could do.

Early the next morning, he handwrote a letter to Clinton. It was designed to serve several purposes. First, it meant to congratulate him for running a winning campaign. Second, it sought to reassure him that Nixon held no meaningful grudges against him for his Democratic politics, his antimilitary and anti-Vietnam past, or his wife's Watergate experiences. Third, it sought to convince him that Nixon admired him. And finally, it was designed to open a direct channel of communication to the president-elect so that his advice would be sought and his influence would be formidable. The letter was the first move in a delicate game of flattery and political maneuvering aimed at getting as close to Clinton's ear as possible. Nixon was positioning himself to be the new president's foreign policy mentor.

In his first written correspondence with Clinton, he congratulated the president-elect on running "one of the best" campaigns he had ever observed. After commending Clinton on his ability to "overcome adversity" during the campaign, Nixon told him that he had the "character" to lead the country and the forces for peace and freedom throughout the world. Nixon extended congratulations to him and to "Hillary," whom he knew was responsible in large part for Clinton's victory.

After I had read a copy of this letter, he said to me, "I know it goes a bit overboard, particularly on the character stuff, but the guy's got a big ego, and you've got to flatter the hell out of him if you are going to get anywhere. I used the word 'character' not in the moral sense—because he has no morals—but in the strength sense. Adversity builds character. A losing team has character. I have to work with the guy, so I might as well start with this. Notice," he said, pointing to the letter, "I just congratulated him on the campaign, not on actually winning, because he did run a first-class campaign. And I referred to her as Hillary and not as Mrs. Clinton. That was a little needle. I hope the message gets across.

"Perot really surprised me by landing nineteen percent of the vote. I didn't think it was possible. It shows you the power of TV."

Two days after the election, he received another call from Dole, who was concerned about the future of the party and his own presidential ambitions. "He must really take over the party," Nixon said. "He's the only one; no one else can do it. They mustn't let it go back to Buchanan and the crazies. And Kemp—well, I like him, but I don't think he has the discipline to be president, and he's got to get off those crazy kicks, like 'deficits don't matter; just cut taxes.' Well, they do matter. But I like him; I'm just not sure he's right for the presidency. Dole, on the other hand, is the leader. If he keeps his voice and his sense of humor, he has the best shot. If he can lead effectively over the next four years, I think the tide will have turned enough away from Clinton's inexperience to favor Dole. When I won in '68, I got a slightly greater percentage than Clinton. I'm working on an analysis I think you will find interesting."

Nixon examined the state-by-state election returns and broke them down into a jumble of raw numbers and percentages. On a small white notepad, he scribbled pairs of numbers, subtracted, added, and compared. On another sheet, he wrote his conclusions: "M.: NOT A LANDSLIDE." The popular vote margin was five million. Two-thirds of this came from a 1.5 million vote margin in California, a one-million vote margin in New York, and 500,000-vote margins each in Illinois and Massachusetts. As Nixon noted, a shift of just 450,000 votes in Ohio, New Jersey, Pennsylvania, Michigan, Wisconsin, and Georgia would have meant a victory for Bush. The 43 percent of the popular vote that Clinton got was slightly "less than RN's percentage 43—in 1968." His analysis reflected the fact that Clinton not only failed to get a majority but won only with a plurality that could have been reversed with a swing of several hundred thousand votes in key states. If Clinton mistook his win for a mandate, he could become a victim of his own political arrogance. Voters wanted change. Clinton asked to lead it; the country was going to demand it. If Clinton failed to produce, he would discover, as Bush had, how fickle the voters can be.

Nixon was more concerned about Clinton's foreign policy than he was about his domestic agenda "because, frankly, I agree with some of what he wants to do domestically—the pro-choice stands, you know. Not the big-government stuff but the social stuff, like abortion and workfare. That's smart," he said on November 6. "But on foreign policy, the guy is just too inexperienced. When Yeltsin called to congratulate him, he already looked in over his head. That's why he's got to appoint someone like [Senator] Sam Nunn or [Senator] David Boren to State and the CIA—someone good and responsible. And also someone I'd have some influence with. Warren Christopher is weak. God help us if he's secretary of state. This is the Vance crowd—irresponsible. Maybe Clinton will be more likely to reach out to me, but I see he's calling on Carter as an informal adviser. He wants to validate Carter's foreign policy and distinguish his own New Democrat style. I don't know if he'll call on me. Republicans are generally more gracious in victory than Democrats. They play hardball. Kennedy and Johnson never invited Mrs. Nixon and me to the White House. Never. I, of course, had Humphrey, Johnson—anyone who was alive. I don't expect that at all from Clinton. If he does, I will be very surprised."

By the end of the week, Nixon had heard from Roger Stone that until three o'clock on the afternoon of election day Bush had believed he was going to win. Such delusion, perpetuated by his aides, did not serve him well. Nixon was disgusted with the Republican blame charade but engaged in some blame himself. "[Robert] Teeter had *four* strategies for a Bush win. My God, you can only have *one* strategy and stick to it; modify it if you have to, but play one game, not twenty. Reagan bitched that he wasn't used enough. Baker ran for the tall grass. They didn't listen to me. Oh well, the whole thing was badly managed; no use beating a dead horse.

"Scowcroft called today," he said on November 7, "to tell me that I went through hell and that that gave them all perspective. Glad I could help!" He laughed for the first time in a long time.

Former presidential candidate Pat Robertson visited Nixon on November 9 in preparation for an upcoming trip to China. He told Nixon that Clinton's "immorality" would be his undoing as president and would prevent him from delivering strong leadership. Nixon, however, was against allowing the far right to overtake the party with a strictly moral agenda. "We must defeat them and then invite them in," he said to me. "I'm not for the mushy moderates either, however—look at what happened to Bush. Principled leadership is the answer. Nothing that goes too far or doesn't go far enough."

He sharpened his message in a speech he delivered, at Senator Phil Gramm's request, to the Republican Senatorial Trust Committee on November 12 in New York. "It's going to be a wake," he said the day before. "I'm going to try to lift their spirits." He gave me a copy of his eighth and final handwritten draft, which he would deliver from memory.

The speech began by deftly placing Bush's defeat in historical perspective. Nixon told his audience that having observed twelve presidential elections and having been a candidate in five over the past forty-four years, he had seen great victories and devastating defeats. He cited Eisenhower's landslide in 1952 and his own in 1972 as examples of shining victories for the party and conservative principles; he cited his loss to Kennedy in 1960 and Johnson's landslide in 1964 as shattering failures for them. And yet, he argued, the Republicans managed to recover from those defeats and emerge stronger and wiser. Learn from defeat, Nixon said, and win the next time.

He implored his audience not to be discouraged, not to engage in the "blame game," to unite behind their candidates in 1994, and to beat Clinton by posing a fundamental choice to the voters: when Clinton argues for more "power to the government," he said, the Republicans must argue for more "power to the people."

After the speech, he remarked to me, "They were depressed, but I think I picked them up by putting the election in perspective. To make it back in '96, we must look to '94. In football, you advance slowly rather than go for the long pass. We gained in '66 and won in '68. We'll come back. At least now they might feel like fighting."

Clinton gave his first press conference as president-elect on November 12, and Nixon watched with grudging admiration. Clinton had an ability to finesse the issues until his answers sounded like erudite solutions to the country's great ills.

"The guy is good. He handles the media so well even though they are all for him anyway. But they are also not going to sit on a story. They'll nail him if he slips up. But what a difference he is from Bush, who was so inconsistent, and Ford, who was such a poor speaker, and Carter, who was smart but not very effective, and Reagan—well, the press conference wasn't his bag. He did better with the prepared stuff. I think I did it pretty well, considering what I was up against. After a good performance, Ziegler would say that they were all grinding their teeth. But with Clinton, I don't know about this early press conference. People can't get bored with him *before* he's sworn in. I'm already sick of him."

Nixon recoiled further when Clinton's first public policy statement as president elect was in support of gays in the military. "I have nothing against gays. We had plenty of them in my administration. I don't care what people do behind closed doors; that's their own business. But life in the military is not life behind closed doors; it's life without doors, literally. As a practical matter, gays do not belong in the trenches. It is not about their ability to fight; it is about living in close quarters without having to worry about—" He paused. "The tension."

Clinton's first big mistake, of supporting the highly controversial concept of gays in the military, forced Nixon to reflect more seriously on the situation that led to his election. "There were three sides to the Reagan revolution," he said as we sat in his residence's study on November 14. He spoke seamlessly, stopping only to sip some tonic water with lemon. "The economic side, with voodoo economics. Cutting taxes would have been OK if he had also cut expenditures. He didn't and left Bush with one hell of a deficit. Second, he strengthened the military; Carter started it, but Reagan did it. And third—which he didn't do but what won him the undying support of the far right—was to espouse those social policies against abortion, for school prayer, et cetera.

"So look at what Bush inherited. The economy is in the pits. The cold war is over, so the military has lost much of its significance. And he was left with the third leg—the weakest of all— the social issues, and he wasn't credible supporting it. He had to face the bad economy and blame Reagan. The 'read my lips, no new taxes' pledge was wrong economically, politically, and personally because after that he couldn't be trusted.

"Bush didn't have any enemies; nobody hates him. FDR used to say, 'It's important to have an enemy'—with his cigarette lighter," he said, waving his hand as if he were holding one. "Dewey used one too, only because Roosevelt did. Anyway, Bush lacked Reagan's mystical appeal, which wasn't his fault, but it ended up defeating him."

Whatever mystical appeal Clinton may have had with the voters, it began to dissipate with his first announcement of support for gays in the military. He campaigned on the issue of the economy and instead launched headlong into a highly sensitive social issue. Whatever Bush's faults, he seemed to have the balance, prudence, and seasoned experience that Clinton now failed to demonstrate.

On November 18, Bush and Clinton met for two hours to discuss the transition of power. Nixon was satisfied that the meeting was lengthy, though he admitted "that Bush didn't look too happy about it. Johnson and I spent hours and hours together. Of course, we had the war then. Johnson showed me the safe and the taping system that Kennedy had installed under the bed. He had every place—every room—taped. Anyway, I was horrified to see that after Bush hosted Clinton so graciously at the White House, Clinton went into a black neighborhood in Washington. That was a direct slam against Bush—that he was not in touch. ABC said that this was the first time a president has done that. That's bullshit. I did it. Pat Moynihan was running the urban program, and Mrs. Nixon and I went to these places. But for Clinton to do it right after seeing Bush was pretty inconsiderate. It sent a bad signal."

On November 21, Nixon invited me to the residence to see the family's Christmas tree and to give me some material to bring back to the office. Christmas carols played softly on the stereo, and Nixon swayed to them as he escorted me to the tree and identified many of the ornaments on it. "Over the past fifty years, in and out of office, you can imagine how many we have collected." He paused for several long moments and seemed to slip into a reverie. His eyes focused on a single shiny ornament surrounded by gold garland, and he continued to sway almost imperceptibly to the music. The peace of the season seemed to find its way to him, even if just for those brief and fleeting moments. Suddenly, he straightened his back and walked to a table in the sitting room, from which he picked up the next day's *New York Times Magazine*. The cover story was about a good friend of Clinton's who had committed suicide after opposing the war in Vietnam.

"This," he said, pushing it at me, "is self-righteous, hypocritical bullshit. They used the war to justify their cowardice. It wasn't class arrogance because Clinton wasn't rich, but it was intellectual arrogance. I am concerned about Clinton and his whole crew—what they signify: the deterioration of moral values. He has vindicated the anti-Vietnam, draft-dodging, drug-taking behavior. Most of that generation was bad, really bad. The Silent Majority was a reaction to that moral decay, but who's going to do it now? The Clintons are going to be our moral symbols for four years, maybe eight. Four years, and maybe we can recover; eight, and the damage will be irreparable.

"The far right is crazy—too bad, because they are saying some of the right things, but they say other things that rational people reject, so who is going to put up the fight? The problem is that too many of our bright conservatives tend to be extremist kooks. The same, of course, is true in spades of the bright liberals. But the double standard accepts their extremism as being idealistically motivated but condemns the extremism of the right as being fascist or worse!"

The Silent Majority brought the country together, but as president, Nixon also had the benefit of the great issues of Vietnam and communism with which to do ideological battle. The three current generations have had completely different experiences: Nixon's and Bush's knew war and generally respected service and country; Clinton's knew war and generally distrusted America; and the youngest—my own—has not known war as profoundly and responds primarily to selfish motivation. Crossing the generational divides was easier for Clinton than for Bush. Bush talked *to* the younger generations; Clinton talked *with* them.

Nixon recognized the seminal importance of Clinton's presidency, though he did not approve of it. "Clinton has opened up the office to all those who otherwise would have been disqualified, as late as '88 with Gary Hart. Most in the media, though, are just like him. They are sympathetic with him on Vietnam; they experimented with drugs and casual sex. The most deadly sin is pride, intellectual pride, and this whole bunch is guilty of that and of losing the ability to distinguish between right and wrong. The late '60s destroyed that ability for many forever."

Nixon saw Clinton's election as an attempt to glamorize that era of false ideals, false courage, and false prophets, when action was compelled by principles based not on morality but on amorality. The higher interest that most like Clinton sought was actually no higher than their own.

Clinton's influence and agenda were tested once again, on the fourth Tuesday in November, with the special Senate race in Georgia between Democrat Wyche Fowler and Republican Paul Coverdell. Both the Clintons had campaigned breathlessly for Fowler, but at the end of the night the race was still too close to call.

Early the next morning, Nixon phoned me with the results. "Well, we did it in Georgia. Our man won, and even though he's kind of a turkey, he's still a Republican body. Dole will be happy. The *Times* gave it front-page play, but the *Post* buried it on page eighteen, although when Clinton campaigned for Fowler, it was front-page news. It's beyond belief. Both Clintons were in there for Fowler, and so was Jimmy Carter, and he still lost. I'm sure Hillary is annoyed. She doesn't want to be associated with a loser. She probably threw a shoe at him." He laughed before changing the subject.

"I see that Clinton is having an economic summit. Ha! Ford did that, and it was a disaster. Remember the WIN buttons? 'Whip Inflation Now!' That lasted two days. Oh, boy, is he misguided. You can't run the presidency by think tank."

Clinton could, however, benefit by talking with Nixon. He had already spoken to Carter and Reagan, both of whom, according to Nixon, "he should see but not expect to learn much from." Clinton's failure thus far to call on Nixon distressed and disappointed him. "If he wants distance from me, fine," he said on November 28. "I won't have to pull my punches like I did with Bush. The press, of course, wants to cut him some slack to protect him, little Chelsea, and poor Hillary, who is such a weak little thing. *Please.* His contempt for the press should make them *want* to go after him, not protect him, goddamn it. If I go after him, I'll be sure that it is covered."

His concerns focused on the Clinton Cabinet beginning to take shape. According to Nixon, Warren Christopher was the weakest possible choice for secretary of state. "He doesn't know anything, and what he does know is wrong."

Anthony Lake, the choice for national security adviser, was "a liberal ideologue. Remember, Henry brought him in because he respected his intelligence but didn't appreciate his desertion on Vietnam. He was wiretapped by Kissinger, and he sued him! He's far to the left. He and Clinton are hooked on three things: the foreign service, the UN, and the Carter obsession with human rights. Disastrous!"

Les Aspin, the choice for secretary of defense, was "a good man. He has character; he's responsible and progressive, but he's from Wisconsin, with a deep tradition of isolationism going back to La Follette. The doves don't like him because he didn't go for the nuclear freeze."

The selection of a personal friend, Thomas McLarty, for chief of staff was a significant mistake: "A president should never choose his chief of staff based on personal friendship. People can say what they want about Haldeman, but he was one hell of a chief of staff. Those who have come after aren't fit to shine his shoes. You need a real hatchet man in there, someone who can say 'no,' not a good friend."

Nixon believed that Clinton was creating severe political problems by choosing for his economic team advisers with disparate ideologies, from deficit reducers like Leon Panetta to activists like Robert Reich. "Look, Panetta will just roll over for whatever Clinton wants. [Lloyd] Bentsen is fine, but he's not like [John] Connally, who was responsible and broad based. Bentsen has his oil and cattle interests. And if [Clinton] appoints a radical feminist as attorney general, that concerns me because she'll take a hard line on our [Watergate] legal matters. Clinton made too many promises. He's going to have a hell of a time keeping them *and* the deficit down. I predict that in eight months he'll have his first resignation. These people don't compromise, and he'll have to settle the issues himself. *That* will demonstrate whether or not he's up to the job. Hillary knows where she's going; I'm not so sure about him."

Nixon thrived on the gossip that swirled around the Clinton's personal life. He pretended that he was uninterested in the salacious rumors but fed off them enthusiastically. Bill's infidelity, Hillary's explosive temper, and their marriage of political convenience were fodder for Nixon's escapist imagination. "I heard," he said, sotto voce, on December 21, "that they can't stand each other, that their marriage is a charade and that she planned to divorce him if he lost. Can you believe that?" he asked with gleeful inquisitiveness. "He'll never dump her now because she is the tower of strength and intellect around there."

He was equally appalled that Clinton complained incessantly about his press coverage. "How dare he bitch about his coverage! They have treated him with kid gloves! He should be kissing their asses—as Johnson used to say—'kissing an ass in Macy's window.' I hope they give Clinton the business, by God!" he exclaimed, clenching his fist in famous Nixon fashion. "This whole thing has put Bush into a terrible funk. Everyone in Washington is saying that he is extremely depressed. Well of course he is! Do they expect him to jump up and down? He just lost the goddamned election. He appears OK on the outside, but he is devastated inside. And the latest word is that Barbara wants to kill Baker. She holds him responsible, and she's really angry." The fist relaxed. "Politics is not for the weak of heart. Even grizzled types like me get bruised." He paused with a smile. "Never admit it, though."

On his eightieth birthday, January 9, 1993, Nixon read a note Bush had written to him from aboard Air Force One en route from Somalia to Moscow. Bush expressed his appreciation to Nixon for his wise counsel during the presidency and the campaign and indicated that he wanted to model his post–presidency role on Nixon's.

"I'm not sure what he meant," Nixon said to me. "Maybe the speech making for free, although I can't see that; maybe the book writing, although I really can't see that either. Maybe he just meant that he would contribute positively where he could. It was a nice thought, anyway."

Bush's vice president also began considering life after office. Quayle contacted Nixon on January 11 and arranged a visit for three days later.

"I will host him at the residence, not the office," Nixon told me. "That way I can keep the press out. The problem with Quayle is that he is so eager that he's not going to listen to me when I tell him that he must lay low for several months. He cannot be too visible. Staying invisible creates mystery and momentum for people to *want* to hear what you have to say when you finally say it. I know that he wants to discuss what he should do with the so-called wilderness years, like I had after 1960, but there really is no similarity. I ran for *president* and lost; he ran for vice president and lost. I don't know what to tell him."

Quayle arrived at the appointed hour, preceded by the bomb-sniffing dogs of the Secret Service. Observing this ritual, Nixon joked, "If someone wanted to blow up either Quayle or me, they would have done it a long time ago!"

Quayle strode into the office wearing a broad smile and a look of great confidence. He addressed the staff with some witty conversation and appeared relaxed and relieved. He related to people well and was incredibly upbeat, considering that he had just lost the election. Nixon escorted him to his residence for lunch and called me after Quayle's departure.

"Well, Quayle was really annoyed that the military leaked that these latest [air] strikes against Iraq weren't so successful. The war turned out great, and they want to keep the aftermath looking great too, and unfortunately it isn't. I did tell him one thing that you might find interesting. I said, 'You can always forgive your enemies, but you can never forgive your friends.' That, of course, was a clear shot at Baker. I told him not to pander to the press; they are not for him. He said he took a hard line on hitting Iraq again, like I told Henry in '73 with regard to Israel—'Send all the planes needed to do the job. We'll be just as criticized for sending ten planes as one. Don't go half-assed.' He took a dim view of Somalia, and he wasn't being racist; he just thought it was a wedge to get the U.S. there and then to allow the UN to take it over.

"I told him he should build up his foreign policy credentials. He has them, but no one knows it. I told him to do foreign travel. Baker kept him out of China, Russia, and the Mideast. Now is his chance to go. He can then return and be an expert. I told him to limit himself to three boards; you don't make a lot of money, and they want him for other purposes. He says he's taking honoraria because he needs the income, but that's not the case. I told him to consider running for the Senate or for governor in Arizona. He said some were urging him to do it. I told him, 'Run.' He said he'll be accused of being a carpetbagger, but I said, 'No way. Reagan wasn't born in California. It's no big deal. Very few Arizonans were born there.' But he's a realist. He knows that he's too damaged to run in '96. He's got guts and heart, but he's just not considered heavy enough for the top job.

"For his memoirs, he needs help—a straight shooter—someone who is for him. He needs someone loyal. I don't know who would read it unless he makes it really controversial. I told him not to kiss the asses of the intellectuals. Take them on. They're not his friends anyway. And take on the media; *make* it controversial. The meeting, though, was good. He's a good man, and I came away with a higher impression of him."

Nixon was so impressed that he wrote a letter to Quayle four days later, offering new insight into his brief initial advice on memoirs. Nixon believed that although professional writers were supposedly objective, most, he told Quayle, were liberals or left-leaning independents. He recounted his experience with the National Security Council staff in 1969, when policy experts such as Morton Halperin, Roger Morris, and Anthony Lake who were appointed by Kissinger for their unbiased professionalism became some of the administration's severest critics. He advised Quayle to find a collaborator who was not simply loyal to him personally but loyal also to his principles.

Quayle replied immediately: "It is very difficult for a liberal to understand and to have a feel for the conservative perspective. You have first hand experience with people who claim to be loyal but who turned out to be disloyal. . . . I admire your wisdom and I will continue to seek your counsel in the months and years ahead."

Nixon was fond of saying that his "advice is worth what it costs," but many in the Bush administration, including the president and vice president, sought out Nixon's counsel after the election. As one who had spent years in the political wilderness and later in exile, Nixon was in a unique position to advise those out of office on either how to get back in or how to use their time constructively. The advised usually acted upon his counsel, to their benefit and to Nixon's; his position as the wise sage of the Republican Party was now uncontested.

The Clintons embarked on a multistate bus tour en route to Washington for the inauguration. It was billed as a trip to express gratitude to their supporters and to reassure them that they would remain in touch with the people who had sent them to the White House.

Nixon thought the idea was absurd. "Are you going to get on the bus?" he asked me, laughing so hard that he dropped the telephone receiver. "For a president-elect to get on a bus and drive around waving to people like some kind of idiot is really too much. During the campaign, he could play the sax and do whatever the hell else he did, but now he is going to be president, and with that comes some responsibility to dignity."

Nixon's disdain for Clinton's pre-inaugural plans reflected a recognition that Clinton was making the same mistake Bush had made: projecting one image while actually being something else. Clinton had campaigned on a pledge to extend the reach of opportunity to ordinary Americans, and yet the team he assembled included more Oxford and Rhodes scholars than people who had fought in Vietnam. His initial Cabinet selections were members of the highly educated liberal elite. The contrast was part of a striking gap between the common people, to whom the Clinton campaign made its appeal, and the well-educated, affluent group who would govern them. As a candidate, Clinton spoke in populist rhetoric, playing to the middle class, appealing for public service, and criticizing the financial excesses of the Reagan years. The Cabinet he put together, however, was composed primarily of people educated at the most prestigious institutions, who escaped the Vietnam War and who in many cases earned wealth in the decade they now derided. Clinton said that he wanted an administration that "looked like America," and yet it failed to represent any kind of economic or class diversity. The difference between this and previous administrations' elite was that it was education and not birth or wealth that elevated these individuals to Cabinet level. Nixon considered them an aristocracy in their own right, with a myopic academic worldview and solutions to problems that excluded people from the equation.

Ultimately, Clinton's fate would depend upon how well he governed, not upon the educational background of his Cabinet members. But for the Clinton elite, relating the government to the people would be made more difficult by the fact that their generation had not experienced what their parents had during the Depression and World War II. Clinton won the right to bring change, but if that change consisted of academic solutions without realistic expectations, it would not be for the better.

Zoë Baird's selection as attorney general was aborted when it was discovered that she had failed to report her household help's wages to the Internal Revenue Service and pay their Social Security taxes. Nixon initially reacted to the pre-inaugural scandal with amusement but then rushed to Baird's defense. "I'm for her now," he said on January 18. "She's in with business, and the alternatives to her are worse. [Consumer advocate Ralph] Nader and his jerks are all over her because she's not radical for them. You see, these bastards go after 'the what' if they can't go after 'the how.' When I got Hiss, Eisenhower said, 'You got Hiss and got him fairly,' and he put me on the ticket. It drove the libs up the wall because they couldn't go after 'the how'; with Zoë Baird, it's the same."

His disappointment with Clinton's choices extended to the president-elect's proposal for an Economic Security Council. "Remember I called for one in *The Real War,* but Clinton's is designed to deal only with the domestic economy. I wanted one to deal with the American economy *worldwide.* His will not do."

Clinton's emphasis on domestic problems to the exclusion of foreign policy caused Nixon much concern. If the United States turned inward and failed to lead internationally, the forces of peace and freedom, which had gained so much momentum with the end of the cold war, would suffer a serious and dangerous setback. Domestic policy and foreign policy were inevitably intertwined; as Nixon often said, the United States could not have a healthy economy in a sick global economy, and we could not have tranquillity at home in a world engulfed by war. Clinton's attempts to separate domestic from foreign policy and concentrate on the former would only create greater problems in both arenas. If we led in peace now, we would not have to lead in war later.

On January 19, the day before the inauguration, I entered Nixon's office to find him sitting in his corner chair, feet propped up on the ottoman, twirling his eyeglasses in the air. "Pull up a chair," he said, "I have a lot to teach you today—this last day of the Bush presidency." I sat down and waited a few moments for him to speak.

"With all of the drivel being written on the inaugural, not one word has been written on the twentieth anniversary of the '72 landslide, the fortieth anniversary of Eisenhower's election, or the sixtieth anniversary of Roosevelt's. Nothing! These are landmark elections. Those who do the political writing in this country have no historical view whatever.

"My heart goes out to Bush for having to ride with Clinton to the inaugural. Hoover did it with Roosevelt, and it was hard on him. And Eisenhower and Truman did not get along *at all*." He crossed his two forefingers together to denote conflict. "It's hard to remain civil with someone who just ripped out your guts in an election.

"Do you realize that in twenty-four hours we will have a new president—'Hail to the Chief' and all of that?" He was interrupted by a phone call on his private line. He answered it, mumbled something, and smirked. "Wrong number," he said to me. "Some guy looking for Ed from Taco Bell. Imagine—calling me thinking you are reaching Taco Bell!"

I burst out laughing and Nixon, invigorated by the comic relief, launched into a stirring and emotional retrospective of his political career. "I think back over the years and am amazed; so much has happened. In 1932, I was a college sophomore. The Depression had begun, but we weren't really affected; there was high unemployment, but you know . . . But then I had my first run against [incumbent representative Jerry] Voorhis, who people in the district thought was too sappy, and I won. The first race was the best. Campaigning was new, politics was new, and the feeling of stepping on Capitol Hill for the first time beat any other feeling in politics. So there I was, a green freshman congressman, and I was on the Labor Committee with Kennedy, and we worked on the big issues, like Taft-Hartley. Then I went to Europe at age thirty-four with the Herter Committee and saw the Communist movements in Britain, France, and Germany. That was my first hard lesson in how the real world worked.

"And then Hiss came along, of course, which gave rise to my critics and drove them crazy because I hit at the heart of the establishment. They never forgave me. Then came the Korean War, and Eisenhower's great line in '52 was 'I will go to Korea.' But before that, in 1950, I beat Helen Gahagan Douglas, who was closely associated with the Communist front organization—not so with Voorhis, who was a socialist but not as far left as Helen Gahagan when I beat him in the old twelfth district. But with her, it was a clear titanic struggle. I am unique in that I'm neither left nor right, but I'm also not a mushy moderate. I always stood for something.

"Nineteen fifty-two was such an exciting time. Eisenhower made the inaugural very formal; he had us wear morning coats and top hats when we took the oath. We went to those glamorous balls forty years ago tonight; I remember them well. I remember one at the Mayflower Hotel, where Lawrence Welk was playing his champagne music. We had some Hollywood types supporting us in our day: John Wayne when he was beginning to be famous and some orchestra leaders whom I had seen long ago at Duke [University Law School]—Johnny Long, who was before your time, and Les Brown. I will never forget those days.

"And then I went to Kennedy's inaugural; that was a *cold* day." He lifted his shoulders with mock chills. "It was difficult for me because everyone around me, including Mrs. Nixon, believed that the election had been stolen and that I should have demanded a recount. The coldness of the day reflected the feeling toward Kennedy's victory on our side.

"I remember in 1968, I left my coat in a room and had to borrow one from a Secret Service agent who later died of cancer. We had thousands of antiwar demonstrators, some of whom were violent, and I insisted that Mrs. Nixon and I stand up. I didn't even think about risking my life. I just did it to show those goddamned protesters that this president was not going to be pushed around.

"Thinking back on it, it is unfair that someone like Clinton should become president tomorrow. Two things about him bother me the most: the draft evasion and the drug use. [Former *Time* editor in chief Henry] Grunwald asked me today about moral decay in America, and I attributed it to the lack of family, church, and decent, safe schools. The 1960s permissiveness—which Clinton played in and now represents—shot this decay upward. The drug problem is a legacy of the Kennedy and Johnson eras. They called the '50s the dull generation, but I *never* made a speech as vice president on drugs; I didn't have to.

"Anyway, Eisenhower asked [in 1953], 'What are you and Pat doing this summer? You should go on a trip.' This is how history is made by incidental events. A man named Holland, I believe, asked me to go to New Zealand, and Eisenhower approved it. A trip that was supposed to be a few weeks lasted sixty-nine days. We covered Asia, except for China, of course, and much of it was still colonial. We went on to Iran, where the young shah [Mohammed Reza Pahlevi] was married to Saroya, whom he later divorced when she didn't bear him a son. They stayed with us and danced into the night. We stayed in a beautiful place, which we really appreciated, especially after staying in some of the places we did, with no air-conditioning and mosquito nets—oh, boy! That was rough going. Mrs. Nixon was such a trouper.

"You know," he added parenthetically, "after thinking back on that trip, it occurs to me that Bush's foreign policy credentials are overbuilt. He was good at the UN, but that wasn't worth a tinker's damn. And he drove his bike around Beijing as ambassador and did some good things there, but that was about it. I really *earned* the respect I got abroad. Well, anyway . . .

"So we won in 1968, and the first term was fine, and we went on to win in '72 by the biggest landslide—bigger than

Reagan's in '84, and he won on the social issues. We didn't have that so much as we had the good guys—us—versus the bad guys—the drug culture. We were going to do so much in the second term: visit all fifty states and concentrate totally on the Middle East. I think back to '73; it was so full of promise. We were getting the war wrapped up, although we couldn't put that in the inaugural speech. Oh! What we could have done. We wanted to accelerate everything, especially the Middle East, where I had great leverage. I told Henry to make '73 the year of the Middle East because we had to do it in a non–election year. He wanted it to be the year of Europe, but I rejected that.

"We were going to go full tilt on the domestic side; we wanted to change the whole establishment, and they knew I had the power to do it, and it scared the hell out of them. I was going to build a new Republican Party and a new majority. We were going to work on attracting more of the Jewish vote; they do better under Republicans than Democrats anyway. And blacks, who needed to be lifted up and given some hope. I was going to break down elitism in the universities, in the news, in the party. People love to see a president paying attention to them. Yes, a new majority . . ." he said, his voice trailing off.

"And we were going to move the southern Democrats to us. They were ready to go, and with Connally at the top we could have done it. Domestically, we had one hell of a good agenda: drug and welfare-reform programs. And on education, I knew we didn't need more money, but we did need to improve quality. The [National Education Association] was never for me. But we started the [Environmental Protection Agency] and the cancer initiative.

"Nineteen seventy-three was a great time. We had a week before the news of the cover-up business came to me, and then the Watergate bullshit came along. Imagine—that silliness! Well, there was the cover-up, but we were protecting our people, which everyone does. One of the biggest mistakes related to Watergate—and I know I've said this to you before—was letting

Haldeman go. He was loyal and tough. Haig was good, but he was nothing like Haldeman. The people around Bush were all self-promoters. We had some, like [John] Dean, but all the Bushies were like that. We have taken the shit ever since—insulted by the media as 'the disgraced former president'—not ever by reporters in person but always in print and broadcast. Surviving is a miracle. [Herbert] Hoover told me when he was in his eighties, 'I intend to outlive the bastards!' I'll outlive some of them, but who knows how much time is left."

He stared at the snow falling outside his window. "I have confidence in the economic future. The problems will correct themselves as long as Clinton doesn't go hog-wild with liberal spending. Americans are competitive people. Foreign policy? We need the leadership to do what needs to be done. It was easy, in retrospect, for Kennedy and me. We had an enemy to unite the country. What is our role now? The danger is in fighting the new isolationism of the right and the left. Clinton may or may not be up to it; he may be a born politician, but that does not necessarily mean he is a born president."

Nixon's stream-of-consciousness recollections on this day were among the most open, emotional, and revealing of any of our conversations. He had seen the cycles of American politics push great and lesser leaders to the top and, in turn, bring them down. His own seasons of ascent and descent brought memories of power and irrelevance, satisfaction and frustration, glory and condemnation. Politics had given him the greatest achievements of his life and the worst defeats, and he remained its most controversial practitioner. His thoughts were not maudlin reflections but a positive exercise in historical perspective. January 19 was a day for Nixon to look forward and back. Ahead, he saw a young man who represented avoidance of duty and selfish interest about to become president. Behind him, he saw his own career interwoven with Republican and Democratic presidencies in a political kaleidoscope of policy and personalities. He sanctioned the past, as he had to, but was wary of a future led by Bill Clinton. Political cycles would eventually move the country in another direction, as they always have, but for Nixon, Clinton's election lowered dramatically the moral gauge not only for the presidency but for the country.

Nixon spent inauguration day 1993 in front of his television set, watching the transfer of power. He called me after the ceremonies with some wistfulness in his voice. "Bush looked awfully sad. It's rough on him. I had many loyalists; Reagan had some; Bush had none. Who knows if Clinton has any? Probably not, especially since even his wife is for him only because he is her ticket to power. Tricia saw them coming down the steps of Blair House this morning, and when they didn't think any cameras were on them, he snapped at her. Now, Monica, I don't think he would be that stupid as to make a blunder like that on inauguration day, but the point is that he should know by now that every time he sneezes, there will be commentary on the evening news. They must at least *pretend* to like each other. They of course need each other: she's the brains; he's the vessel. He's a good speaker but not particularly sincere. He loves himself, though, and that comes across. He *loves* the adulation.

"His speech was far too partisan. Inaugurals should not be campaign speeches. His applause lines were totally inappropriate. These speeches should be almost religious in their vision and sweep. Clinton's was not. Inaugurals are for leaving politics at the door and lifting the nation. Clinton failed that first test."

His final comments that night were to be his last on any presidential inauguration. "I've been in five inaugurals: forty years ago, and the same drill in '56, and in '60 as the outgoing vice president, and of course twice as president. I am saddened that someone like Clinton can assume the presidency. I am saddened that the country has come to this politically. And I am saddened by the fact that I probably will not live to see the tide turn. I seldom look back, but it's amazing how much has changed."

The vision that new presidents should bring into office and that should sustain them once there was becoming an endangered commodity. Of all the campaigns Nixon had lived through, he considered 1992 one of the most vacuous. Vision and inspiration mattered less than tactics and strategy. The minutiae of the issues prevailed over transcendent themes, and polls prevailed over messages. Neither the incumbent nor the challenger imbued his campaign themes with enriching notions of country and mission beyond his plans for the next four years.

Democratic government requires more than a tactical approach to the issues. It demands a presence of spirit that elevates the people and inspires them to care not only for their country but for themselves as part of a higher cause. A campaign without vision may teach the voters what the candidates will *do* in office, but it does not teach them what they will *be*. Inspiration cannot be manufactured; it must be projected with true belief. Neither Bush nor Clinton had the ability to infuse substance with long-range vision and therefore had difficulty inspiring eloquent campaigns, passionate followings, and messages worth heeding.

Nixon relished watching a presidential campaign for the thrill of the game. The race to an uncertain outcome is fraught with all the excitement and caprices of high-stakes competition. Ideas and ideologies are on trial; personalities are tested and scrutinized. The election is subject to historical forces that push the candidates and the voters in unforeseen directions. Choices are made. The selection of a president heralds a new political season and another chance to define an era. As both a presidential winner and a presidential loser, Nixon understood that vision is the key to effective leadership. Without it, the 1992 campaign denied the American people a choice based upon inspiration. The result was an ambiguous call for change and a tentative vote for an untested challenger. Nixon's frustration, disappointment, anger, amusement, and enthusiasm as an observer of the campaign recalled his memories of those emotions as a candidate. His own campaigns had been won or lost on their merits, but he had always tried to elevate those whom he sought to lead.

The last campaign Nixon observed failed to inspire on a grand scale, creating a yearning in the former president not for office but for the arena. Of all the privileges and allowances of power, Nixon most missed the opportunity to move people. The 1992 campaign had shown him that despite his defeats, his abilities as a candidate and as a leader surpassed those of most of his contemporaries. Watching Bush, Clinton, and Perot compete for his old job reaffirmed to him that he had been destined not only to be a candidate but to be president.

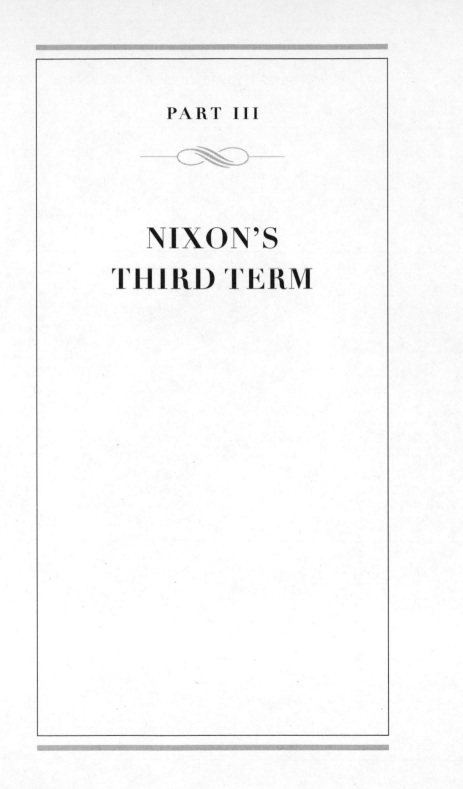

PART III

NIXON'S
THIRD TERM

Bill Clinton's presidency officially began on January 20, 1993, but Clinton had made enough mistakes as president-elect that Nixon had already prepared himself to be both amused and tormented by his performance. Nixon held out a slim hope that the office might have a moderating effect on the president's and the first lady's liberal views, though he believed she would be less willing to compromise than he. His eagerness to bring fresh ideas to Washington as a New Democrat with a New Covenant for the American people seemed to overrun responsible government. And that Clinton surrounded himself with political novices reflected poorly not just upon his judgment but upon his ability to lead. The advisers he chose failed to rein in his tendency toward overzealous politicking and overpromising. And since national debate would certainly alter the tenor and content of policies he promised to effect in their purest form, disappointment, frustration, the perception of political weakness, and vulnerability to criticism would inevitably result. Nixon was torn between wanting to advise him in order to save him from future mistakes and wanting to savor the political satisfaction of watching him stumble. He did both.

"He could be a great president," he said two days after Clinton's inauguration. "But I doubt it. It's clear that the guy can be pushed around. Remember with Roosevelt they used to say, 'Clear it with Sydney'? Well, Clinton must clear everything with Nader, the NEA, Hillary, and God knows who else. The guy is susceptible to pressure, and that will cripple his presidency.

"But you know, brain power is a given with him. A president must have it, and he does. The problem is that he believes in the wrong things. He has deep-down liberal beliefs, primarily because of his relationship with Hillary. She's good—articulate, crisp, and decisive. But he's also shrewd and savvy. If he can get away with it, he will go as far as he can with his liberal ideas. He is indebted to too many; the NEA isn't worth a damn, and on health care—well, I think reforming it is almost impossible politically because he has too many constituent groups to please; let's see what she does." He stopped, realizing he was referring to the first lady and not to the elected president.

"What can *he* really do? I'm afraid not much, though he really thinks he can. It's good that he won't succeed because his ideas—which are really hers—are so out there that we'd have the Johnson presidency all over again. Communism and socialism have failed, and here we are with a president who wants to move in that direction. Not only is it irresponsible, but it is wrong."

Since Nixon's expectations of Clinton's presidency were so low, he approached it with a mix of political curiosity, some fear, and healthy doses of skepticism and humor. Shortly after the election, Nixon received a form letter from the president-elect, asking for Nixon's financial help in Clinton's efforts to "put people first." Enclosed was a pledge, preprinted with Nixon's name, that announced: "Yes! I accept Bill Clinton's invitation to join in a nationwide effort to support our agenda for change. To help make a dramatic difference in people's lives, I am enclosing my Putting People First contribution, made payable to the Democratic National Committee, in the amount of . . ." He left it on my desk with a comic note that said he assumed the appeal was meant for me. Nixon knew that Clinton's impulsive enthusiasm for domestic issues, as seen in the "putting people first" theme, and his inexperience in foreign affairs would result in a lopsided and quickly untenable presidency. Nixon laughed at Clinton's solicitation but knew that eventually the president would truly seek his help.

The world, looking to America for leadership, demanded Clinton's boundless energy. His most serious errors, according to Nixon, involved mistaking conversation for leadership and personal interaction for decision making. His self-indulgent, emotive style made Nixon uncomfortable, not just because Clinton used it for political purposes but because it inhibited effective leadership. Clinton needed to cultivate decisiveness and self-restraint. His impulse to handle everything at once would not serve him well in foreign affairs, and this is where Nixon hoped to step in: by offering steadiness, a tenacious opinion, and by counseling against overcommitment, Nixon thought he could get Clinton to prove that he had greater designs than those on his own political survival. Steer the country and the safety of the world, Nixon wanted to advise him, and your political position will be secure. His opportunity approached quickly.

Nixon intended to visit Russia in mid-February and expressed some concern that Clinton might resist his plans. On January 28, he said, "Mrs. Nixon brought up the fact that he isn't going to like it that we are going to Russia, but I said neither did Bush and Reagan." He paced slowly in the office while considering the issue. "They can't stop me. I'm glad I'm seeing [Strobe] Talbott. It will keep Clinton's gang from pissing on the trip. [Warren] Christopher is a nonentity; [Tony] Lake is OK, but he was wrong on Vietnam. His crew is not strong. He's got a State of the Union in mid-February—I didn't do one in '69; I put out a written thing—so I don't think he'll meet Yeltsin before that. Besides, it's in their interest to have me go. After all, they don't know shit from Shinola on foreign policy."

Nixon relished the idea that Clinton might defer to him on international affairs and permit him greater latitude than either Reagan or Bush had. Clinton might grant more weight to his opinions and advice and perhaps even act on them. He was a clean slate with regard to foreign policy, and Nixon intended to fill it with his own lessons.

Advising on domestic policy, however, did not present a similar opportunity. Their views were so far apart that Nixon could offer only measured criticism and more conservative alternatives without endangering his ability to counsel on international affairs. He would keep his opposition to Clinton's policies private unless he felt the welfare of the nation was threatened. Clinton's first policy statement, in support of gays in the military, though not grave enough to warrant Nixon's public criticism, caused the former president concern. Supporting such a controversial policy meant courting political disaster, and Clinton stumbled right into it.

"It is such a mistake for Clinton to have this as the first issue out of the gate," Nixon said on January 27. He had just returned from a luncheon with Rev. Billy Graham when he called me to complain about the raging debate over gays in the military. "I don't go for this 'outing' business. If someone is gay, that's their business, and they should have the right to protect their privacy about it. But gays in the military is a whole other issue. The reason Clinton is for it is because they were so vocally for him. He had a lot of support in Hollywood, where gays are everywhere. It's not just the gay lobby but because of Hollywood that he's going forward with this. I'm surprised to see that it's the lead story on ABC. The Republicans should not compromise on this; they should force the Democrats to a vote. But I can't believe that he is so stupid as to go with this issue first. It's a loser."

The next day, he summoned me to his office as soon as he arrived. I found him sitting in his usual corner chair, trying to clean his eyeglasses. He put them on and opened his eyes until they were as wide as saucers. "I look terrible in these glasses! Don't you think they make me look old?"

I removed my own glasses from their case and put them on. "Not at all, sir. Do you think mine make me look old?"

"Well, of course not. But you're not eighty." He shook his head. "Eighty! Jiminy crickets!"

He pointed to a newspaper article about the controversy over gays in the military. "Do you see this? This is great ammunition for us if we only don't let them off the hook. This is not bigotry, as [*New York Times* columnist] Tony Lewis suggests; this is realism. Letting gays in the military is just not a very smart thing to do, militarily or politically.

"I am disappointed in Clinton. I thought he'd be wiser about these things. Most of the people I talk to think he's not up to the job. I don't know. The jury is still out. He could go over like gangbusters because he starts with a lot going for him and he's a smooth talker. But it comes down to the tough call: can he make it? I think if he can, he can sell it effectively."

Two days later, he turned his attention to the Republican strategy. "What it all comes down to is economics. If the economic news is still flat a year or a year and a half from now, we could have another '66, but not as big because we started so low. And those who say we need another Goldwater are nuts; he destroyed the party. I made the speech in '66, and the braveless [Republican National] committee could have run it again, but they didn't."

Then he made his first remark about the next Republican presidential nominee. "Dole is the only one who can lead. He is by far the smartest politician—and Republican—in the country today. He is the last great hope for the party in this century. If he gets some big wins next year, he will be the nominee and have a great shot at winning.

"But taking the long view, we need more young people running. This party has lost it. We need to appeal to young people, or we are going to end up being the party of the crazies."

Nixon's relationship with Senator Robert Dole spanned decades. As political colleagues and friends, they looked to each other for a kinship that very few other politicians could provide. They were of the same generation and shared similar experiences in military and political warfare and similar political values derived from nearly identical social and economic backgrounds. Dole was from Russell, Kansas; Nixon was from Yorba Linda, California. Dole had served in the European theater in World War II; Nixon had served in the Pacific. They had both been vice presidential candidates. They had both run for the Republican nomination for president. That Nixon had won the nomination and the office led Dole to him for guidance on how to get there. That Dole was the leading Republican in the Senate when Nixon was out of power led Nixon to him for the inside track on shaping policy. It was a complementary relationship that both valued, and Nixon felt so strongly that Dole should be the next president that he devoted his partisan activities to helping Dole toward that goal. A vote for Dole would be a vote for a smart, savvy, responsible moderate, not unlike Nixon himself. A Dole presidency would be not only the best thing for America but the best thing for Nixon.

Later on the evening of January 29, Nixon called me with Clinton's first poll numbers. "He's at fifty-six percent approval, but his disapproval number is significant. He's at twenty percent! My first approval numbers were much higher. I had fifty-two percent, but only five percent disapproval—*with* the war and all of the haters. You see, Clinton has a very small core of dependable support but a pretty big core of people who really can't stand him. It will be interesting to see how this plays out. He's already getting into trouble trying to please everyone."

On February 1, Nixon had lunch with Dole, whom he had already begun to advise informally on his 1996 presidential run, and a small group of freshman senators. "No great stars," he said to me, "but they'll be loyal soldiers, and that's all Dole really needs. He's going to run. I told him privately that he will be the nominee if he just picks up a few seats next year and continues to be the voice of the party. The character issue will help him tremendously against Clinton, basically because Clinton has little to no character."

He cleared his throat before emitting a stream of disconnected thoughts. "By the way, did you see his little Cabinet meeting out at Camp David? It didn't amount to a tinker's damn. An academic approach to the presidency simply doesn't work. I see that he is now hell-bent on the economy—good luck. And he shouldn't be so goddamned available to the press.

Bush was, and look at what happened to *him!* He's thrashing around, but the press is all for him. The economic news is better, but unemployment must come down to five percent; as long as it's at seven, that's no good. The recovery we see now reflects what Bush did six months ago. Dole is the only one making this point, but he's not getting any media on it. Damn them! Clinton has been in office for a grand total of two weeks, and he's taking all of the credit for the economic upturn? Please. Well, at least Dole is out there swinging."

As we prepared for our upcoming trip to Russia, Nixon grew increasingly concerned that the Clinton administration would oppose it, if not try to stop it. The previous Republican administrations had sanctioned Nixon's trips abroad and requested his insights, but the former president could not predict how a Democratic administration would react. He rationalized that the inexperienced Clinton would see his journey as an opportunity to glean some advice and guidance without appearing to ask for it. And yet Nixon feared that Clinton and his advisers might try to prevent him from wringing the fullest effect from the trip.

On February 4, I traveled with Nixon to Washington, where these fears were quelled. We met with Strobe Talbott, Clinton's adviser on Russian affairs, to alert him to the mission and to hear the administration's position. Talbott indicated that Clinton supported the trip and that the administration appreciated Nixon's taking the lead on the Russian issue. Clinton, he said, was inclined to accelerate the aid process but wanted Nixon's insights on the matter upon his return.

As soon as Talbott left the room, Nixon turned to me with a glare. "I am so disappointed that he was so wrapped up in the details of the U.S.-Russian relationship, like nonproliferation [of nuclear weapons], that he was missing the broader picture. If democracy and the free market fail in Russia, you can forget about the proliferation issues. First things first. Let's help get democracy stabilized first and the economy out of the toilet before we worry about that kind of stuff."

He shook his head. "I kept struggling to get him to see the mountaintop stuff, but he kept sliding back down into the nitty-gritty. All of Clinton's people are so detail oriented. Well, at least they aren't going to cause any problems for our trip."

"Sir," I said, "implicit in your remark to Talbott that you wouldn't criticize Clinton *on the trip* was that if Clinton does not step up to the issue in due time, you would go after him."

Nixon clenched his fist and slammed it on the armrest. "Whammo! And I am freer to do it with a Democratic president, and I *will*."

At Washington's National Airport, we boarded the flight for Newark. Nixon sat by the window and I sat on the aisle, an empty seat between us. The passengers and crew delighted him with autograph requests and general goodwill. As the plane took off, he instructed me to write thank-you notes on his behalf to the people with whom we had met in Washington and to prepare memoranda on the conversations to refresh his memory. When I took a notepad from my briefcase, Nixon leaned over.

"Do you have enough light? Here, take this pillow for your back." He handed me the pillow and then ripped into a bag of peanuts. He waved down a flight attendant and asked for two glasses of grapefruit juice.

"Monica, don't kill yourself over these memcons," he said, using the shorthand term for "memoranda of conversations." "Just do a stream-of-consciousness thing. That's how people talk anyway, and it will make them easier to read."

He downed one of the glasses of juice. "I want you to know that I am going on this trip at my advanced age to save Russia but also to have you see the world and how a former president interacts with a current one and those of other countries. You have already seen how Clinton sent out Talbott to get our pulse, and I was able to get his. That's the way it works." He drank the other glass of juice, then closed his eyes for the rest of the flight.

We left for Europe on February 7. The trip was remarkably free of any discussion of Clinton's presidency, but it was marked by the profound relief of knowing that the president supported the mission and by the hope that upon our return he would contact Nixon to request a debriefing. Upon landing back in New

Jersey on February 22, we learned that Clinton had arranged to meet the Russian president.

"I see that Clinton and Yeltsin have announced a summit for April 4. He'd be wise to talk to me before that," Nixon said to me over the phone on February 25. Influenza had struck all of us during the last days of the trip, and he choked out his words. "This damn cold! The doctor told me that it will last a week. You can take that because you're young, but at my age, I can't afford a week! But getting back to Clinton—I don't know if he will call on me. He should, but the newspeople are slobbering all over him, so he may not want to alienate them by talking to me. We'll see. And you know, Hillary's people are lulus. They are really radical. She is something else." He sneezed and coughed. "In the meantime, drink a lot of liquids, and try to sleep."

Nixon rarely complained, but he finally grumbled, "I'm feeling pretty bad. It's a miserable goddamned thing. I haven't been sick like this in five years! I know you have the same thing, so I'll let you go. Besides, I'm on codeine, and I feel like I'm walking on the ceiling!"

On February 28, a recuperating Nixon received a signal that Clinton had been affected by his visit to Russia. News reports indicated that the president planned to increase aid to Russia by $300 million, to which Nixon responded, "That's pennies."

"He probably did that to preempt any criticism from you on the issue," I said.

"True, but it's still tokenism. He needs to do more, and if he doesn't, I will come after him. All of this other crap he's consumed with—gays in the army, health reform—none of it matters compared to having to fight another cold war.

"Speaking of colds, how is yours? Mine is a little better, but my fever came back because I went off the medicine, which I probably shouldn't have done. I could only eat scrambled eggs and dry toast today, which I had to make myself because Heidi [Retter, the housekeeper] broke her ankle roller-skating with [Nixon's granddaughter] Jennie. Actually, Mrs. Nixon and I made it together, but I think she picked up a touch of what we had. She thinks Clinton will call." I agreed, and he shrugged off my response. "Maybe," he said.

Nixon's defense mechanisms were charged. A call from Clinton would not only validate Nixon in the view of the president's advisers, many of whom came of age during the Vietnam era, but would set a precedent of cooperation between the two men that would grant Nixon significant influence. He hoped for this result but knew that ideology and the first lady might prevent it. If Clinton did not call, Nixon planned to hide his disappointment, cling to a rationalization, and lash out with a well-directed criticism. A late-afternoon conversation with Dole on March 2 crystallized this approach.

"Dole told me something very interesting," he said to me. "He said that Clinton may go to [Senator] Strom Thurmond's party next Tuesday, and Dole told him that I was going to be there and that we should meet prior to it. And Clinton—I don't know how serious he was—said, 'Well, I guess I'll call him about Russia or something.' We'll see. The guy overcommits on everything. I doubt he'll call."

Clinton called that day, and their unexpectedly close relationship was born. Later that evening, Nixon left a one-sentence message on my answering machine: "I just had a forty-minute conversation with your friend who lives in the White House."

The next morning, Nixon was eager to share the substance of the conversation. He sat in his office, twirling his eyeglasses and sporting a wry grin. "Have a seat," he said to me. "Well, it was a surprising thing, but your prophecy was correct. He did call. I waited five minutes on the line, and then eight minutes, and they couldn't find him. The White House operator asked if he could call me back. At about ten minutes to ten o'clock, he called again. Frankly he sounded very tired, and—most surprising—he confided in me; he said things that he absolutely would not want made public. I wonder if his wiretaps are working!" He chuckled.

"He was very respectful but with no sickening bullshit. To give you a quick overview, he only spent one third of the time on foreign policy, mostly Russia, but he asked about China also. He said that he was worried that his defense cuts may be too steep; of course he may have just said that because I'd be against cutting defense too much. But he likes to talk, and he was candid on aid to Russia. I gave him the highlights of what we found. He asked what I thought of Yeltsin, and he said he admired his guts for seeing him when Clinton was a candidate. After all, Bush was president. He admired the fact that Yeltsin was so straightforward; I told him that with Yeltsin what you see is what you get. He said that he has spoken to Yeltsin twice and Yeltsin sounded worried. Clinton suggested that they meet earlier than the April 4 date, but Yeltsin wanted to wait until after his struggle with the parliament had been resolved. He said that Yeltsin told him to see me."

Nixon raised an eyebrow. "That was something! But Clinton asked me, 'Will he last?' I told him that it will be a very tough thing. And he won't survive unless he has U.S. support. He is the best politician in Russia, the most popular—and elected. We cannot leave any distance between the United States and him. He asked about sending technical assistance and so forth. But what is amazing is that two thirds of the conversation was about domestic policy."

He bit one end of his eyeglasses. "He said it was a tough call as to what to do. I told him that I am almost solely concentrating on foreign policy, because I didn't want him to feel that he had to listen to me on that score; we are, after all, on different sides of most domestic issues. So I reassured him that I don't engage in partisan politics anymore but that any criticism I give is meant to be constructive. He appreciated that."

He leveled his gaze right at me. "He never brought up Hillary. Not once. And I gave him several lead-ins. He didn't respond to any of them. Strange." He paused.

"He said that he gets up at six, jogs, has breakfast with Chelsea and sees her to school, and gets to bed around eleven. He wanted to know if that were typical. It was great to hear him ask that because I used to observe Eisenhower's schedule for that same reason. When you are in that job, you want to know that even your schedule is right, or at least typical.

"Anyway, it was the best conversation with a president I've had since I was president. Better than with Bush, because Baker was always looming around, and I *never* had such a conversation with Reagan. Clinton wanted to be reassured. It was never a dialogue with the others. I used to have to force things into the conversation with Reagan and Bush. This was a different cup of tea. He really let his hair down. This guy does a lot of thinking."

Nixon was impressed with Clinton's intellectual curiosity and the political risk involved with the call. "I think that his call is significant." He stopped, put his glasses on the end table, and folded his hands together. "He invited me to the White House."

The sentence hung in the air before he continued. "In twelve years, neither Reagan nor Bush *ever* put me on the White House schedule or put a picture out. We would get the story out on occasion, but you know . . ."

He was clearly satisfied and relieved. Clinton's call was a signal that the president wanted to work with Nixon, and since the conversation was so productive, substantive, and cordial, Nixon's influence would only grow. A true working relationship with Clinton would give Nixon not only the gratification of advising the president on a serious scale but the ability to affect the course of events as he once had.

The next day, he continued to gauge the conversation. He put down his handheld tape recorder when I entered the office and waved me in. "I'm just dictating my thoughts on the conversation with Clinton. It was very interesting. I think he overruled Hillary on calling me, because you know that she wouldn't have approved. Why do *you* think he called?"

"I think he realized that he had more to gain by talking to you than by ignoring you," I said. "Obviously, he can use your advice on foreign policy, but the fact that he wanted to discuss domestic policy as well is significant. He probably didn't get very far with the other former presidents and now realizes that you are the source for responsible advice. I give him credit for calling you because he has opened himself up to criticism from your opponents, who also happen to be his supporters."

"That's true. The guy is secure that way," he said.

"I also think, though, that by drawing you in personally, he was making it more difficult for you to criticize him."

"That's right," he said. "Disarm the enemy. I know it. I think he doesn't want to have to worry about me upstaging him. You know, he said he comes from a small state and didn't realize the enormity of the job. But I tried to get it through to him that he needs to spend more time on foreign policy because—well, look, he's starting to be criticized in the press for it, and he must tend to it before a crisis forces him into it. Besides, foreign policy is just more interesting. As long as he is talking to me, he'll be OK. If he relies on his Carter-type advisers, he will run into trouble."

That evening, he had dinner with former ambassador to Russia Robert Strauss, after which he called me to recount the conversation. "Bob told me that he had just spoken to Clinton, who told him that his conversation with me was 'the best conversation he has had as president' and that he learned more from his talk with me than from all of his advisers. Clinton is trying to learn, and he told Bob that he wants my recommendations on Russia. He told him that the letter I sent him after the election was the most moving he received. Now the guy could just be full of crap, but at least he knows how to be diplomatic! In any event, Clinton is a listener, and my sense is that he has a profound fear of failure. It took guts to call me, but maybe those guts came from that fear."

A snowstorm raged all day long on March 5. Nixon's article urging more significant aid to Russia, "Clinton's Greatest Challenge," appeared that morning in *The New York Times*, to his great satisfaction. It directed Clinton to address the need for U.S. aid to Russia with the same zeal with which he tackled domestic issues:

> If [Clinton] demonstrates the same leadership qualities in addressing the major foreign policy issue of our time, he can secure his place in history as a great President. That issue is the survival and success of political and economic freedom in Russia.

Nixon reviewed a litany of danger signals emanating from the Russian republic: skyrocketing inflation, plummeting living standards, astronomical crime rates, and bloody civil conflicts. He followed with hopeful signals that, if nurtured, might permit the reforms to take root: increased privatization and growth in private industries, a free press, fewer shortages, and a workforce responsive to economic incentives. He argued for an immediate increase in Western financial aid to Russia, a restructuring of its debt, and a single coordinator to organize the flow of money, goods, and services to the country. Nixon leveled the challenge directly at Clinton:

> The demise of Soviet Communism was one of mankind's greatest victories. But the victory will not be complete until Russia and its neighbors can enjoy the benefits of political and economic freedom. It would be tragic if, at this critical point, the United States fails to provide the leadership only it can provide. By leading abroad as he has so effectively at home, President Clinton will establish himself as the world's preeminent statesman.

Nixon looked at the article approvingly. "Well, it's a little over-the-top, but the point is to get the guy's attention."

He hosted William Safire for lunch and asked me to come to his residence for a meeting about his upcoming visit with Clinton. He was standing by the large picture window in his study, and he turned quickly when I alerted him to my presence.

"Come in! Sit down! Wow! Have you seen this snow come down? Pretty, isn't it?" he said and sat down. "Well! The meeting with Safire went well. He might put out something; he's loyal that way."

"And trustworthy," I said.

"Right on. He's a thoughtful guy. And he's just good."

He cleared his throat and paused dramatically. "Clinton wants to see me at the White House Monday at three. Not in the Oval Office—in the residence—but he has his reasons." He was clearly pleased. "If you can think of anything I need to tell him—although most of it is in the *Times* piece—let me know."

"You may want to tell him that one of the most surprising things we found on the trip was that the Eastern European leaders were less fearful of the Russian democracy collapsing and of having an authoritarian regime installed than they were of an

American withdrawal from Europe leaving them vulnerable to a resurgent Germany," I said.

"Ah, that's right," Nixon replied. "That is something he should hear. The Germans are of course not a threat, but he needs to take the Eastern European concerns seriously."

He switched gears. "Clinton asked me why the Chinese have ten percent economic growth. I said that there were three reasons." He counted them off on his fingers. "One, Deng [Xiaoping] started with agriculture, which Gorbachev didn't do and the Russians still haven't done. Two, they have political stability, which is unfortunate because political stability is too high a price to pay for growth without freedom. And three, because they're Chinese. Clinton understood it. I see that he said in his press conference that he agreed with 'President Nixon's general thrust of his op-ed on Russia.' At least he read it."

Nixon spent the weekend preparing for his meeting with Clinton. He wrote extensive notes, primarily about Russia, and reviewed them until he felt comfortable with his points and how he would structure the conversation. He met with Clinton at the White House on March 8 and remained in Washington for two additional days, during which he delivered a rousing speech on the House floor. News coverage of these events was positive and extensive. Nixon, the headlines proclaimed, was back once again. On March 11, he returned to the office and called me over the intercom.

"Monica," he said. "Remember me? Come on in."

When I opened the door to his office, I found him beaming from behind his desk. He stood up, moved to his corner chair, propped his feet up on the ottoman, waved me into my usual chair, and smiled. "This trip," he said, "was probably the best one I have had to Washington since I left the presidency." He tried to restrain the smile. "The House speech was really something. I did it from the well, because I wanted to talk *with* them, not at them. I told them that the last time I was there was forty-three years ago, when I briefed the chamber about the Alger Hiss case. Who would have thought I'd be back in 1993, talking about a democratic Russia? They loved it. And I said that I heard [Douglas] MacArthur speak after he was recalled by Truman from Korea. He said, 'Old soldiers never die; they just fade away.' I said, 'Old politicians sometimes die, but they never fade away.' The place roared!" Nixon clapped his hands together. "Oh, boy! It was really something."

He recrossed his legs and assumed a graver tone. "The meeting at the White House was the best I have had since I was president. Clinton was late greeting me—which I understand is a big problem for him—because, he said, he was on the phone with the Filipinos. I said I understood. Clinton took me up to the residence, and he said that we had almost met once in 1978 in Hong Kong, but he said he was just a governor then and it didn't work out. Incidentally, I'm a little annoyed that Bush turned the Treaty Room, which was Lincoln's Cabinet Room, into an office. Why do people do such stupid things?" He rolled his eyes.

"Anyway, Clinton is very earthy. He cursed—'asshole,' 'son of a bitch,' 'bastard'—you know. He's a very straightforward conversationalist. Up in the residence, I saw Chelsea, who was very shy, and Hillary. The kid ran right to him and never once looked at her mother. I could see that she had a warm relationship with him but was almost afraid of her. Hillary is ice-cold. You can see it in her eyes. She is a piece of work. She was very respectful to me and said all of the right things. But where he was very warm with Chelsea—he's touchy-feely, anyway—she wasn't at all.

"We discussed health care, and Clinton said how difficult it was because of all the vested interests. Hillary did say that our administration had the best health program—and we did. [Attorney General] Elliot Richardson put together a hell of a deal. She also said that we did great things on the domestic side—although compliments coming from her are like—I don't know what! Both of them are very smooth. Clinton was casual. We both drank diet Cokes. As an aside, he told me that he got fattest in New Hampshire when he was defending himself. I think the first phone call broke the ice, because he really let his hair down with me.

"I told him that on Russia the risk of action is great but the risk of inaction is greater. He took it. He was also very interested in China. He told me to tell the Chinese that he's an OK guy, because he's nervous about what they think of him. I told him to hit the Japanese on aiding Russia and to hammer them all on the IMF [International Monetary Fund]. He brightened up when I told him about the grain-barter deal. He made a note when I said that Russia must develop an entrepreneurial class and do it at the grass roots—that's the Peace Corps mentality, which is why he picked up on it. He also agreed that it will take more money than what he put forward.

"He said he's only been to Camp David once because he wanted to get to know the White House first. I was impressed that he didn't engage in flattery—none of this backslapping bullshit on the op-ed or the great contribution I've made. A politician's capacity for flattery is boundless, but there is no time for it in a conversation like this. He wanted to talk seriously; I like that. Although," he said, pointing a finger in the air, "he didn't send best wishes to Mrs. Nixon when I mentioned that she was ill. But anyway, he was poised, intelligent, imaginative, and very self-confident. He's president, and he knows it.

"He also said that the domestic issues are very difficult." He lowered his voice. "Monica, history will not remember him for anything he does domestically. The economy will recover; it's all short-term and, let's face it, very boring."

"Sir," I asked, "did you sense that he is getting frustrated with domestic politics?"

"Yes! He's getting more interested in the foreign policy stuff because he realizes getting the domestic stuff through is just very hard—pretty thankless too. For the last six months of the Bush administration, foreign policy was an orphan. Clinton has got to seize this."

He radiated youthful enthusiasm. "I wish you didn't have to go to school this week," he said, referring to my graduate-school course work at Columbia University. "I wish you could have been there. The conversation with Clinton was more than either Reagan or Bush ever gave me. It has been quite a week,

hasn't it? But always remember that you never top a performance. I won't go back to the House. Let them remember that
performance. Sometimes you get the best media by doing none.
I think that Clinton showed real guts by having me there. And I
think we could work together on the Russian thing and on
whatever he wants. I got a good sense from all of it."

Nixon was clearly gratified. Clinton took a political gamble
by seeing him, and Nixon made it worthwhile. He now had a
positive working relationship with the sitting president, which
gave him what he had sought: the power to affect the course of
events and greater legitimacy in the eyes of those who had opposed him. Clinton's Republican predecessors had been unwilling to bestow such visible recognition on Nixon for fear that the
association would tarnish them; it took a Democratic president,
unencumbered by the Republican hesitation, to do it.

Toward the end of March, however, optimism that Clinton
would act more forcefully on Russian aid turned to skepticism.
Nixon had urged Clinton publicly and privately to do more to
support Russian democratic and free-market gains; Clinton had
acted only in a limited way. As Nixon debated his next move, he
took a call from Canadian prime minister Brian Mulroney, who
mentioned that he had just spoken to Clinton and urged him to
convene a special G-7 meeting on the Russian situation. The
problem, as Nixon saw it, was that there was no one person
outside the government with the ability and stature to act as a
coordinator on a Russian-aid program. Even if Clinton moved
forward with a plan, organizing it would be exceedingly difficult.

"I got the sense that Clinton was committed to doing more on
Russia, but I hope he wasn't just telling me what I wanted to
hear. Bush and Baker suffered from a great lack of creativity in
foreign policy; it was a damn shame that they were in charge at
the end of the cold war. But here Clinton has a historic chance
to do something, and I don't see it happening," he sighed on
March 19. He removed his pocket tape recorder from his briefcase and pointed it at me. "I'm dictating a memo to Dole on the
Russian thing. Maybe he can do something."

Nixon's limited ability to effect policy disturbed him, particularly because he thought he had made an impact on Clinton at the White House. The idea that his advice had been diluted inspired rage, disappointment, and frustration. If Clinton did not want to act on the advice, Dole could use it against him.

Dole took the bait. Several days later, the senator indicated that it would be better for Clinton and Yeltsin to hold their summit in Moscow than in Vancouver, British Columbia, because the danger of a coup increased with Yeltsin's departure. The summit remained in Vancouver, but Dole had scored a political point.

"Dole was right-on!" Nixon said. "At least he sees the importance of this issue. You know, if it weren't for us, this issue wouldn't be number one. The domestic stuff Clinton is so obsessed with has a very limited ability to change America. The Russian situation has the ability to change the fate of the world."

On March 23, Clinton held his first press conference, and Nixon pronounced himself "very impressed" with the performance. "He handled it very well, not just on Russia, where his statement in support of greater aid was strong and correct, but on everything. I have to say that the guy has stood up well so far. I agreed with almost everything he said today. But the reporters—and God knows I've encountered the worst—were really nasty. That's a hazard of the job, but goddamn it, are they rude!"

Clinton must have sensed Nixon's sympathy, because he called him the next day. When I went to his residence at four o'clock in the afternoon on March 24, Nixon was eager to share the contents of the conversation. First, however, he recounted his phone conversations earlier in the day with Dole ("I told him that the most important thing he needs to do is to keep hammering home that the Russian constitution is illegitimate because it was written under the Communist regime, and so is the congress") and with political consultant Roger Stone ("Stone says that both Clintons have bad tempers and that it is an explosive situation").

Then he turned in his chair and said quietly, "Well, enough
about that. At about two-thirty, I got a call from Clinton, and
we spoke for about twenty minutes. He came for straight advice—no bullshit. I sensed he was really panicked about what to
do on the Russian thing. I told him that I thought what he's
done so far has been outstanding and that he must meet Yeltsin
carrying a significant aid program. I reiterated that it's a risk to
support Yeltsin, but if he goes down without U.S. support, it
will be far worse. He must see Yeltsin alone—no secretaries of
whatever or other assholes along. If I had waited for the bureaucracy, we never would have had the China initiative. He
gave me the four policy options on Russia he has, two of which
are ludicrous. And you can't do anything at the ministerial level.
I sent him a fax on this, which I think is pretty good. I told him
that he must deliver a real program, and he must stand up for
Yeltsin unequivocally. He must enlist the G-7 at the presidential
level to make the package big enough. He should meet Yeltsin in
Vladivostok and then go to Tokyo and stroke the Japanese.
They should be doing more for Russia."

There was a long pause. "He asked if I thought he should talk
to Kissinger. I couldn't tell him not to, and although Henry is
brilliant, that's just what he wants." The prospect of Kissinger's
preempting Nixon's special relationship with Clinton vexed
him. "So I told him to talk to Scowcroft first. Anyway, he's
probably seeking advice from others, so I gave him a bit of additional advice. I told him that when he talks to others, he must
tell them what he is going to do and *then* ask for their advice,
because if you ask first, then do something else, they'll be upset.
Clinton likes to talk to everyone, but when you do, your thinking gets watered down. But how do you like that?"

Nixon tried to contain his joy. Despite his insistence that flattery not pollute the relationship, he was flattered by Clinton's
attention. And although he prided himself upon his ability to
remain unaffected by it, he submitted to it, if only momentar-
ily. The mutual adulation reached new heights on March 30,
when Nixon received an inscribed photograph of Clinton with
a request for one from Nixon, and Nixon returned the favor

with a humorous note commending Clinton's courageous decision to aid "China."

"The China reference was pretty funny, I think. He'll get a kick out of it," he said, stoking the relationship with that much-maligned flattery. "By the way, I thought you'd be interested to know that I received a nice note from [communications director George] Stephanopoulos, thanking me and asking me to let him know when he's doing something wrong. I suppose everyone in that administration sees the benefits of kissing up to me!" He laughed. "As long as Clinton doesn't renege on the Russian-aid thing, he'll be OK with me."

The following day, Clinton delivered a speech focused almost solely on the issue of aid to Russia. Nixon was satisfied that much of what he told Clinton survived in the speech.

When I told him that CBS News gave relatively favorable coverage to the speech but then followed it with a poll showing that most Americans did not support Russian aid, he spewed contempt: "Goddamn loaded poll. Look, Clinton really stepped up to this issue, which is more than we can say for Bush. The only negative is that he is stopping in Portland, Oregon, on his way to the summit to talk about logging or the spotted owl or some damn thing. I think he feels that he has to offset the foreign policy with something domestic."

Nixon, once again, took it upon himself to refocus the nation's attention on foreign policy. When we returned from Russia in late February, he decided to make another journey to the Far East. The Russian situation was urgent and deserved priority, but relations with China, Japan, and Korea were languishing dangerously. Nixon's mission was to tend to the crucial economic and political relationships with the thriving Pacific Rim in the hope that the administration would again follow his cue.

During the April 3 flight to Anchorage, he remarked to me that he had received a call from Clinton's national security adviser, Tony Lake, who wanted him to carry some messages to Beijing. Nixon put on his eyeglasses and removed from his briefcase a yellow legal pad on which he had made notes of the conversation. "I told him that I appreciated their gutsy call on Russia, and he said that it couldn't have been done if I hadn't taken the lead. He brought up some things he wanted me to discuss with the Chinese—primarily on human rights—so that they can go after those who oppose MFN [most-favored-nation trading status]. Also on Russia, he said that the top-level G-7 meeting was still a live idea." He put the legal pad back in the briefcase and took the glasses off. "I don't like—or was not impressed by—what he did on Vietnam or to Kissinger, but I've got to get along with these people, and he was very helpful."

The Clinton-Yeltsin summit took place while we were in Anchorage, and Nixon wanted constant updates on the tone of the meeting and on how Clinton handled Yeltsin. My positive assessments reassured him. "If Clinton continues to step up to this and follows through, Yeltsin just might survive. And Clinton will have a triumph of historic proportions." The trip consumed his energy and prevented any further serious examination of Clinton's activities. Now that he was satisfied that his relationship with the president was sound, he resumed his private criticism.

"When I met with [Governor Pete] Wilson during my stopover in California," he said to me back in the office on April 24, "we decided that Clinton tries too hard to please everybody and ends up pleasing nobody or very few."

Nixon had stayed in California for several days on our way back to tend to some functions at his library and to speak with Wilson. He returned with fresh insights about the president and first lady. "He does what's expedient. Hillary is the true believer. The whole bunch of them are just learning on the job; it's a terrible way to run the White House. But of course people will say, 'Who is Richard Nixon to criticize?' "

His voice dropped. "You know, last night I had insomnia, so I turned on one of those late-night comics. He said something to the effect that Clinton had his first one hundred days and his first one hundred lies and that we should bring back Richard Nixon—he was an honest man! You see what I mean? This is what we are up against. The audience didn't really laugh, but it just reinforces what's out there. Clinton can be as dirty as they come, and we will get the arrows."

Despite the positive relationship he had built with Clinton, he still resented Clinton's ability to thrive despite transgressions that would have severely damaged another president. The press, he felt, protected Clinton as it had protected Kennedy, and Clinton himself was masterful at dodging the political bullets. Nixon at once admired him and scorned him. The next phone call from the White House illustrated these dueling opinions.

"You will be pleased to know that I got another call from Clinton today," he told me on April 26 with thinly veiled satisfaction. "He thanked me again for taking the lead on aid to Russia, and he was delighted with the [Russian] election results, although he agreed with me that the media have been disgusting by downplaying Yeltsin's victory. Naturally, I'm not for Clinton, but I will side with him when the media pack comes after him. Anyway, I told him—again—that it was a gutsy call on aid but the right one, and he said he'd just talked to Yeltsin; Clinton said [Yeltsin] was pleased with the aid program, but he was having difficulty getting the goddamned bureaucracy to carry it out. And these are his own people! But they have a socialist mentality and move like snails. I told him that I completely understood. Look, if we had relied on the bureaucracy, we never would have gone forward with ninety percent of what we accomplished with regard to China, Russia, Europe, and the Middle East.

"Well—the main reason he called was to ask what I thought about Bosnia. It's obvious that he's leaning toward lifting the embargo and using limited air strikes against the Serbs. I told him that I agreed, but whatever he decided I'd support. He's on the right track with this since we have got to have a balance of force on the ground before a peace agreement is even an option, but I didn't want to push it in case he goes with something else. To reinforce this point, I told him that you can only negotiate at the table what you win on the battlefield. And I said that if the Serbs aren't stopped, they may go after other parts of Yugoslavia. He made a good point. He said, 'Yes, or in other parts of the world.'

He is tilting toward action and thought that Britain and France would go along. I also told him that he cannot win the war there, but he can provide a correlation of forces that may bring some sense to their heads.

"He listened, but who knows what we will hear tomorrow? He's very susceptible to pressure from the press. And it burns me up to see that Tony Lewis—who went through a male change of life over our bombing in Vietnam—is for our involvement in Bosnia. With a Democratic president, I guess military intervention is OK." He smirked.

"Oh, I also told Clinton that Yeltsin should attract private investment like China has, and he said he wanted to talk to me about China at a later time, so that's in the mix."

"Clinton is very clever," I said.

"He sure is, but what exactly do you mean?" he asked.

"Well, by mentioning China at the end of the conversation, he leaves you tantalized, waiting for the next call—and prepared once it comes."

Nixon shook his head in agreement. "Of course. The guy knows how the game is played."

Clinton's one hundredth day in office came and went on April 29 with little fanfare. Nixon groused over a *Washington Post* poll showing Clinton's approval climbing to 59 percent and dismissed it. Despite his action in behalf of the struggling reform process in Russia, Clinton had done little to convince Nixon that he belonged in the job. Clinton's agenda overflowed with promises made that would inevitably unravel unkept. On May 1, Nixon commented on the trap Clinton had set for himself.

"The guy is all over the place," he said. "Health, education, welfare reform, God knows what else. What he has put out there is enough to fill a two-term president's agenda, never mind the first three months! The problem is that he has no steel. He's totally unfocused. I'm surprised that Hillary doesn't have more control over disciplining him. Where he's sloppy and undisciplined, she's strong and decisive. Where are *our* women?" He waved a hand in the air. "She's just good. But looking back on these first months, I think that the decisive step—what will reflect well on him—is that he bit the bullet on Russia."

"Assuming," I said, "that he follows up and gets the Congress to pass the program."

"True," he replied, "but even so, at least he did it." He paused. "And I hope he has a better appreciation for the gut-wrenching decisions presidents have to make, like the kind he protested against when I was in there. I doubt he'll do anything on Bosnia. The libs in his party are after him to do something, but I don't think he will.

"You know, in a few days, on May 8, we will celebrate the anniversary of the second hardest decision I had to make, the first, of course, being the resignation. It was the bombing of Haiphong [in 1972]. We were worried about the Russians. It was an extremely difficult decision. No one—except for Connally, really—was with me. Richardson was ready to resign. Kissinger was waffling. I don't think Clinton has it in him to make the tough call.

"I remember so well when [CIA director Allen] Dulles came to see me during the Cuban missile crisis. I put all of this in *Six Crises*. He told me he told Kennedy 'not to let it fail.' My God, you've got to go all the way or [do] nothing. Clinton must not go halfway on Bosnia. All of this Hamlet-like deliberating over Bosnia makes him look weak. We've got to get our allies, the Congress, and the people to go along. Instead of *telling* them what we are going to do, he's looking for their permission! This isn't leadership! He doesn't scare anybody, and neither does Christopher. Hillary inspires fear. You've got to put fear in these people or scare them with silence—just don't say anything and leave it uncertain. But I find his vacillation on this frankly shocking."

His disappointment in Clinton began to escalate; what originated with low expectations reached heights of frustration and anger. His advice was being watered down. His experience was being drawn upon but not used. The lessons of his presidency were being wasted. Clinton weighed and reweighed his options without issuing firm decisions. Indecisiveness in a candidate usually signals weakness; in a president, it signals dangerous ineptitude. Nixon believed that if Clinton did not begin making the hard decisions, he would be marginalized as president. His falling approval ratings and the disavowal by some in his own party bore this out.

"I'm afraid our friend in the White House is in big trouble," Nixon said on May 20, when he heard that Clinton had been heckled in California. "He can't go too far left, but if he doesn't, Hillary will kill him. I heard that he had the airport in Los Angeles closed so that he could get a two-hundred-dollar haircut on the runway. Two hundred bucks? That could cause a serious problem. People don't understand the big numbers, like the deficit, but they do understand a two-hundred-dollar haircut. I remember so well when we went after the Truman administration for extravagance for getting a 'deep freeze'—you know, a freezer. No one could afford it in those days, and it had an impact. Clinton played the average guy on the campaign trail, but now he's straying into elitist territory. He'd better watch it. It's like he's not thinking. If he keeps this up, he will be so vulnerable by '96 that we could run anybody and win."

A call from Roger Stone later that day inspired a review of the possible Republican challengers of Clinton in 1996 when we sat down for our daily meeting. "I like Kemp," he said, "but he has the Clinton problem in that he is pretty undisciplined. He's got some good ideas, but he is all over the map. Besides, if he plans to run, he's got to get over that Johnny-one-note crap on the supply-side stuff. People want more from a presidential candidate. He's got the charisma, and he's a real charmer, but I just can't see him in the top job. Stone likes [Massachusetts governor] Bill Weld, but, Monica, he cannot be nominated, not by the party. The party does not nominate elitists from the Northeast, and he's too liberal on the social issues, which isn't necessarily wrong. Bush was an elite, but he was helped some by Reagan. Frankly, a Buchanan appeals more to that crowd, but he is totally unelectable when it comes to the general election—too far out there.

"Pete Wilson has a shot. If he can create a miracle in California, he might do very well, but I just don't know. He's very good on foreign policy. I like [Lamar] Alexander; he's very bright and responsible. If he can raise the money, he might do something. [Richard] Cheney is smart as a whip and would probably be a responsible and strong president, but I don't know if he is likable enough—you know, with the personality—to be elected. Besides, he's another one who skipped out on Vietnam. The others who gas around about running, like [Phil] Gramm, don't have a chance.

"This leaves Dole. He is by far the top choice. He is smart, responsible, experienced—and can leave the others in the dust. If he can keep his voice and pull up some wins in '94, he will be perfectly positioned to be the nominee in '96.

"Clinton, of course, will run again, but the chances of him winning a second term are slim unless he stops making stupid mistakes, starts looking presidential, and makes some tough calls on foreign policy."

Nixon was referring to the upcoming annual debate over extending most-favored-nation status to China. The designation permits countries to trade normally with the United States and is restricted only in the case of nations that openly sponsor terrorism, such as Libya and Iran. Those who argue to revoke China's MFN status contend that China's human rights violations should preclude it from enjoying the economic benefits of normal trade with the United States. Supporters of continuing China's MFN status, like Nixon, argue that the best way to promote human rights reform in China is through the open door of trade. Clinton, under pressure from members of his party to revoke MFN status, remained silent on the issue as the vote approached.

"If he lets [U.S. Representative from California Nancy] Pelosi control foreign policy, he'll have a hell of a mess," Nixon said, referring to the outspoken critic of China's human rights record. "If the administration is leaning toward slapping conditions on MFN, they are playing with dynamite. The Chinese will say, 'to hell with you,' and they should. I think that the reason Clinton hasn't called me on this is because he knows where I stand, and he doesn't want to hear it because he's made up his mind. He doesn't want to have to overrule me.

"I remember when I was running for Congress, I got excellent advice from an older member, who told me never to ask an older politician for advice unless I was prepared to take it," he said, restating one of his favorite anecdotes. "That's why he hasn't asked me. Adding conditions will be a terrible mistake, and I will make it known what I think if he does it. China is a giant, and the United States can't be screwing around with it. The nuclear-weapons sales are an important issue, but trade must be separated—make it a *political* issue. If he doesn't step up to this, I swear I will go public against him."

If the issue of aid to Russia inspired urgency in Nixon, the debate over MFN status inspired rage. He would not tolerate a regression in the Sino-American relations he had done so much to advance since his triumphant opening to China in 1972. If Clinton intended to attach conditions to MFN status for political reasons, Nixon would break with him publicly. Trade was too important—not just for U.S. relations with China but for U.S. relations with others—to be overtly politicized. The debate over the North American Free Trade Agreement, which promised to open up the economies of Canada, the United States, and Mexico to unimpeded trade, offered a similar example.

Clinton supported NAFTA and tried to enlist the former presidents to co-sign a letter endorsing it. When Nixon received the request from the office of the U.S. trade representative, he sent it back out to me with a note instructing me to prepare a response since he did not intend to sign a "joint" letter. I responded to the request with a simple reply: "President Nixon is not in a position to co-sign an op-ed with the other former presidents. On several occasions, however, he has publicly stated his full support of NAFTA. Please be assured that he supports all efforts to implement the agreement."

Free trade and the benefits that it brings to the U.S. economy, to our relations with other countries, and to the forces of democracy and free-market economics were too important to be sacrificed on the altar of partisan politics. Clinton could score a political point by adding conditions to China's MFN status, or he could engage in higher statesmanship. When he finally refused to attach conditions and "delinked" Beijing's human rights record from the annual decision on whether to grant China MFN status, Nixon was surprised, relieved, and gratified. The rationale was that previous attempts to deny this status had not only made China more recalcitrant but had also threatened to hurt the fifty-billion-dollar trade flowing between the United States and China. By reinforcing trade ties, the administration argued, the United States would be in a better position to influence China on human rights. Nixon's arguments became Clinton's policy.

Unfortunately for Clinton, however, some Nixonian drama seeped into domestic political management. On May 19, the entire White House travel office was fired and replaced by staffers handpicked by the Clintons.

Nixon was incredulous. "Imagine if I had done that? I would have been through right then and there. He's a mess. He pissed off the press with this because they were affected. Their planes were affected, and they get to be friends with the travel staff. You'd be mad too if your friends were fired. He'd better cut his losses with this and not let it drag on for days."

Clinton's management style—detail oriented, personal, and hypercommitted—created internal problems that began to escalate into political problems. Having had his presidency terminated prematurely by such a situation, Nixon was sensitive to the mistakes Clinton was making: trusting the wrong people, making decisions without considering the leapfrogging consequences, and making excuses for his actions instead of explaining them. The travel-office scandal pointed to Clinton's belief that his personal style would save him from political disaster. Implicit in this was an arrogance that had the power to produce the opposite effect.

I entered Nixon's office on May 27 to find him pacing behind his desk. A copy of *The New York Times* lay on the ottoman. "Did you see this? Did you?" he asked me, pointing wildly at the paper. He referred to a front-page story detailing the unlimited White House access enjoyed by television producers Harry Thomason and Linda Bloodworth-Thomason and the angst they felt as the president's and first lady's best friends and in which they compared themselves with Nixon's good friend Charles "Bebe" Rebozo.

Nixon was enraged. "Like Bebe? He *never* asked for anything, like these people [have]. He didn't have an office in the White House, like these people [have]. He never tried to affect policy. These people do. It burns me up."

He sat down, carrying his anger to the next subjects of conversation. "Bosnia is screwed up beyond belief. He should have either said, 'We'll do nothing or something.' Instead he has the worst of both worlds. And Christopher is so bad; he's like [former secretary of state Cyrus] Vance times two! Brzezinski told me this is the weakest foreign policy team since the Herter days [1959–60, when Christian Herter was Eisenhower's secretary of state]. Christopher, [State Department Undersecretary Peter] Tarnoff, and the nice boys like Talbott are great analysts but no executives. [State Department Assistant Secretary] Winston Lord is a good second man but not a top man. The NSC is nothing. And there is no one really in charge of Russia."

He reacted strongly when I told him that Clinton planned to speak at the Vietnam Veterans Memorial on Memorial Day. "My God!" he exclaimed, throwing his pen down. "That is obscene. I will never go to that memorial. I don't like it. It's so mournful."

Nixon's experience in prosecuting and ending the war was an agonizing memory that for him was symbolized by the monument. He felt that the memorial reinforced the negative sentiment on Vietnam and rather than honoring those loyal soldiers' ultimate sacrifice, touted their losses as part of a mistaken enterprise. "No, I won't go—but Clinton? That makes me want to puke! His demonstrations prolonged the war. He's a brazen bastard." He ran his hand over his hair.

"Oh, by the way, I got a haircut this morning. Can you tell?" he asked. "Dominic, my barber, was interviewed after Clinton's two-hundred-dollar haircut and was asked how much I pay for one. I pay him twenty dollars every time, which is what a haircut *should* be, for God's sakes." His scowl turned into a smile.

"Well, from Vietnam to hair; we've covered *a lot* of ground today."

On May 29, Nixon found a new reason to be irritated. He called me, appalled that David Gergen had received an appointment to Clinton's White House as a counselor to the president and director of White House communications. Nixon considered Gergen a talented opportunist, a shrewd man without political convictions who knew how to manipulate the press and the people to showcase his boss and, therefore, himself in the best possible light. Nixon used him when he wanted positive spin; Gergen gave it to him and claimed the credit for himself. Clinton hired him for a different reason: to restore the image that had gotten him elected and to make the president appear as the candidate had once appeared.

"Gergen has no problem prostituting himself," Nixon said. "He's sucking up to power, and that's really all he's ever done. He's good, but he's no loyalist. Clinton will be making a huge mistake if he thinks Gergen is there to help him. He's there to help himself. He can handle the media. He was OK with us. Some say that he pulled me, Ford, and Reagan to the center. He did nothing of the kind. He didn't move *me* anywhere. [Political commentator] Bob Novak said he was never a Reaganite. You can't really consider this a defection because the guy was never a Republican. In fact, he believes in nothing. Well, as long as Clinton knows what he's getting, he'll be OK for him. Of course, this is an inside-the-Beltway type thing. No one else cares." He shrugged. "Clinton needs *something*. His poll numbers are down to about thirty-six percent—that's damn near terminal."

Clinton did not make Gergen's job any easier by appearing at the Vietnam Veterans Memorial on May 31. His speech was heckled by veterans and others who considered Clinton's draft evasion reason to deny him the respect afforded to other presidents.

Nixon reveled in the controversy. "I didn't want to watch him, but it was all over the channels, so I had no choice," he told me by phone after the speech. "The media downplayed the draft dodging during the campaign because they were all against the war. All of them are from that era. ABC and NBC said it was a small minority who turned their backs on Clinton and booed him during the speech. I say, 'Great.' But there *were* a lot more of them than the media let on. Julie and Tricia have similar reactions. It was revolting and disrespectful for him to be there."

"Didn't it surprise you that Mrs. Clinton wasn't there?" I asked.

He paused. "She *wasn't* there. I hadn't even noticed because I was so disgusted with *him*. Of *course* she should be there. We always did those things together. Maybe they had a fight. Maybe she threw something at him!" He laughed.

"He looked uneasy at Arlington [National Cemetery] after the disaster at the memorial," I said.

"I know. I think it shook him up. He likes to be liked, and when he's not—well, I think it shocks him."

If Nixon had been advising Clinton on his schedule, he would have told him to exercise greater restraint in choosing his appearances. His avoidance of military service did not need to be highlighted at the memorial to the war he condemned. He could have saluted all soldiers' contributions without acting as a lightning rod for his critics. Modesty and shame were noticeably absent from Clinton's actions. Nixon knew that his presidency would suffer if he did not weigh more responsibly what he did and what he said. As Nixon found and as Clinton was learning, experience can be a hard teacher.

"I'm surprised that the Clinton collapse happened so soon. Hillary must be climbing the walls. Where are the *responsible* women in America?" he asked with a wink on June 4. "Hillary is so clever. She's invisible when the negative stuff erupts." He pointed at me. "Always judge people in power by the people they choose to be around them. The people around her are all to the radical left. They are going to doom her.

"I see that he revoked Lani Guinier's name for that post [assistant attorney general for civil rights] in the Justice Department. You know, he still hasn't learned that it's better to fight and lose sometimes than not to fight at all. And all of the columnists hung him for withdrawing the nomination. He gave the worst excuses: that Hillary played no role in the selection and that he hadn't read her writings—now, please! This shows bad judgment and incompetence. He should have just said, 'I don't have the votes.' It's better to be honest." Nixon had learned his lesson well.

"I saw Guinier rebuke him for withdrawing her name, and she was good. He screwed her by not standing up for her, so she screwed him. He just can't be decisive. If the economy improves, which is questionable, he may be all right. If it doesn't improve, he's dogmeat."

Clinton's approval rating held steady at about 40 percent. Nixon asked me to list all of *his* approval numbers from 1969 to October 1973, and he compared his annual averages, which never fell below 51 percent before Watergate, with Clinton's.

"We were so much higher *with the goddamned war,*" he said on June 2. "People want strength and decisiveness in their leader even if they disagree with his decisions."

Of Clinton's many problems, Nixon thought that his tendency to talk too much was the most devastating. To govern is to choose. Clinton overpromised and underdelivered. His meltdown by early summer indicated that he could neither master the competing forces in domestic politics nor follow through with clear action in international affairs. The scandals, from the haircut and the travel office to the hiring of Gergen and the withdrawal of Guinier's nomination, led *Time* magazine to cover the "incredible shrinking presidency." The depths of his problem reached into the depths of the man himself. If he did not lead from his gut, he would self-destruct. And Nixon, having experienced it, knew that Clinton had to correct himself before the wreckage spread to the rest of the country.

Whatever points Clinton had scored with Nixon, he lost many of them when neither he nor Mrs. Clinton attended Mrs. Nixon's funeral in June. The administration was represented by the Clintons' friend Vernon Jordan, who held no formal position in the administration.

Nixon, rocked with grief, exploded after the service. "Vernon Jordan? The Clintons sent Vernon Jordan? He's a fine man, but come *on*. Hillary should have been there. That was inexcusable. He comes to me for advice to save his ass, and he can't even send a Cabinet member to Mrs. Nixon's funeral? What the hell was he thinking?" He shook his head and then, as if looking for a revenge he had no control over, asked, "Are his polls still in the toilet?"

Nixon's attitude about Clinton went through a marked change after Mrs. Nixon's funeral. Disappointment evolved into hurt, anger, and eventually hostility. If Clinton wanted advice, Nixon would provide it, but without the cordiality that had characterized their previous relationship. From that point on, Nixon disabused himself of any illusion that Clinton came to him for any reason other than to help himself.

Nixon's view of Clinton's upcoming trip to Asia reflected the change. Without his previously positive manner, Nixon speculated that the trip would provide no political lift for the president and make very little news. Since summits between allies are important but lack the drama endemic to meetings between adversaries, Clinton would reap few political benefits. But Clinton, elected to tend to domestic issues, found himself relying more and more on foreign policy to boost his approval ratings at home. The press, said Nixon, was his accomplice.

"The press is trying to build him up for Tokyo," he said on July 4. "And then they'll say that he dazzled them with his knowledge of every little thing. It's all bullshit. The trip—this *debut*," he said disparagingly, "won't help him at home one bit."

The summit produced a communiqué reiterating the importance of the Japanese-American economic and political relationship, which Nixon denounced as "fluff," and positive press for the Clintons, which he derided as "pathetic slobbering." "For all of Clinton's bitching that he's gotten bad press, I don't see how he can complain now," he said. "They've killed themselves to build him up. And look at the way they've deep-sixed the travel-office thing. Poor Dole kept at it, but they buried it. And here they are, lavishing praise on him every time he sneezes. Look, we had China and Russia. They hated to give us credit for anything, but those were *real* accomplishments. They have already begun their orgy: 'Clinton is back,' " he said on July 16.

His astonishment was fueled by the news that Clinton intended to nominate Dr. Joycelyn Elders for surgeon general. "They must be gushing over him because of the people he has been choosing. Apart from cronyism, what makes the head of the Arkansas health commission qualified to be surgeon general of the United States?"

"Well, what makes the governor of Arkansas qualified to be president of the United States?" I asked with a smile.

"Ah, ha! But that's a different matter," he said. "But really— who is picking these people for him? He's got to stand by her, but I heard that her ideas are way out there. He's really stacking them on the left."

Nixon's frustration with Clinton's selections stemmed from his disapproval of their ideas as well as from his fear that they could undo the accomplishments of his and his Republican successors' administrations. Nothing, however, prepared him for the news of the July 20 suicide of Vincent Foster, White House deputy counsel and former partner of Mrs. Clinton's at the Rose Law Firm. U.S. Park Police discovered Foster shot to death in Washington's Fort Marcy Park, a tragic development that intensified the air of mystery and depravity surrounding the Whitewater affair.

What has come to be known by the label "Whitewater" relates to the ongoing investigation of an Arkansas real estate venture dating to the late 1970s and its connection to a now-defunct Arkansas savings and loan institution. The Whitewater Development Corporation, founded in 1979, included as investors Governor Bill Clinton, Mrs. Clinton, then employed by the Rose Law Firm, and James McDougal, a businessman and subsequent owner of the Madison Guaranty Savings and Loan Association. The company purchased a tract of land as a real estate development project and opened an account at Madison Guaranty. The venture proved financially unrewarding, and Madison Guaranty went bankrupt in 1989 at an estimated cost to the taxpayers of sixty-eight million dollars.

In the fall of 1992, the Resolution Trust Corporation, an agency responsible for the disposal of the assets of failed savings and loans, asked the Justice Department to investigate the failure of Madison Guaranty, including payments it had made to Whitewater. No action was taken. In December 1992, a month after the election, McDougal had bought out the remaining Whitewater shares of president-elect and Mrs. Clinton, a transaction in which the Clintons were represented by Vincent Foster. In October 1993, when it was learned that documents pertaining to Whitewater had been removed from Foster's office shortly after his death, the RTC again asked the Justice Department to investigate the failure of Madison Guaranty.

As the investigation unfolded, an array of complex questions emerged pertaining to the nature of the Clintons' connection to McDougal, the possibility that funds from Madison Guaranty were improperly diverted through Whitewater to cover debts from Clinton's 1984 gubernatorial campaign, the possibility that the Clintons received income tax benefits from the failure of Whitewater to which they were not entitled, the suspicious circumstances of Foster's suicide, and the possibility that federal regulators had improperly shared information with White House staffers regarding the ongoing civil and criminal investigations. Clinton continually denied any illegal or unethical conduct involving his wife or himself in their real estate and financial dealings. Mrs. Clinton followed suit and publicly defended herself. The complex web of allegations, players, and interests initially kept the public's curiosity at bay.

It did not, however, bore Nixon. Foster's death and its suspicious connection to the Whitewater affair intrigued him on a visceral level. The slow accretion of self-doubt and anguish leading up to the suicide was something that Nixon himself had not only experienced but had overcome.

I delivered the news to him, and he paused, stunned.

"This could affect Clinton in unseen ways," I said.

He looked at me blankly. "You may be right. He's a *personal* type of guy. Not Hillary; she's cold. But why do you think he did it? I don't think it was the pressure of the White House. Do you? I mean, there's got to be more here than meets the eye." He was clearly disturbed. "Why would he crack? What sets people over the edge? He had a family. He had a good job . . ." He looked away.

"As you know, sir, people have different thresholds of tolerance, and things often run deep. He looked like a decent man. Perhaps he was being asked to do things that he found . . ." I paused. "Well, unethical."

"That could be," he said and hesitated. "Imagine the kind of pressure we were under! We had the war, hundreds of thousands of demonstrators, the press kicking us every night. And this was well before Watergate! What this administration has to deal with is nothing in comparison." He stopped. "I don't mean to minimize what Foster was going through, but you know what I mean. Maybe, coming from Little Rock, he just wasn't ready. And it could've been [Chief Counsel Bernard] Nussbaum. He's a Watergate guy and a tough shit. Chiefs can treat deputies like crap. I just hope that that wasn't the reason. Nothing in life is that bad—where suicide is the only option. Believe me, I was under enormous pressure in the Watergate period, but not once did that ever, and I mean *ever*, cross my mind."

Several days later, his suspicions that the White House was involved in a cover-up of the details of the suicide intensified. On July 29, Nixon called me into his office and handed me the newspaper, which he had folded back to a story on Foster. He raised an eyebrow. "Something is very fishy here. I don't think it was murder, as some have suggested. But I do think there is more here than they are letting on. I can't believe that it has taken this long to announce the discovery of the suicide note. The first place they must have looked was in the son of a bitch's briefcase, and only now they are saying that they found it! Please. Files had been moved, the police were restricted from the office—what the hell. It smells like a cover-up, and they went after us on it, but look at the way they have handled this—terrible! They should interview Nussbaum. They can't hide behind attorney-client privilege because [John] Dean knocked that out with Watergate."

"The entire tragedy is suspicious, but I doubt that they will investigate beyond what they absolutely have to," I said, then tried to change the subject. "I cannot believe that Clinton said that the United States would furnish air cover in Bosnia if formally asked. The United States does not wait for an invitation! We consult our allies, then act. Period," I said.

"Damn right. But that's the Clinton way," he said, then slipped back into his analysis of the Foster suicide. "I think that what we have here is a major political problem. This death must cut right to something else, like that land deal, or their taxes, or something. There's a reason why they are being secretive and maybe even—well—obstructing the investigation."

Nixon was torn between panic for the president and a gratified sense of revenge as the Foster suicide cracked open many of the secrets of the Clinton White House. Having endured Watergate, Nixon knew the damage that could be wrought on the presidency; having been a Republican target, however, he knew it was time for political justice. He was neither shocked nor angered to learn that the dark suspicions swirling around the death had more to do with Foster's responsibilities than with any personal trauma he may have experienced. One of Foster's jobs was to prepare the tax returns for the Whitewater project, and ominously the files pertaining to the land-development deal were turned over to the Clintons at the time of Foster's death. That Mrs. Clinton may have played a role in directing these maneuvers was no surprise to Nixon.

"Hillary handled the finances; that much is clear," Nixon said. "He was too busy worrying about the next election. Besides, he is a people person; she is a master behind-the-scenes manipulator. He can't be bothered with the numbers stuff, but she loves it. The problem is that she represents everything she claims to condemn: all of that money-making greed and opportunism she and her gang criticized the Reagan era for—well, they are just as guilty of it. Hypocrites! Their hearts bleed for the poor just as long as *they* aren't poor."

Mrs. Clinton was even more dangerous, according to Nixon, because her covetousness was so often cloaked in a vaguely defined higher moral purpose. She was suspect not simply because she was the wife of the president but because she appeared to be at the center of every dubious episode spinning around the White House. She had initiated the Clintons' involvement in the Whitewater investment and managed it for over a decade. She had, reported later, parlayed one thousand dollars into almost one hundred thousand dollars in less than a year by trading cattle futures and claiming, incredibly, that she based her decisions on *The Wall Street Journal*. She was said to be behind the firings in the White House travel office and the fired employees' replacement by Clinton cronies. And she brought her close friend Foster to Washington and was now suspected of having his Whitewater files in her possession. Instead of being paralyzed with grief at the loss of her friend, Mrs. Clinton apparently acted swiftly and furtively to spirit from Foster's office anything related to the Clintons' Arkansas dealings. Nixon's sensitive antennae were clued in to culpability at the highest levels by her damning tendency to protest too much.

Foster's suicide affected Nixon on many levels. He was moved by the finality of the act. He was forced to reflect on his own past bouts of depression brought on by the pressures of the presidency. He compared what he perceived as a cover-up of the matter with his own Watergate experiences. And he had to confront mortality once again, for there is a fraternal relationship between politics and death. A political death, like the one he suffered after Watergate, could be overcome; a mortal death could not. Foster's suicide wrapped both in a tragic package, leaving Nixon dispirited and unsettled. Government was supposed to bring the country up, inspire, direct, lift with vision; it was not supposed to provoke personal devastation and death. With each fallen public servant—Nixon included—the nobility of the profession faded further from view.

Despite the warning signal of Foster's death, politics continued unabated. In the heat of early August, Clinton gave a speech advocating strategies for reducing the deficit.

Nixon called me immediately after hearing the speech and Dole's response to it. "It was just a warmed-over campaign speech on deficit reduction—too many charts—and he's too smug. Phony."

"He was marginally persuasive," I said.

"True. And his reference to [Arizona senator Dennis] De Concini was shrewd since he's counting on his vote. But I think it was much ado about nothing. Watch—it will be a Pyrrhic victory. Dole's response was great. He's a class act. I like him anyway, but he was good because it was simple and honest. Clinton lost his audience with too many facts. He tries to cover too much—like health care! There's a whole speech right there! The problem with Clinton is that he's too available, tries too hard with the press. Look at where that got Bush. And Johnson invited the press into his bathroom! No, Clinton should lay low, but that's not in his nature. He'd rather just gas around."

He called Dole the next day to congratulate him on his response to Clinton and to tell him that he looked so good on television it was difficult to tell whether the president or he were older. Nixon's 1996 campaign for Dole was under way.

"Dole is coming to see me next week," he said with a smile on August 18. "He wants to talk about his own strategy: if he's on the tube too much, if he's answering Clinton the right way—that type of thing. You know, the media gave him a reputation for being mean in '76, but he was right then. Dole can be tough, but he can also be a warm, funny guy. That should come across more. We had that problem. You can't be something that you're not, and you want to come across as strong, but he's got to let his human side come through so that the people *like* him enough to vote for him as well as respect him. That's what it takes to win."

Dole arrived at the office at four o'clock in the afternoon on August 25. Nixon reintroduced us, and Dole, remembering that I had been with Nixon at a Kansas fund-raiser for his 1992 campaign, began to ask me about Nixon's latest project.

Nixon interrupted him. "Monica," he said, "the senator was wondering if he is overexposed on television. You watch the shows and the news. Tell him—what do you think?"

Nixon knew that my answer would reflect a genuine admiration, fondness, and respect for Dole. I told him that I did not think he was overexposed but rather shone as a responsible counterweight to the parade of administration mouthpieces.

Dole replied with a smile, "They're trying to run up my negatives!"

Nixon and Dole retreated to Nixon's office for an hour-long meeting. They emerged laughing, and Nixon walked Dole downstairs so they could leave in their respective limousines at the same time. Dole's car was waiting, but unfortunately Nixon's was not. I came downstairs to go to my own car and noticed Nixon standing by himself in the heat, waiting for the limousine as the summer sun set behind him. I walked up to him and put my briefcase down.

"Monica!" he said, slightly startled. "You don't have to wait with me. You worked hard enough today. It's late. Get going home."

"I'm not going to leave you standing here by yourself, sir," I said.

He smiled. "Well, if you insist! I was going to fill you in on the Dole conversation tomorrow, but since you're here . . .

"I told him to wait until after '94 and then kick the hell out of Perot. And I told him not to just be *against* everything, but to be *for* things, like NAFTA and aid to Russia. Dole is just damn impressive. I told him that I would draft a memo of strategy for him, so I am going to go into the tank for the next few days and just do the damn thing. It will be highly confidential. I'll let you read it when I'm done, but not sooner!"

The limousine pulled up, and Nixon stepped in. As I closed the door behind him, he waved and shouted, "There is no one but Dole!"

On September 3, he completed his memorandum to Dole and placed it on my chair in his office. "That's your copy of the 'Dole Game Plan,' " he said, pointing to the nine-page draft. "Read it, and let me know if I've missed anything."

I took the memorandum back to my office and was struck by its straightforward approach. He evaluated Dole's current position, telling him that since he was the most important legislative and political leader of the Republican Party, Dole could not be defeated in 1996 for the nomination should he decide to run, and no one could win without his support should he decide not to run. According to Nixon, none of the possible candidates—including Kemp, Cheney, Weld, Gramm, and William Bennett—could challenge Dole successfully, but he would need their support in 1996.

Nixon focused Dole's attention on two particular potential threats: California governor Pete Wilson and the former chairman of the Joint Chiefs of Staff, General Colin Powell. Wilson had strong foreign and domestic policy credentials, Nixon wrote, and Powell was a wild card. Both could make significant runs for the nomination. Nixon advised Dole to maintain open and constructive relationships with both, but particularly with Powell since he had the power to change the dynamics of the race by joining either party.

The vice presidential nomination should go to a "heavyweight," and Nixon suggested [South Carolina Governor Carroll] Campbell, [Wisconsin governor Tommy] Thompson, and [Lamar] Alexander. They were progressive and serious Republicans who would lend additional gravitas to the ticket.

On the religious right, Nixon advised Dole to maintain a good relationship with its members but to avoid allowing them to dictate his policies or his campaign. Since they needed Dole more than Dole needed them, Dole could resist advocating their more extreme positions and avoid giving them power over his own agenda.

On media coverage, Nixon reassured Dole that he did not suffer from overexposure and that in order to compete with Clinton for air time, Dole had to lead forcefully and get coverage wherever possible.

On Perot, he instructed Dole to withhold criticism about him until after the 1994 elections, since Perot could still influence the outcomes of several House and Senate races. After the elections, however, Dole should actively and aggressively campaign against any Perot candidacy.

Nixon turned his attention to policy, where he advised Dole to be "conservative" on the economic issues but "compassionate" on issues such as welfare and health care reform, without appearing to go along with Clinton's views on these issues.

Nixon could have been advising himself with his next remarks to Dole. He told him to ground his message in the experiences of his modest background, to champion the "underdog," to remind voters that he is neither wealthy nor part of the Eastern elite, but that he comes from the "heartland" where he will always derive his personal and political strength.

He advised Dole to be pro-NAFTA, pro-reform in Russia, supportive of Yeltsin and patient with the Chinese, responsibly supportive of Israel and the restructuring of NATO, and tolerant of but not dependent on the United Nations. Dole should remain an idealist without allowing that idealism to overrun crucial American interests.

On choosing a campaign team, Nixon told Dole to accept everyone's support but to limit his circle of closest advisers to those who would be qualified to serve in his administration should he be elected. There was, Nixon wrote, no room in a presidential campaign or in an administration for lightweights. Nixon cited members of his own administration in support of this argument: Kissinger, Haig, Scowcroft, Schlesinger in foreign policy; Arthur Burns, Moynihan, Herb Stein, Paul McCracken in domestic policy; Ray Price, Bill Safire, Dave Gergen, Pat Buchanan in speechwriting; and Tom Korologos in congressional relations. All were—and remain—heavyweights, Nixon wrote, and Dole should follow the same example.

Nixon turned to Dole's "personal factors," including his age and how it might affect his candidacy. Nixon told him that his age would not be a liability after four years of Clinton and his administration of "baby boomers." He reminded Dole that many of the world's most preeminent statesmen, including de Gaulle, Adenauer, Yoshida, and Chou En-lai, remained brilliant, sharp, and effective well into their seventies. Dole should not disregard the age issue but embrace it as a way of pointing to Clinton's inexperience.

He whetted Dole's appetite with some prescient predictions. If the economy did not improve significantly by November 1994, he said, the Republicans would gain at least five seats in the Senate and twenty-five in the House. And if the economy remained a serious issue, Nixon foresaw the possibility that Republicans might win the House.

Although he did not predict the results of the 1996 election, he told Dole that the race was winnable, even if the economy improved. Clinton could be beaten, but he should be defeated with his own record. He instructed Dole to attack Clinton's policies and not him personally. Any criticism leveled at Clinton should be directed toward his woeful inexperience and inability to attract centrist voters because of his close ties to the extremely liberal left wing of the Democratic Party.

Nixon wished him good luck and, in a parting note of personal camaraderie, he appealed to Dole to "stay young."

Nixon's memorandum to Dole accomplished several objectives. It offered Dole sound advice on how to win the nomination in 1996. It solidified Nixon's position as Dole's chief, though shadow, adviser. It guaranteed Nixon tremendous influence in a Dole White House. And it reassured Nixon that he was still a player in the presidential game. Advising Dole, someone so similar to Nixon generationally and philosophically, was the next best thing to Nixon's running for the office himself.

With Dole counseled on how to wrest the office from Clinton, Nixon turned his attention back to the president. On September 2, Gergen called to see whether Nixon would attend a White House ceremony with the other former presidents to honor the signing of the peace agreement between Israel and the Palestine Liberation Organization. Nixon, completely opposed to such "dog-and-pony shows," refused to attend. He believed that his support of the agreement precluded any obligation to be there. "Gergen must know that I wouldn't go to one of those events where they trot out the former presidents like some sideshow, whether it's for NAFTA or the Middle East thing. If Clinton wants to call me on it, fine, but I will not go," he said, agitated.

"Carter deserves to be there. I do too, of course; we saved the place during the Yom Kippur War. The peace thing wasn't Reagan's bag. Bush should be there because the Gulf War was significant. But if this agreement is going to stand, we need to pour money in right away. The Israelis make twelve thousand dollars a year and the Arabs in the territories make one tenth of that. They need to even it out, or they are going to have enormous problems. But I've made my support for this agreement clear, and I will not attend the ceremony. I've done enough of them as president."

He called me Sunday morning, September 5, ecstatic that *The New York Times* had run an article arguing that neither Clinton nor Christopher had any real influence over the agreement between PLO chairman Yasir Arafat and Israeli prime minister Yitzhak Rabin. "I love it!" Nixon exclaimed. "Look, with the end of the cold war, it was inevitable that they'd come together with or without Washington. I told Rabin he was the only one who could do it because of his military background; people trusted him not to give away the store. It was genius. And here is Clinton claiming a huge victory for American foreign policy." He paused. "Well, I suppose he's got to claim *something*. He's got a full fall, full of messes: NAFTA will be a battle, and health care is going to be disastrous even with Hillary in charge. It's just too complicated to try to socialize it the way they want to. Those who want to keep the good benefits they have with their companies that go further than the minimum the government is going to offer will have to pay taxes on it. And I love it. We are going see a big rude awakening!"

Nixon declined invitations to the ceremony on September 13, 1993, that formalized the peace agreement and, later, to the NAFTA-ratification ceremony. His rationale was that he had advised the parties privately and made his positions public, so his presence would be nothing more than window dressing for the incumbent president.

Nixon watched the historic handshake between Rabin and Arafat on television, then remarked to me how relieved he was not to have been there. "I can't tell you how glad I am that neither Reagan nor I was there. It was like a three-ring circus. And I don't know how Bush could sit there and watch Clinton go through all of this, grinning up there like a Cheshire cat. And by the way, Kissinger showed up after telling me he wasn't going to go! And [former secretary of state George] Shultz did the same thing to Reagan! They are something else. I don't think they just decided at the last minute to go; I think they chose not to level with us. But anyway, at least Clinton mentioned the Norwegian foreign minister, who was responsible for negotiating the goddamned thing, but he should have made him a signatory."

He lowered his voice. "I thought you would like to know that Rabin called me from the White House about fifteen minutes ago. It took a while for him to get on the phone because he had to take a call from Israel. But what a class act! He thanked me for the thoughtful note and for all my support then and now. I told him it was risky, and he said he knew, but he also knew that it was necessary. I told him that it takes a brave one to make peace but an even braver one to keep it. He thanked me for all I have done from 1973 to today. Isn't that something? Once again, I tell you I am glad that I didn't go, but it would have been worth going just to see Rabin.

"This foreign policy 'triumph,' as Clinton likes to call it for himself, won't help him at all in the polls. It didn't for Carter, though it should have. He is still very low."

"This is so important to the Middle East and to the United States," I said, "that it *should* help him politically."

"I know," he replied. "But the public is just so focused on what's happening at home that they aren't paying any attention."

"Presidents have a hard time getting their attention without an enemy," I said.

"Bingo." He paused. "I see where Bush is going to stay the night at the White House. What is wrong with him?" He clenched his teeth. "I can't understand why they all want to go back to the goddamned place."

A presidency is over the minute the new president takes the oath of office. For Nixon, this meant no return visits unless requested by the incumbent for a limited amount of time and for a serious purpose. To go back was to admit that you missed the power and the privilege. Nixon missed both but would never make a public example of it by frolicking at the White House.

On September 17, he returned to Washington but stayed several blocks away from the White House. I arrived the next morning as David Gergen and White House Chief of Staff Thomas

McLarty were leaving Nixon's hotel suite. Nixon introduced us, escorted them out, then called me back in to give me his impressions of both.

He looked tired and drained. The trip to Washington the night before and the early meetings with the two members of Clinton's inner circle seemed to have sapped his usually boundless energy. He remained seated throughout our conversation, carefully sipping coffee and smoothing his tie.

"McLarty is soft-spoken and seemed like a real gentleman. Gergen is the same as he always was: shrewd but opportunistic. I told him that Clinton has to do a better job of projecting strength and of standing for something even if that means losing some support. I told him he doesn't have to worry about Gore usurping the spotlight, but Hillary is a problem. Gergen agreed. I told him to rein in her sharp sides. She can't continue to appear like those Frenchwomen at the guillotine during the revolution, just watching and knitting, knitting . . ." He did a scowling impression of Mme. Defarge.

"Clinton is good with people, which makes him a good politician but not a good statesman. He must take on an issue and lose. Losing sometimes means a win. He should take this approach when it comes down to the health thing."

"I think Clinton hates to lose anything, which is why he is more inclined to compromise than to stand up for something," I said.

"True. The guy *needs* to win all the time, which of course never happens." He paused. "Meeting with them really gave me a sense of what Clinton is thinking and doing, which is actually too much for a president at any one time. Of course, that assumes he's working by himself, which he is not." He paused again. "She is always there, working with him, working apart from him, pushing him to take on more, taking it on herself. Gergen knows he can't control her; no one can. But the point is that when Hillary gets going on health care, she will control *everything*. It will be fascinating to watch."

Nixon's trip to Washington reinforced for him the idea that while Clinton needed Gergen's services, Hillary was the mistress of her own spin. Her ability to charm her way around controversy seemed to outshine even her husband's. Through sheer force of will, she intended to get some semblance of health reform passed. When Mrs. Clinton and her commission studying health-care reform finished their work, they passed their recommendations to Clinton, who then gave a speech on September 22 in support of a complete overhaul of the health-care system. Nixon watched the speech and called me immediately afterward with an enthusiastic reaction.

"It was a hell of a speech," Nixon said. "He's just damn good out there. He was full of passion and conviction. He moved people. He used the TelePrompTer, but he did it as well as Reagan. He wove in the anecdotes, and he was able to hold people's attention for fifty-three minutes. Some people have a problem giving credit to our opponents—not me. And when our people are jerks, I say so! He brought the goddamned house down.

"I was surprised to see that he mentioned my health program." He paused. "Did you know that that was the first time a president ever mentioned me? Ford, Reagan, and Bush never did. It took a lot for him and drove the critics crazy because now they'll have to pay attention, particularly the press. But he did it. He said we had a plan, and had we survived, it would have been better than this one.

"You know, I've always been a liberal on health issues because I lost two brothers to TB and an aunt to cancer. And during my years in Congress, I helped put together a modest plan, and it didn't go anywhere. Eisenhower didn't want to do anything, and we didn't survive. But Clinton acknowledged my efforts. Remember when I was at the White House and saw Hillary, and she said to him, 'Richard,' then she corrected herself and said, '*President* Nixon had the best plan'?" He laughed. "Isn't that something? Maybe she put it in his speech; she's so shrewd. The liberals will go, 'President *Nixon* had a plan?'!" He chuckled again.

"Well! Look at that Cabinet. Aren't they an awful-looking group? My God! [Health and Human Services Secretary Donna] Shalala and [Attorney General Janet] Reno? They are so far to the left that I don't know what they are. And Hillary!

She's so steely. She even *claps* in a controlled way. She's a true-believing liberal.

"But I do give credit to Clinton for taking on foreign policy at the end and standing up for the Russians. Look, the Europeans fell in line after Clinton supported Yeltsin yesterday. See what a little leadership can do? If he had a Kissinger or a Brzezinski, he might be better. But Christopher is just weak. Clinton communicates so well; if he could just get it together. In any event, the health plan the way it is will never pass, but at least he—or I should say *she*—gave it a shot."

"The problem with the plan is the problem with most solutions Clinton's advisers advance," I said. "It's all pure theory, which doesn't translate well into real practice."

"Agreed," he said. "But something needs to be done. He's right on that. He thinks it should be a government solution. I don't. In any case, I don't think that the health issue is going to be big enough to make a real impact in '94."

As Nixon expected, the first lady began an aggressive campaign to sell her program to the Congress and the people in order to force an impact on 1994 and beyond. Health-care reform was one of the principal promises made by the Clintons during the campaign and the one for which they would be remembered. In an attempt to offer equal health-care opportunities for all Americans, the administration sought to institute price controls and compulsory conscription of every doctor and every patient in a government-controlled, government-directed, government-regulated system. A vast new bureaucracy would have to be created to run the industry, reducing efficiency and quality of care for all in the name of access for all. Centralizing health care was less about health than it was about government power. Mrs. Clinton set out to persuade the country that this liberal prescription was the correct one.

On September 28, she went to Capitol Hill to testify about the details of the administration's plan. She defended the plan as the fairest, most comprehensive approach to reforming the system, in which everyone would have access to quality health care regardless of economic status or other extenuating conditions.

The plan she advocated had its critics, but there were not any in the hearing room as she testified.

"Goddamn it! She has the gift of dazzle," Nixon said after watching her testimony. "She knocked them dead up there. They swooned over her and gave her standing ovations and just went gaga. Can you believe it? She takes the gloves off but does it with such sickening sweetness that it makes me want to gag. Liberals *love* government," he said, extending the pronunciation of the verb. "Hillary doesn't give a shit for people." He stopped. "Well, that's not fair. She might shed a tear now and then; we all do. But she and her crowd all see government as the first resort when it should be the last. And here are our idiots, cheering her on. They threw softballs at her when they should have been aiming for her head!"

His frustration with the Republicans' deferential treatment of Mrs. Clinton on Capitol Hill spilled over to his dismay that the other half of the Clinton partnership had let foreign policy slip into disarray. In his preoccupation with domestic issues such as health care, the president had allowed the humanitarian, peace-keeping military mission begun by George Bush in Somalia to evolve into a dangerous and more committed nation-building exercise. A minor operation like the one in Somalia drained attention and resources from the more important foreign policy issue of Russia. If Clinton were distracted by it, he could not give Russia the priority it deserved.

"The Clintons are spinning out of control," Nixon said to me at his residence on October 8, waving a pen in the air. "They are running around with their little pet projects, but no one has their eye on the ball. Maybe I will write him a note."

Clinton, however, preempted him with a call, which Nixon missed. "Oh, God," he sighed to me. "I hope he's not going to rope me into another former-president thing. Maybe he wants to talk about Somalia. I'll just say, 'Look, you inherited this, so just complete the humanitarian mission, and get the hell out.' The United States cannot be in the business of seeking a political settlement there. It's a mistake. And I suppose I will stroke him on Russia."

He got up, went into the kitchen, and returned carrying a cantaloupe. "I'm going to the Bahamas tomorrow, and I don't want it to go bad while I'm gone. Here, enjoy it. Now go on home, and think about what you are going to do for your country tomorrow! I'll call you after I talk to him."

My phone rang at nine o'clock that evening. "Monica? Well, he called at six-twenty-five from Air Force One. It was a terrible connection. I never used that phone. Anyway, I had read that some of his aides described him as cranky and tired because he had to focus on foreign policy, and I sort of got that feeling. He started right out, 'What do you think of Somalia?' I said in confidence that 'you inherited it, which began as a humanitarian mission. You endorsed it, and you continued it. But now it has changed its character, and now we are into nation building.' He told me that he was 'blindsided' by this, which I thought was very interesting, because he implied it was by his own people!

"I told him that his speech was excellent, but I was concerned that he implied that the goal would be a political settlement. The main thing is that that must *not* be a consideration. He must get those troops out. He knew it. Somalia is a mess, and it will still be a mess when we leave. He said that [United Nations secretary general Boutros] Boutros-Ghali was obsessed with [Somali] general [Mohammed Farah] Aidid, but I said that the United States can't be fighting this pipsqueak, although he did overthrow the previous dictator. But the goal must not be changed. He used the example of Cambodia, but the UN failed there, and it will fail again.

"I hit hard the point that we should use the UN, not be used by it. I hope it sunk in. We'll see. I also told him never to let Americans serve under a UN commander; we never have since World War II. He didn't react. I told him to limit the engagement but don't stick around.

"He said he'd been working on Russia and Japan, but he did say he would never let Somalia happen again. He was hit by the spectacle of a dead American soldier being dragged through the streets, and even though he dodged the draft, he's an Arkansas boy, and maybe some of that southern patriotism came through.

"Anyway, I congratulated him on Yeltsin, and he said there were some who felt he shouldn't go as far as he has to support him. At least he's standing up on that. It was a good conversation, but he sounded troubled and hectic."

"Did he seem at all insecure in discussing foreign policy with you?" I asked.

"Maybe a little. But this is a very confident guy. I'm sure he called others for advice, but at least he's calling me. He's very affected by editorials and press reports. My God, if I worried about all my press reports, I'd be dead by now! He did ask how I was feeling; maybe Gergen put him up to that. In any event, if he takes any advice, I hope he listens to me on the UN."

Nixon spent three quiet days in the Bahamas and returned on October 12 to find that Clinton had not listened to him. In his quest to return to power, exiled Haitian president Jean-Bertrand Aristide requested—and received—a pledge of potential military support from Clinton, sending Nixon into a tailspin. "What in the *world* is Clinton doing now in Haiti? He's gone crazy on the UN! I just talked to Scowcroft about Somalia, which of course began under him. But Haiti? Aristide is not our friend; he's anti-American and a little bit of a nut. But we're supporting him because he got two thirds of the vote and wants to get back in power? What are we talking about? And if we're going to nation-build, we picked the two worst cases! Haiti is impossible, and Somalia was an artificial state created by the British." Nixon seethed. "He must be going crazy, having to put health care and the rest on the back burner for Haiti!"

Clinton's frustration must have been a growing source of insecurity for him, for he called Nixon again on October 19. "The point of the call, I suppose, was Haiti," Nixon said after the conversation. He crossed his arms and legs in a self-satisfied pose in his office chair and waved me into my usual seat. "It's clear that he's driven to distraction by the foreign policy stuff. Today, he just sounded irritated, but he was great with me and even said how nice it was that he had me to talk to about these things. The guy knew his stuff. He's a quick study. If he could only learn—" He stopped. "Well, I guess the presidency is a little late to be learning foreign policy. He doesn't know foreign policy, but he's smart enough to reach out. He's sort of unorganized. The White House operator placed the call, and he wasn't there. Again. Oh, boy." He rolled his eyes.

"When he finally made it to the phone, he gave a monologue on Haiti, and it was obvious that he had studied it. He said he made a mistake criticizing Bush on the Haitian refugees. He tried to cite the drug connection—trying to make it into a national interest of the United States. That drug stuff is bullshit. All those islands are full of drugs; that's no reason to break relations with them. I told him, once again, not to get into nation building and not to reassure them that we would use force. Carter made that mistake with the Iranian hostages.

"I also told him that Dole's proposal for the president to be required to get congressional authorization to send troops is wrong. The War Powers Act was wrong in '73, and this is wrong now. He realized that Dole had to protect his right wing, but I think he appreciated my comments.

"When I told him I planned to go to Russia, he didn't react. He may be planning a summit or something and didn't want to tell me. I don't know. He calls me, but I don't know if he listens. I hope I got across that Haiti and Somalia are peripheral issues and don't amount to a tinker's damn compared to Russia; Russia is the big one."

He assumed a mocking voice. "Monica, shall our next fact-finding trip be to Haiti?" He burst out laughing. "Well, it *is* warmer than Russia!"

Nixon's instincts about a Clinton trip to Russia were correct. Several days after Clinton's evasive comments to Nixon, the White House announced that the president would be traveling to Moscow for a summit with Yeltsin, about which Nixon commented that the trip was "totally political. He needs a victory, but even this could lose for him." Polls indicated that the public was losing faith in Clinton's ability to lead on the economy and in foreign affairs. There was a prevailing sense that foreign crises had not been handled well, and that in turn had created serious doubts about overall Democratic competence.

With the November elections fast approaching, Clinton needed to regain the momentum that originally put him in the office. Polls indicated that the Democrats were running ahead of the Republicans in the gubernatorial races in New Jersey and Virginia and in the mayoral race in New York City. Nixon predicted that the races would be far closer than the polls suggested but that the Democrats would win in New Jersey and New York City. I, however, was more optimistic. On the night of the election, Nixon left a brief but merry message on my answering machine: "It was a clean sweep. You were right, as usual! I'm glad you're on *our* side!"

As he scanned the returns the next morning and analyzed Christine Todd Whitman's victory in New Jersey, George Allen's in Virginia, and Rudolph Giuliani's in New York City, delight flickered in his eyes. He handed a heavily marked newspaper to me. "Look at these results," he exclaimed. "It gave me a great lift. Clinton and Hillary were active in all three places, and they lost them all. I love it! We actually *won* all three races. The sentiment against him must run far deeper than I had thought. Now he *really* needs something to give him a boost."

Ironically, the president who campaigned on domestic issues now relied upon foreign policy ones to resurrect his flagging popularity. The summit with Yeltsin in January 1994 would allow him to appear presidential on the world stage, and the impending vote on NAFTA would earn him a reputation as a genuine free trader, which would help him with conservatives. Clinton had Gergen call Nixon's office to see whether Nixon would be willing to place persuasive phone calls to several senators who had not yet decided how to vote on NAFTA. Nixon, of course, was delighted to be part of the game.

The day before the November 17 vote, Nixon remarked, "It should pass, but he's had to buy the goddamned votes. The Democrats will take a pass until the final call, and then they'll change their votes in the well. It's a cynical business. This made me laugh: as soon as it was clear that Clinton was going to win on this, the media started saying, 'This is a defining moment in his presidency. He's big on the world stage.' Meanwhile, he couldn't even deliver a majority of his own party!"

Press coverage of the vote the next day further horrified him. "They have gone hog-wild. And for Clinton to bash the press proves he's a whiner. He has faced nothing like I faced. My God! But did you notice that he didn't thank any of the Republicans? And now he's back pandering to labor. He just gets out there and emotes all over the place, telling each audience what they want to hear."

Vice President Al Gore called Nixon on December 2 to thank him for the note he'd sent praising him on his debate with Ross Perot over NAFTA. "It was good of him to call," he told me immediately after the conversation. "I got along well with his father. He wanted advice for his upcoming trip to Russia. I told him that what he will not hear from the State Department people is to see the opposition. And Yeltsin's people won't like it either, but he must do it because opposition today could be leadership tomorrow. I didn't tell him that I thought it was a mistake for him to go only three weeks before Clinton is to go, but what the hell. Gore is pretty responsible. His ideas on the environment go overboard, but overall he's a good man."

He turned his attention to Gore's boss and showed me a recent poll. "Clinton's polls haven't moved at all, despite all of these so-called victories. Nothing will help if the guy isn't more decisive."

In late December, an issue returned with a vengeance to haunt the Clintons and make them even more *indecisive:* Whitewater. Some details had emerged during the campaign and more were exposed after Foster's suicide, but with congressional hearings set to begin, Whitewater commanded a greater share of the public's attention. The complex situation involving the infamous land-development deal in the Ozarks, Arkansas savings and loan scandals, and Clinton's gubernatorial war chest entered a new and more treacherous phase.

Although we had discussed Whitewater previously, Nixon's first remark about it as a serious presidential issue came on December 15. "This is a mess. There is so much corruption involved here that they are all up to their eyeballs in it, particularly Hillary, since she handled all of their finances. The Foster suicide smells to high heaven, but they probably won't reopen that investigation. The taking of his files was definitely obstructing justice. Look at what they did to us! My attorneys—[Jack] Miller and [Stan] Mortenson—have been fighting Watergate-related crap for twenty years now. I've spent over two million dollars in legal fees. None of it was worth it. Do you think that in twenty years the Clintons will still be fighting Whitewater?" He shook his head sadly and pointed a finger down on his desk. "Anything the Clintons turn over now will have been totally sanitized." He lowered his eyebrows. "If our people don't step up to this, so help me—" He made a fist. "Of course I can't say anything, for obvious reasons, but they had better go after them on this."

Nixon implied that if the Republicans did not investigate, they would be just as responsible for the double standard they always complained about. Whitewater was a serious enough issue with grave enough implications to warrant a full investigation of the president's and first lady's activities. If the Republicans failed to press it, Nixon would lose all faith in his party and its ability to fight back.

Nixon began his final year, 1994, ruminating about the political maneuverings related to Whitewater. On January 4, he told me, "The big news is that there is a follow-up on that Clinton savings and loan scandal and the Arkansas connection. The *Times* called for a special prosecutor—so did *USA Today*—can you believe it? There must really be something to it if *they* are calling for a prosecutor, not that anything will come of it. Janet Reno said no; she gets high marks, but she's a partisan witch. She's about as political as Bobby Kennedy was in that job. But I must say that the media so far have been pretty fair on this. They smell a scandal, and that's better for them than writing the good stuff. But with a Republican, they would be all over this, and I mean *all* over this. To think that Hillary came after me! They are making the same goddamned mistakes we did."

He lowered his voice. "It isn't that they are stonewalling—although they may be—it's the *appearance* of stonewalling or having done something wrong. That was our mistake: giving the *impression* of wrongdoing. It's really between the two of them. She's telling him he can't have the special prosecutor, and he knows he has to. She's up to her ass in it, and they are both guilty as hell."

Shades of Watergate colored his analysis of the Whitewater affair. From Nixon's unique vantage point, the Clintons' situation had the complex anatomy of a potentially explosive scandal. The appearance of stonewalling, the obstruction of investigations, the policy of appeasement in assenting to a special prosecutor, and the repeated denials of wrongdoing flowing from the White House brought back enough negative memories for Nixon that he felt compelled to ask me a desperate question: "Didn't anyone learn anything from Watergate?"

Mrs. Clinton, active on the impeachment committee, apparently did not. Her equivocations on the matter and her refusal to offer immediate and open cooperation gave the impression not only of lack of judgment but of guilt. For Nixon, Whitewater represented a scandal whose time had come: players who had worked to remove him from office, now in the nation's most powerful positions, were at the center of their own twisted scandal. If the Republicans pressed the investigation with as much ideological zeal as the Democrats had done during Watergate, Nixon's own mistakes would be compared with Clinton's with some sense of fair play.

He remained skeptical, however, that an investigation on the scale of Watergate would develop. "I see that Bob Fiske is going to be the special prosecutor on Whitewater," he said on January 21, tossing his newspaper in the wastebasket. "I don't know much about him, but if he turns out to be a Baker type, we're doomed. We don't need a softy or an elite intellectual type on this; we need a tough son of a bitch. But I still don't think anything will come of it. His friends in the press will protect him no matter what. We didn't have that advantage."

Clinton, like Nixon before him, continued to operate as if the scandal had never erupted. He worked hard to appear undistracted, sidestepping the Whitewater political follies and traveling the world. He went to Russia in mid-January for a summit with Yeltsin and returned to give a State of the Union address that focused mainly on health-care reform and show-cased his formidable speaking abilities and ambitious domestic agenda.

"Clinton is effective," Nixon said the day after the January 25 speech, "just wrong. But the press will play it up so they don't have to cover Whitewater. It's as dead as a doorknob.

"And when he talks about foreign policy, I shudder for the guy. He's just so *uncomfortable*." He raised his shoulders in a mock tremble. "It wouldn't be so noticeable if he weren't so confident with the domestic stuff. He's pretending not to notice Whitewater. Of course I tried that, and it doesn't really work. The best thing to do is to confront it, explain your position, then try to move on. In their situation, it's a case of protesting too much. They are guilty, but now they *look* it."

On February 10, Nixon received a call from former president Bush, thanking him for signing pictures for his grandchildren. As the Whitewater investigation gathered additional steam, Bush must have been privately pleased, as was Nixon.

"He was very frank," Nixon said to me. "I asked what he thought of Clinton. He said Clinton is a charmer but, well, not Bush's cup of tea. He told me he was speaking a lot, mostly overseas. And he said that Scowcroft was writing their book about the end of the cold war. He said, 'Dick, *you* can write. I can't.' I don't know about that, but it was a good conversation. He sounded sad, particularly when he was discussing Clinton."

"Did you sense that he still cannot believe that he lost to him?" I asked.

"I think that's it. Bush is such a decent guy that I think he has trouble accepting the fact that the country chose Clinton. He's the kind of guy who really takes these things to heart. He didn't mention the Whitewater thing, but you know he's got to be secretly jumping for joy. Unless, of course, our people flush the thing down the tubes. They did it with [Commerce Secretary] Ron Brown and [Illinois representative Dan] Rostenkowski. Those guys are guilty as hell and corrupt up to their eyeballs, and they're all still at the trough. It's our own people's fault; they are just not up for the big play. My critics used to say that

Watergate was a gift to them; here we have a gift from the Clintons, and no one is up to using it.

"The point has to be made that unlike this situation, no one ever profited in Watergate. Here you have financial gain *and* abuse of power. I remember when they went after [Commerce Secretary] Maury Stans for one thousand dollars; meanwhile, Ron Brown takes millions, and nothing is done.

"And here was Hillary, on the impeachment committee, screaming about the eighteen and a half minutes, and now she's in Little Rock, shredding."

Nixon's fixation on Whitewater had little to do with the actual scandal. Instead, he used it as an excuse to vent his frustration with a double standard that he perceived as protective of Democrats and persecutory toward Republicans. Unethical behavior was not exclusive to Republicans, but Democratic presidents seemed mostly immune from its consequences. This infuriated Nixon. If Watergate were a manifestation of Republican corruption, then Whitewater deserved to be treated as the Democratic version. Anything less would be an unfair act of selective prosecution. Nixon's frustration stemmed from the fact that he could rely neither on the press to investigate nor the Republicans to advance the inquiry. If Whitewater were going to fade away, it would be because the president's opponents did nothing.

Nixon's concerns began to affect his relationship with Clinton. On March 2, the White House called to inform him that Clinton would be calling the next day, probably, Nixon speculated, to discuss Nixon's upcoming trip to Russia. Nixon responded with characteristic nonchalance. "The guy is doing what's in his interest, which is only right. But I think I'd like some distance from that crowd at this point."

He was far less enthusiastic about his March 3 conversation with Clinton than he had been about their previous discussions. "I got a call from Clinton this morning, as expected," he told me with a broad smile that left his face as quickly as it came. "We spoke for about fifteen minutes. It was a good conversation. He wanted to know what my itinerary was going to be in

Russia. I told him that I was going to see the opposition: [former vice president Aleksandr] Rutskoi and [nationalist Vladimir] Zhirinovsky. He thought that was great because his people can't see them. He was worried about Ukraine, as he should be. He said he was glad that I'm going to see [German chancellor Helmut] Kohl; he said Kohl was one of America's best friends.

"This conversation was more limited, but it was still good. He was respectful, always referring to me as 'Mr. President.' With Reagan, I started that, and he said, 'Now, Dick, we've known each other a long time.' Bush was always like that. But with this guy, it's just not right. We're of two different generations.

"But you know, at least we are getting support from the administration on our trip. Remember Shultz? He gave us nothing. And Baker instructed the embassy to treat me as just another businessman. Insulting. At least this administration has treated me the right way."

Nixon went to Russia on March 4 and saw Yeltsin's opposition before seeing Yeltsin, sending the Russian president into a furious fit of revenge that included revoking Nixon's invitation to the Kremlin and pulling his government limousines and bodyguards. Nixon responded with his usual artful flair. He expressed disappointment at being unable to meet with Yeltsin but praised his commitment to political and economic reform. The additional media attention generated by the controversy gave Nixon an unanticipated global audience to whom he could direct his appeal for action. In Washington, Clinton defended Nixon with a positive statement of support.

Nixon called me from Moscow on March 9. "Monica? I can't believe that I got through to you. I just punched in your numbers and hoped for the best!" I pictured him crouched over an antiquated Russian phone, praying that the numbers on the rotary matched the ones he was trying to dial. "Well, it's five A.M. here, but I've got insomnia, so I thought I'd call and fill you in. Yeltsin, of course, had had a few when he erupted at me. That's well-known. But we got some good news coverage and managed to get through to the White House. Clinton gave a good statement; of course he *had* to. I understand that both he and Dole sent Yeltsin notes urging him to see me. Both of them have been *very* good. Seeing the opposition has always been my practice. These are the men who will be running for the presidency. It doesn't matter if Yeltsin won't see me. We are not canceling this trip. We will see everyone else we came to see."

After telling me that he had been violently ill the day before and was battling simultaneously a high fever and the brutally cold temperatures of Moscow, he bid me good night, only to call me back ten minutes later. "I forgot to ask you about Whitewater," he said breathlessly.

I told him that the independent counsel did not want the Congress to hold hearings before he had a chance to complete his initial inquiry. "That was the same pattern with Watergate," he responded. "The reporters covering me here asked me to comment, and I said, 'No, when I am traveling abroad, I do not comment on domestic matters.' They were trying to pry a comment out of me, but there is no way I'm going to be in a position to comment on that or anything else related to that goddamned mess."

Upon his return to the United States, Nixon dictated a memo to Clinton on the Russian situation in order to avoid having to meet with Talbott and Christopher. "I should report only to the man, anyway," he said on March 21. "I was brutally honest in this memo; I told him he needs a new ambassador in Kiev because the situation is very dicey. I don't want to tell the State Department idiots because they won't do a damn thing. Maybe if he hears it from me, he'll get on the ball. He'll need a foreign policy victory since this Whitewater stuff is dominating the news. I think he must be worried that Whitewater could weaken him so much—not to the point of impeachment—but enough to weaken him immensely. He defends her all the time on this stuff because she defended him on the womanizing crap. They are both very smart and totally cynical."

In early April, the press continued to pursue the story, much to Nixon's surprise. His expectations that the story would be followed were so low that any coverage at all delighted him.

"The double standard is still at work," he said on April 4, "but at least they are following it up. They can't like doing it; Clinton is their man. But when they smell a story, they will climb over anyone and anything to get it. Tony Lewis's column gave away their bias: he said that the media blew it out of proportion. Can you believe it? They said it's nothing like Watergate. I say, 'It's worse. In Watergate, we didn't have profiteering, and we didn't have a body.'

"I remember the night before the resignation [Nixon's son-in-law] Eddie Cox said, 'These people hate you,' and he was referring to Hillary and Nussbaum and their crowd. Our people today don't have the passion to go after him or her. You know, in the early months of 1973, Watergate didn't affect the polls, but when the Ervin Committee got started and it got on the tube, that's when it took off. When these hearings begin, it will get more attention. At least let's *hope* that it gets more attention."

Then he took a step to interject himself into the Whitewater scandal. "I'm going to call Dole and tell him to put someone good on the select committee. We can't have a bunch of dumbos asking the questions." Nixon's concern was that the hearings would backfire, expose nothing, and end up helping Clinton politically. The hearings needed to be dynamic, explosive, and revealing in order to keep the nation's attention. A president in the middle of a scandal should have been enough to command extensive press coverage, but without damaging evidence, the hearings could prove to be a tiresome exercise, forcing public sentiment to Clinton's side.

Four days before a stroke that would silence Nixon forever, he made his last comments about Clinton and the Whitewater investigation. It was April 13, and he called me after the evening news to complain about its tediousness. "No wonder Whitewater is hot. It's not because the press wants to cover it necessarily, although they love a scandal. It's because the rest of the news is so damn dull."

He was neither angry nor bitter but reflective. "Clinton and Hillary are guilty of obstruction of justice, maybe more. Period.

Our people must not be afraid to grab this thing and shake all of the evidence loose. Watergate was wrong; Whitewater is wrong. I paid the price; Clinton should pay the price. Our people shouldn't let this issue go down. They mustn't let it sink."

That last remark was a cryptic reference to Nixon's critics who refused to let Watergate sink. That Nixon's last words about the incumbent president were an exhortation to have Whitewater pursued is a telling reference to his own demand that his mistakes be put in context. Desperation and frustration drove this plea for fairness. He did not consider himself a victim; he took responsibility for the actions of himself and others in the Watergate affair. He did, however, consider himself a casualty of a fierce political double standard that protected Democrats and punished Republicans, a double standard enforced by the press and the institutions of government that were supposed to guard against it. Nixon, though he could not control the Whitewater investigation, tried to will it to a satisfactory conclusion. He did not hold a personal grudge against Clinton, although Clinton's avoidance of military service during the Vietnam War disgusted him, but he did think that Clinton should be held as responsible for his misdeeds as Nixon had been for his. Suffer the consequences, Nixon pleaded, and be fair.

It is interesting, then, to consider Clinton's gracious remarks two weeks later, at Nixon's funeral. They had shared a mutually beneficial relationship: Clinton got solid advice from an old pro; Nixon got access to a president that he had not had with either Reagan or Bush. Nixon appreciated the fact that it took a Democratic president to grant him the public credibility that had been denied him by Ford, Reagan, and Bush. He admired Clinton's political courage. With several phone calls and an invitation to the White House, Clinton had done more to restore Nixon to the center of power than anyone else had apart from Nixon himself.

Their unique relationship was apparent in Clinton's speech, when he stated, "May the day of judging President Nixon on anything less than his entire life and career come to a close." Clinton was part of a generation whose members, in their youth, protested against Nixon and everything he stood for and, in their middle age, sought his advice and guidance. The wheel of history had turned; time had changed perceptions. Nixon was too large a figure, too complex, and too great an influence on the twentieth century to remain a persona frozen in 1974. Clinton added impetus not only to the reexamination of Nixon's career but to his relevance as a historical dramatist. Nixon did everything on a grand scale, sometimes with the fine precision of a master, sometimes with the blunt force of a steamroller, but always with a vision in mind. His ability to take the course of history and mold it according to his will did not end when he left the White House. He wrote, spoke, gave interviews, and traveled, but he wielded the most influence when he advised his successors, and of those successors, he advised Bill Clinton the most extensively.

That it was Clinton and not Reagan or Bush who elevated Nixon above the ranks of shadow advisers was an irony not lost on him. Two different generations, two different political philosophies, and two different views of personal virtue came together to help each other. In his youth, Clinton gave President Nixon grief as a protester and a useful political target as an enemy; in his presidency, Clinton gave former president Nixon a measure of redemption and respect as a student-in-power.

Nixon had lived through only one year of the Clinton presidency but had determined that, barring spectacular leadership in an unanticipated crisis, Clinton would not meet the standards of greatness. He had intelligence and the ability to communicate but could not make the difficult decisions or "go through the fire," as he said, without vacillating; he lacked the steel that makes up truly great leadership. Bush had failed the test as well. As president during the quietly epic end of the cold war, Bush had pronounced a "new world order" but could not capitalize on it. Crisis management was not enlightened statesmanship. Neither Bush nor Clinton had proved himself capable of initiating and sustaining great change; both had made some difference simply by being president, but they had not moved the nation or changed the world. The nation and the world were changing *around* them, not *because* of them.

Looking ahead, Nixon saw that Dole had the potential to be a great leader. Where Clinton was equivocal, Dole was decisive. Where Clinton was learning on the job, Dole had hard-won experience. Where Clinton had tried to decipher the challenges of the end of the cold war, Dole had recognized and seized them. Where Clinton acted impulsively, Dole acted responsibly. Where Clinton was plagued by scandal, Dole remained untarnished. Where Clinton lacked personal character, Dole had it in spades. For Nixon, these were compelling enough reasons to turn out another incumbent president after one term and replace him with Dole. The country was not better off under Clinton but remained as directionless and anchorless as it had been under Bush. Nixon therefore saw Clinton, like Bush, as inevitably a single-term president, unable to inspire the country to higher deeds and loftier goals beyond the base ones driving his own political survival.

Dole, in Nixon's view, had the unique opportunity to define a new era through an older generation. If elected, he would have the chance to breathe new life into the values that had always defined leadership but seemed to have gotten lost: service for a higher purpose, patriotism, integrity, and vision. Nixon saw Dole's candidacy as the last best chance to restore the traditional pillars of leadership to the American presidency. Dole could initiate a recovery of old truths: that government should inspire people without interfering in their lives, that character matters, and that leadership requires a judicious balance of style *and* substance, compassion *and* toughness, idealism *and* pragmatism. For Nixon, Dole had the power to remind Americans that their commonly held views and values remained relevant and legitimate and had not, despite a rising amoral tide, been washed away from the presidency.

The art of politics is seldom the art of leadership. Clinton is an elitist cloaked in populist garb, but Dole is a true but quiet populist cloaked not in illusive image-making but in the certainty that comes from experience. The contrast between Clinton and Dole cannot be more stark. Unlike 1992, the 1996 election is to be a contest not about just the next four years but about the next century, when leadership of the kind Nixon spoke of will be required to make it the second American century. Nixon saw clearly from Clinton's first year that Clinton is not the one to lead America into the new millennium. Dole, however, is the one, and if he succeeds, Nixon's lessons about leadership will not only endure but live.

Fallen statesmen rarely rise again. A long life, however, serves them well. Nixon, like his old hero, Herbert Hoover, survived almost all his enemies. Few leaders have been more successful at subsuming the past into an unwavering look to the future. Clinton, to his credit, took advantage. Nixon's advice was solicited not out of mere courtesy but out of a genuine need to know what path to take. Considering the depths of degradation from which Nixon had climbed, this was an extraordinary achievement. It was truly his last—and most remarkable—campaign. Courage, endurance, persistence, patience, skill, and generosity with the lessons of his own experience lifted him back to the center of power. But the question of whether history will give him the justice his contemporaries denied him remains unanswered.

Nixon himself believed he would not see that justice delivered. His post-presidential contributions would grant him some historical compensation, but not enough to erase completely the tarnish of scandal. In 1993, Nixon tore out a feature in *The New York Times* entitled "How the Public's View Changes As the Presidents Become History." It profiled each president's average approval rating from Roosevelt to Bush, his rating at the end of his term, and his most recent approval numbers. Nixon's average approval rating was 48 percent; at the end of his term, it was 24 percent; and the most recent rating, measured in 1990, was 32 percent, far below that of any of the other presidents with the exception of Lyndon Johnson. He left the article on my desk with a moving appeal for an explanation.

"M—," it said, "Not surprising on RN." He asked me to explain why Ford and Carter had higher ratings than he did and suggested that it was due to their constant availability to the media. He pointed out that Johnson's low rating stemmed from the "drag of Vietnam," which, he acknowledged, contributed to his own low rating "apart from Watergate." He wanted an answer: were his low ratings irreversible?

The poignancy of the note was not based in self-pity. Rather, it was based in Nixon's sincere belief that he had been one of the hardest working and most visionary, intelligent, and productive presidents of the century and therefore deserved a higher rating than those leaders he considered inferior, Vietnam and Watergate notwithstanding. His expectations of a climbing approval rating were so low that even a slight improvement in his standing surprised him. But when he compared his rating with his predecessors' and successors', he knew that he had only very limited control over how he would be remembered. He contributed when he could, where he could, and to whom he could; beyond that, the wheel of history would turn again without him.

If great leadership required "head, heart, and guts," as he so often claimed, then Nixon demonstrated his intelligence, compassion, and courage as often as he could with the hope that he would eventually be included in the ranks of the great leaders. His career testified to both the positive power of will and endurance in public life and the destructive power of institutionalized ideological opposition. His post-presidential years were spent trying to affect the course of events and guide American policy so that what he had accomplished for the country during his career was not squandered. His own restoration was a secondary but no less important goal. Great leaders did not wallow; they thought and acted. Nixon's contributions in the twenty years from his resignation to his death guaranteed him a historical reevaluation and gave the distant promise of a day when he would qualify unequivocally as a great leader. He knew he would not see that day, but perhaps his great-grandchildren and their contemporaries would, and the wheel of history would be given a final and just turn.

INDEX

ABOUT THE AUTHOR

MONICA CROWLEY was editorial advisor and research consultant for President Nixon's *Seize
the Moment* in 1992 and *Beyond Peace* in
1994, and traveled to Europe and Asia with
him, participating in his meetings with heads of
state and other government leaders. She is currently a doctoral candidate at Columbia University. She lives in New Jersey.

ABOUT THE TYPE

This book was set in Sabon, a typeface designed by the well-known German typographer Jan Tschichold (1902–74). Sabon's design is based upon the original letter forms of Claude Garamond and was created specifically to be used for three sources: foundry type for hand composition, Linotype, and Monotype. Tschichold named his typeface for the famous Frankfurt typefounder Jacques Sabon, who died in 1580.